MANCHESTER
1824

Manchester University Press

Politics Today

Series editor: Bill Jones

Devolution in Britain today

Second edition

Russell Deacon

Manchester University Press

Manchester and New York
distributed exclusively in the USA by Palgrave

First edition published 2002 by Manchester University Press

This edition published 2006 by
Manchester University Press
Oxford Road, Manchester M13 9NR, UK
and Room 400, 175 Fifth Avenue, New York, NY 10010, USA

Distributed exclusively in the USA by
Palgrave, 175 Fifth Avenue, New York,
NY 10010, USA

Distributed exclusively in Canada by
UBC Press, University of British Columbia, 2029 West Mall
Vancouver, BC, Canada V6T 1Z2

British Library Cataloguing-in-Publication Data
A catalogue record for this book is available from the British Library

Library of Congress Cataloging-in-Publication Data applied for

ISBN   0 7190 7527 0 *paperback*
EAN   978 0 7190 7527 8

This edition first published 2006

15 14 13 12 11 10 09 08 07 06   10 9 8 7 6 5 4 3 2 1

Typeset
by Helen Skelton, Brighton, UK
Printed in Great Britain by
Biddles Ltd, King's Lynn

This book is dedicated to my nephews, Samuel and Nathan Deacon, Thomas Barnes and Morgan James and my Politics students at UWIC who have read my previous academic works and have told me they will also now read this one.

Contents

Preface

Back in 1997 the political conversation was of ever larger structures of government, the growing role of supranational bodies like the European Commission and European Parliament, and a general march towards globalisation in all things governmental. In that same year, however, the United Kingdom took a dramatic step in the opposite direction. The New Labour government brought in a series of devolved political measures that resulted in the world of British politics never being quite the same again. In all four of the national capitals, Belfast, Cardiff, Edinburgh and London, there were soon new, devolved Assemblies, or even a Parliament to take the credit or blame for how government services were delivered. People protesting about hospital closures or demanding better public transport no longer needed to go to Westminster but instead could protest in their own capital's devolved body. Although events in Northern Ireland soon put devolved events there into political stasis, elsewhere in the United Kingdom events continued to evolve. Politics in this age of globalisation was now becoming more local. For academics, such as myself, it provided the first chance to study the birth, and subsequent development, of national and regional government. Politics across the nations of the United Kingdom were then examined in greater detail than they had ever been analysed before. Much of this fascinating material has subsequently found its way into the book.

This second edition of *Devolution in Britain today*, therefore, is a book which combines material from many contemporary political studies together with a great deal of historical material on devolution and the history of the nations which make up the British Isles. It also importantly builds upon the late Colin Pilkington's original text for *Devolution in Britain today*, the predecessor to this volume. Colin had provided a great deal of material on the period leading up to the establishment of the devolved bodies and their first two years. As he fortuitously noted in the first edition, devolution is a rapidly changing process, and since his book was written in 2001, so much has occurred in devolution as to warrant a full updating of this book. In this respect, part III of this book has been entirely rewritten and the first two parts of this book have also been substantially updated with additional material.

Devolution is of course constantly evolving, and events and processes can sometimes occur on a daily basis which changes the path of devolution. The advantage of this book being mainly a historical text, therefore, is that it will always prove a useful and relevant text on devolutionary developments regardless of what events occur after it has been written.

The media coverage of devolved government outside, and even sometimes within the regions they serve, is very limited. This isn't because devolution is boring or dull, far from it. Its proceedings are often fascinating to watch and examine, and its policy output literally shape and can even save the lives of all of those they seek to serve. Devolution isn't covered to any great extent because we have on the whole a London-based media which pays little interest in politics beyond the personalities that inhabit Downing Street and Westminster. Many students of politics and the wider public are therefore unaware of what has been happening across the United Kingdom and Northern Ireland unless they seek to work their way through the plethora of websites, academic texts and government reports that detail what is happening. This book will enable students to skip a lot of that tedium and instead update themselves with all the more important points from within this book.

There are some necessary thanks to be made for the writing of this book. Firstly to the late Colin Pilkington and his family for making the first edition possible and setting such a high standard to follow. There are also a number of other thanks firstly to Tony Mason and Rachel Armstrong at Manchester University Press for their help and support with this book. Secondly, to Dr Bill Jones, the series editor for allowing me to contribute to this excellent series. I should also like to thank Gareth Thomas, Helen Skelton and Alys Thomas for their help in determining the accuracy of this book. Those anonymous civil servants in the devolved institutions that so readily supplied information are also owed a debt of gratitude. My final thanks go to my wife Tracey Deacon and daughter Alexandra Deacon who took on my much of my burden of household duties whilst I was writing this book.

List of abbreviations

AM	assembly member
AMS	additional member system
ASPBs	assembly-sponsored public bodies
BIIGC	British-Irish Intergovernmental Conference
COR	Committee of the Regions
CSA	Campaign for a Scottish Assembly
DCA	Department of Constitutional Affairs
DfEE	Department of Education and Employment
DUP	Democratic Unionist Party
FPTP	first-past-the-post
GLA	Greater London Assembly
GLC	Greater London Council
GO	government office
GOL	Government Office for London
IMC	independent monitoring commission
IRA	Irish Republican Army
MLA	member of the legislative assembly
MP	Member of Parliament
MSP	Member of the Scottish Parliament
NAAG	National Assembly Advisory Group
NESNO	'North East Says No' campaign
NHS	national health service
NICRA	Northern Ireland Civil Rights Association
NIUP	Northern Ireland Unionist party
NIWC	Northern Ireland Women's Coalition
NSMC	North-South Ministerial Council
ODPM	Office of the Deputy Prime Minister
OMOV	one man one vote
PC	Plaid Cymru
PPP	public-private partnership

PR	proportional representation
PUP	Progressive Unionist party
Quangos	quasi autonomous non governmental organizations
RC	regional council
RDA	regional development agency
RIC	Royal Irish Constabulary
RUC	Royal Ulster Constabulary
SDLP	Social Democratic and Labour party
SF	Sinn Fein
SNP	Scottish National party
STV	single transferable vote
UDA	Ulster Defence Association
UDF	Ulster Defence Force
UKIP	United Kingdom Independent party
UKUP	United Kingdom Unionist party
UUAP	United Unionist assembly party
UUC	Ulster Unionist Council
UUP	Ulster Unionist party
UVF	Ulster Volunteer Force
WDA	Welsh Development Agency
WLGA	Welsh Local Government Association

1

Introduction:
the wider meaning of devolution

For a biologist the term devolution would refer to the degeneration of a species and would be viewed as a mainly negative occurrence. For a British political scientist, however, the term devolution has become synonymous with the evolution rather than degeneration of the political system. On a European scale devolution of political power is the rule rather than the exception for those nation states of a comparable size to Great Britain. Over the last century political devolution or 'Home Rule' as it was also described has reached the top of the political agenda on three main occasions. In the period preceding and following World War I this was the case in respect of Ireland. Some fifty years later it remerged as an issue after the suspension of the Ulster parliament and devolution referendums of 1979 in Scotland and Wales. Finally at the end of the twentieth century, in 1999, it reached a more definite form with the arrival of forms of devolved government in all of the nation states of the Britain. The last period of devolution also represented one of the central planks of the New Labour government's first term's constitutional reforms.

The issue of devolved power is therefore at the very heart of a whole cluster of constitutional devices, each of which impinges upon and influences the others. At the heart of this tangled knot of political arrangements is the key concept of the nation state and the means by which the political, legislative and administrative integrity of that national polity might be assured against both internal and external threats. In order to understand devolution in this first chapter it is therefore necessary to examine closely the concept of national sovereignty and the related topics of nationhood, nationality and subsidiarity.

Sovereignty

The *Oxford English Dictionary* definition of the word sovereignty is 'supremacy or pre-eminence in respect of power, supreme domination, authority or rule' (1992). More precisely it is the legislative or judicial entity that has no superior body able to override legislative or judicial decisions made for the territory over which it is sovereign. Until recently in the United Kingdom the Westminster parliament was held to be sovereign because no other body had the right to pass and implement laws. So jealously did parliament guard the right to be the only legislative body that other governmental or quasi-governmental bodies which needed to pass laws, rules and regulations, such as local government authorities or transport authorities, could only do so through the device known as delegated legislation. Through delegated legislation, parliament grants to other bodies the facility to pass laws, but only laws specifically related to the jurisdiction of the authority concerned. In strict legal terms they are not laws, but by-laws. As the nineteenth-century constitutional writer, Professor A. V. Dicey, himself an ardent opponent of Irish Home Rule and dedicated upholder of the Union parliament, put it: 'The sovereignty of Parliament is the dominant characteristic of our political institutions ... [Parliament] has, under the English constitution, the right to make or unmake any law whatever, and, further, that no person or body is recognised by the law of England as having a right to override or set aside the legislation of Parliament' (cited in Adonis, 1993, p. 8). The sovereignty even stretches to the laws made by the European Union (EU): the Westminster parliament retains sovereignty over the determination of these laws but cedes its authority to determine these laws to the EU.

With a view to what we shall be discussing later, it is worth bearing in mind the way in which Dicey used the expressions '*English* constitution' and 'the law of *England*' in the passage quoted above. In 1885 Dicey was of course talking about the sovereignty of the United Kingdom parliament in Westminster but, by equating Britishness with Englishness, he manages to ignore the claims of Scotland, Wales and Ireland to a share of that sovereignty in what after all has been claimed to be a United Kingdom of nation states. Dicey was reflecting many of the commonly held views of the time which saw Scots, Welsh and Irish as component parts of an overriding English sovereignty. The debates on sharing sovereignty between the various nation states in the British Isles were to remain at the forefront of political thought for much of the later part of the nineteenth and the early part of the twentieth century. During this time and afterwards an argument put forward by unionists was that Britain can be regarded as a nation primarily based around the ability of the people living in Britain speak English (Budge *et al.*, 1998, p. 140). Issues concerning the existence of the Celtic languages were ignored. The shared issues of all of the nations being separated from the European mainland continent, interweaving populations, economic unity and single currency, joint monarchy and sharing ever-changing borders helped ensure further cohesion.

Defining sovereignty

For a word in regular use by politicians and political commentators, sovereignty is very difficult to define with any precision, simply because it can mean different things to different people at different times. And that imprecision over the meaning of the word implies that a skilled politician can make it mean whatever he or she wishes it to. However, according to elementary political theory the many and varied meanings of sovereignty can be summarised under just two headings, distinguished as:

- **Legal sovereignty**, which is usually vested in the legislature but which in federal states is usually said to rest in a sovereign constitution. British parliamentary sovereignty is typical of the former, while the governance of the United States is typical of the other.
- **Political sovereignty**, which is vested in a person or persons. At one time the monarch often in combination with the church and aristocracy were sovereign but with evolution of democracy has come the belief that sovereignty is vested in politicians only with the endorsement of the *demos* or people.

To some the more times that the electorate is directly asked to endorse a political decision the healthier the democracy. To this effect the outward manifestation of political sovereignty is that determined by the nation's constitution, which is often altered by the referendum. This is a Swiss invention of the nineteenth century, devised to match a provision of the Swiss constitution of 1874 which states that, if 30,000 citizens can be found to sign a petition against an act of the federal assembly, then that act must be voted on by the entire electorate. Following that early example many states now have provision for referendums written into their constitutions for when legislation threatens to alter it. Consider, for example, the six or more referendums held in Denmark over the years concerning Danish membership of the EU. Denmark is not alone, however, since of the fifteen EU member countries Austria, Denmark, Finland, France, the Republic of Ireland and Sweden all require referendums before changes are made to their constitutions. Referendums in Europe have not always been benign, however. The referendum or 'plebiscite' was the method used by Hitler to expand a Greater Germany prior to World War II. The Swiss themselves used it as a method of preventing women from either voting or taking part in Swiss government until 1974. It can be seen therefore as a method by which the majority can been seen to legitimately suppress a minority. Referendums can also be no more final in their endorsement that statutes. The federal Canadian government in Quebec has held numerous referendums on independence for the province, all unsuccessful. In Britain despite the Conservative party accepting the result on the 1997 referendum in Wales, endorsing a Welsh assembly, by 2005 it had become official Conservative policy to hold another referendum on whether it should be scrapped.

In Britain sovereignty is said to be vested in 'the crown in parliament' rather than a codified constitution. The term 'crown' no longer refers to the literal crown of the monarch but to the body which now exercises the royal prerogative on behalf of the monarch: in other words, 'the crown' equals 'the government'. It is only fair to say that what is called by ministers *parliamentary* sovereignty might be rather more accurately described as *executive* or *governmental* sovereignty. It has been claimed that this blurring of distinctions is the 'contradiction at the heart of the British Constitution: the principle of parliamentary sovereignty being used by executives to minimise their accountability' (Judge, 1993). The claim made by upholders of parliamentary sovereignty is that referendums are unnecessary, under the principle of representative democracy, 'since everyone has a representative in parliament and those representatives can be mandated on policy matters through election, there is no need to undermine the sovereignty of parliament by approaching the electorate direct' (Pilkington, 1997, p. 127).

Despite the general support for the principle of parliamentary sovereignty, the mainstream political parties in Britain have found that any large-scale political change which would prove to be politically divisive particularly in their own political party or in the popular press should be dealt with by a referendum. Therefore the Human Rights Act, which has profound constitutional implications over the way that British law is made and enforced, was not endorsed by a referendum. It was mainly non-controversial politically and therefore there was no real political pressure to have it endorsed. Devolution for Scotland, Wales and Northern Ireland was, however, politically sensitive. There was the possibility that a future Conservative government would abolish the devolved bodies in Scotland and Wales if they were not endorsed by referendum. It was thought that successful referendum would remove this prospect. Because Westminster maintains political sovereignty, however, it does not in reality prevent any referendum being overturned either by parliament or another referendum. In essence all political parties support referendums if they suit their own aims. Even the unionist politicians who see the influence of Brussels and Europe overriding British sovereignty at every turn support the notion of a referendum if can be seen to return some of that sovereignty to parliament.

Britain as a nation which has relied on international trade for its economic survival since the middle ages has long been aware of the limitations of the nation state to hold sovereignty over all aspects of socio-economic events that influence it. Trading depressions and world wars and the arrival of the EU have only confirmed the limitations of British sovereignty to influence matters which have a great impact upon it. As a partial compensation to this, successive governments weakened by the decline of empire and sterling have been unable effectively to exert their sovereignty over the global economy but have nevertheless sought to ensure that this centralised sovereignty would still remain pre-eminent within the United Kingdom.

For the United Kingdom today the concept of a nation state raised upon the solid foundation of parliamentary sovereignty appeals to some politicians in the Conservative party, Labour party and particularly the United Kingdom Independent party (UKIP), even though it is quite evident that it is squeezed between the conflicting demands made by the pooling of sovereignty represented by the EU and the sharing of power demanded by devolution to the nations and regions of the United Kingdom. Under attack from two different directions the very notion of sustaining a unitary nation state would seem to be in terminal decline. Yet for them the battle still remains to be lost.

The nation state

In medieval Europe, even in the British Isles, the concept of a politico-geographical entity composed of people with a common ethnicity, religion, language or culture was unknown. Everyone in positions of power paid lip-service to their version of Christendom, within which the dukes, princes, kings and emperors represented secular power and the Pope spiritual dominion. Within that dual hegemony, loyalties and allegiances were personal, made up of the reciprocal oaths, duties and obligations of the feudal system. When the nation state began to emerge, as early as the fourteenth century, it was largely due to a breakdown in feudal relationships through disputed allegiances.

The dispute between France and England over the overlordship of Aquitaine, known as the Hundred Years War, transformed a feudal quarrel between two kings into a bitter war between two countries, each of which developed a strong sense of national identity as a result. It also brought Welsh soldiers into active participation in an English–French war. All the early examples of nation states came about through war, revolution, or the expulsion of an alien power. For example, England, Scotland and France discovered their national identities by fighting one another in a series of wars spread over more than two hundred years, while Spain and Portugal emerged from the rise of those Christian kingdoms who took joint action to expel the Moors from the Iberian peninsula.

Yet, although a handful of nation states including both England and Scotland existed prior to the fifteenth century, the development of the nation state to the point at which it was perceived to be a part of the natural order of things is a fairly recent development. Essentially it can be claimed that contemporary nationalism as we understand it today was created by the French Revolution. In a post-Napoleonic Europe the oppressive Austro-Hungarian Empire or the crumbling Ottoman Empire led to the rise of liberal nationalism in the nineteenth century among their subject peoples in Italy and the Balkans, leading to outcomes such as the independence of Greece and the unification of Italy, in the creation of what Mazzini called 'a sovereign nation of free and equal beings'. Basic Liberal ideology in the nineteenth century naturally included a belief in national self-government and this implied support by the Liberal party for national independence movements abroad and Home Rule for Ireland and possibly Scotland and Wales in the notion of 'Home Rule all around' (cited in Coxall and Robins, 1995, p. 69).

The heyday of the European nation state based on linguistic and cultural identity, however, undoubtedly came after 1918 when the collapse of the Austro-Hungarian, German, Russian and Ottoman empires created a wealth of new nations in Central Europe and the Middle East. That was followed by the many newly independent states created by the period of decolonisation that followed World War II, with even more to come after the collapse of the Soviet bloc in 1989. As Peter Alter said in a survey of Europe taken at the time of Maastricht in 1993:

> Between 1870 and 1914 there were only about 50 sovereign states in the world, 16 of them in Europe. The figure barely fluctuated over the period. By the end of the First World War the community of nations had grown by 10 as new states emerged in Europe. When it was founded in 1920 the League of Nations had 42 members: its successor the United Nations, was established in 1945 with a membership of 51. By 1960 this figure had grown to 82; by 1973 it was 135 and in 1992 it stood at 183. (cited in Keegan and Kettle, 1993, p. 121)

It would be convenient if all those political entities we generically call countries, states or nations were homogeneous in having populations that are religiously, ethnically, linguistically or culturally united, within clearly defined geographical boundaries. Unfortunately, this is almost never the case since most countries, whether by conquest, amalgamation, annexation or mutual interest, are made up of divergent and sometimes conflicting groups: there are Catholics and Protestants in Ireland and Scotland; Serbs, Croats, Bosnian Muslims and Kosovan Albanians in the former Yugoslavia; Flemings and Walloons in Belgium; Jews and Palestinian Arabs in Israel; Kurds in Turkey or Iraq and so on. Virtually every state in the modern world has significant minorities within its borders that are so different ethnically, linguistically or culturally that they could well form separate national entities themselves.

Many of these so-called multinational or multicultural states have sections of the population, usually the majority sections, which regard themselves as the 'rightful' inhabitants of that country. These feelings can sometimes lead to the minority populations feeling repressed in their own cultural and ethnic expression. The lesser or minority groupings in this situation naturally resent being placed in an inferior position and this in turn leads to feelings of resentment and alienation on the part of the minority groups. And it is these feelings that have helped create those nationalist parties that take up the cause of separatism in an attempt to achieve autonomy, self-determination and freedom of domination by the 'superior' nation. Often these groups work to achieve their aims through political, democratic or parliamentary means but, in some instances, as with the Basque Euskadi Ta Askatasuna (ETA) separatists in Spain, Corsicans in France, the Kurds in Turkey or the Irish Republican Army (IRA) and Ulster Defence Force (UDF) in the UK, these nationalist groupings can employ violence to pursue their ends in the so-called 'military option': whereupon these nationalist activists become 'terrorists' to their enemies and 'freedom fighters' to their friends.

One of the criticisms levied against an upsurge in national self-determination is that it is like a set of Russian *Matrioshka* nesting dolls: when one is opened, another is revealed within. In this 'me too' syndrome minority groups seeking separation from the larger body may well achieve that separation only to discover that they too have minorities within themselves, also clamouring for separation. This was a problem that soon became apparent in the break up of the former Soviet Union. In the United Kingdom the same problem occurred in Ireland, where a section of the population sought independence from Britain, only to find when they achieved that independence that there was a Protestant minority in the north-east which wanted to preserve the union with Britain and who were willing to fight to maintain it. And then, when the Protestants were granted their own unionist state in Northern Ireland, they in turn discovered that a Catholic nationalist minority was unwilling to accept the authority of Stormont and they too were ready to take up arms against the majority (Budge *et al.*, 1998, p. 141).

One of the principal functions of a constitution is to counter such fragmentations by reconciling the different social, ethnic and political groupings living within the state or other sovereign body. There are largely two ways of creating a political union out of a regional cultural diversity, these two ways being known as unitary and federal systems.

Unitary systems

In a unitary system there is one sovereign authority with the ability to enact primary legislation, administer and adjudicate for the whole of the state or society. If power is devolved to the regional components of that society it is with the consent of the central authority, which supervises such devolution and can revoke it at a time of its own choosing. Various areas or districts of the country can pass and administer their own local laws but those secondary laws can only be passed because the national legislature has delegated that right to that devolved body.

Any move away from the power of the centre to determine laws has been resisted at the highest levels in both the past and the present. There are those former party leaders, like Baroness (Margaret) Thatcher, Lord (Neil) Kinnock, John Major, William Hague and Michael Howard who can be described as 'unionists' and who campaigned vigorously against what they saw as the 'break-up of the union' by these movements of nationalism or devolution and to whom any hint of federalism is an anathema. This pro-unionism political stance has deep roots. At the end of the nineteenth century the fervently unionist A. V. Dicey believed that 'the nations of Great Britain have historically expressed a desire for unity and a sense of common interest and national feeling' (Evans, 1999, p. 45). To unionist politicians like Dicey or Baroness Thatcher the United Kingdom was a good example of a successful unitary state, with one sovereign parliament controlling all aspects of the governance of

Great Britain and Northern Ireland. And it is a defining feature of a unitary system is that it should have one sovereign body made up of just one central executive, one legislature and one judiciary. Of course since the Acts of Union between England and Scotland in 1707 there had been different legal systems in both England and Wales to that in Scotland. There had also been a devolved parliament in Northern Ireland between 1922 and 1973 also with its own executive and judiciary. Wales and Scotland also had devolved executives covering a variety of areas. Yet the notion that the United Kingdom remained in essence a unitary state based around Whitehall and Westminster continued to be pre-eminent. To this effect in 1997, when framing the bill which would create a devolved parliament in Edinburgh, a clause was included which related to the importance of preventing the fragmentation of the civil service in Scotland by stating that, 'this ensures that all the staff of the Scottish Administration should be civil servants in the Home Civil Service. Maintaining a unified Home Civil Service is considered to be essential for the preservation of the Union.' The same White Paper, describing the nature of the Scottish parliament, stated quite clearly that 'the United Kingdom Parliament is and will remain sovereign in all matters' (White Paper, 1997). In the actual Scotland Act which followed, it was made clear that the Scottish parliament's legislative powers 'do not affect the power of the Parliament of the United Kingdom to make laws for Scotland' (Scotland Act, 1998). The same is also true of the Welsh assembly for which Westminster plays an even more dominant role (Government of Wales Act, 1998).

Federal systems

In a federal system the component provinces or regions within the national state each possess their own supreme authorities which have legislative and executive jurisdiction within their areas of competence; the central authority or federal government merely retaining the most important functions like economic planning and defence. To maintain relationships within the conflicting interests of federal component states means that a federal system must be regulated by a written constitution and controlled by a supreme court. It is these regulating bodies which decide the dividing lines between federal and subsidiary (state) authorities; which apportion responsibilities, and which determine the extent to which the component states of a federal body have the right to pass their own primary laws.

The problem for a federal government is where the component states are very different in geographical size, population, wealth and power. In such a situation the representatives of the smaller and less powerful states feel oppressed and overwhelmed by their colleagues from the larger and more powerful states, while the larger states in their turn feel frustrated and held back by having to consider their smaller colleagues. In the United States this anomalous situation was resolved by federalists like Alexander Hamilton who, when drawing up the constitution, created a congress in which members of the lower house, the House of Representatives, are elected to represent geographical constituencies of approximately equal population, while the upper house, the Senate, represents the interests of the states, with each and every state having two senators, regardless of size, the confederation thereby becoming a federation (Brogan, 1985). Other federal states have consequently developed their own mechanisms to cope with the potential imbalance between the weaker and more powerful states within their system of government.

The union state

The majority of modern states in the world operate a system of unitary government in which they vest sovereign power in a single institution (Heywood, 1997, p. 129). For much of its history Britain has been viewed a unitary state, but in fact strictly speaking it is neither unitary nor federal but rather what is known more simply as a union state:

- Like a unitary state it has a single sovereign parliament, although that parliament did not originate as a single body but grew from the merger of previously separate assemblies, as the English parliament united with the sovereign councils or parliaments of Wales (1536), Scotland (1707) and Ireland (1801). Compared with a federal structure, therefore, the component legislatures within a union state had combined their jurisdiction and sovereignty. Where some political power has been re-devolved across the United Kingdom it can be taken back again by Westminster when it sees fit. Such a move was made with the Stormont government in Northern Ireland in 1972 and the Northern Ireland assembly in May 2000 and October 2002. Therefore any devolved body in Britain can never be similar to the state government in a federal system. There is no constitutional protection over its sovereignty or its functions and it remains subordinate to the national parliament.
- Unlike the traditional unitary state, on the other hand, the component nations of the UK continue to possess pre-union identity, some rights and institutions peculiar to themselves, which maintain some degree of autonomy. This is even reflected in the constitutional terms given to the component parts of the union: England and Scotland being kingdoms, Wales a principality and Northern Ireland a province. The most obvious example of differing political institutions is the Scottish legal system, which is distinct from the English system in enacted law, judicial procedure and the structure of the courts. In Scotland and Northern Ireland the banks are able to issue their own bank notes. The education systems of the four nation states are also distinctly different. Even linguistically English is not the only official language in the system of government in the United Kingdom. Wales is a

bilingual nation with the Welsh language having had equal status with English in the courts since 1942, and within public institutions and local councils since 1967. Northern Ireland is the one part of the United Kingdom which up to now has regularly used proportional representation in elections and which has its own distinct civil service. And these three national entities within the UK have had their own government departments for some time in the Scottish, Welsh and Northern Ireland Offices, providing administrative devolution in a number of discrete areas. For these and other reasons, the UK cannot be regarded as ever having been a single monolithic structure of government.

It is interesting to compare the United Kingdom's status as a union state with two other European states that were created in the nineteenth century by a much more rapid process of unification: Germany and Italy. Germany grew out of the merger of the North German Confederation and the southern principalities like the Kingdom of Bavaria and, although the act of unification was the result of machinations by the Prussian chancellor, Otto von Bismarck, the German Empire proclaimed in 1871 was essentially an association of separate kingdoms which chose to recognise the king of Prussia as emperor. It therefore possessed a federal constitution from the start and the structure put in place at that time can still be recognised in the Federal Republic of Germany that we know today. Italy on the other hand was unified by the merger of various states with the Piedmont-centred Kingdom of Sardinia, under King Victor Emmanuel II. The other Italian states were either annexed and absorbed, as was Lombardy after the Austrians had been expelled by Franco-Sardinian forces; or they voted to join Piedmont in a plebiscite of the people, as was done by the Grand Duchy of Tuscany or the Kingdom of the Two Sicilies. Ultimately the united Kingdom of Italy was proclaimed in 1861, the parliament of the Kingdom of Sardinia became the parliament of the Kingdom of Italy and Turin, capital of Piedmont, became the capital of Italy. Italy therefore, like the United Kingdom, is a union state, created by merger and absorption (Taylor, 1954).

The German, Italian and British states have one thing in common: all three have formed a union of peoples in which one particular people is dominant. In Italy it was Piedmont, in Germany it was Prussia and in Britain it was England. One is reminded of the final slogan proposed by George Orwell in *Animal Farm*, 'All animals are equal but some are more equal than others.' (1945, p. 114). Alternatively it is possible to consider the position of the dominant states within the union state in the context of a term borrowed by Tom Nairn from the world of natural history and speak of the UK as 'consociational'; a term which means a community of animals living together in which one species is dominant (Nairn, 2000, p. 155). What this means in practice is that when a system of union government evolves it is not a marriage of equal partners.

Devolution or subsidiarity?

Devolution is defined as 'the process of transferring power from central government to a lower or regional level' (Robertson, 1986, p. 84; Heywood, 1997, p. 131). Bogdanor defined it more simply as 'the transfer of powers from a superior to an inferior political authority (Bogdanor, 1999, p. 2), Many others have defined devolution in a host of different ways, perhaps most accurately summed up by the Irish nationalist leader, John Redmond, who, in defining Home Rule in a speech of 1883, said: 'The idea at the bottom of this proposal is the desirability of finding some middle course between separation on the one hand and over-centralisation of government on the other' (quoted in Bogdanor, 1999, p. 20). The original concept of devolution was put forward by Edmund Burke at the end of the eighteenth century and formed part of his solution to the problems of the British government in dealing with the revolutionary American colonists and the Irish Catholics who were disenfranchised by the 1801 Act of Union. He based his ideas on the fact that the Westminster parliament had two functions – a legislature for the United Kingdom and an imperial parliament for all British territories. If these functions were separated so that the various British possessions such as America or Ireland had their own local legislatures while owing overall allegiance to the imperial parliament in London, then the circle could be squared (Bogdanor, 1999, p. 23).

In terms of national governments it can be seen as the process by which political power is transferred from the centre to local or regional bodies, which thereby carry out governmental functions while leaving sovereignty in the hands of central government. There are, however, three forms of devolution:

- **executive devolution**, which devolves the power to make decisions, and is typified by the Greater London Authority and the central work of the Welsh assembly;
- **legislative devolution**, which devolves the power to make laws, and is the form of devolution represented by the Scottish parliament;
- **administrative devolution**, which devolves the power to carry out specific functions, and which was practised by the Scottish, Welsh and Northern Ireland Offices, as well as the various English regional government offices.

Devolution has been supported as a concept because it allows the dispensation of governmental powers across a wider area than that of Whitehall and Westminster. During the 1997 and 1998 devolution referendums this concept of alienation from the British centre of power was at the heart of many of the 'yes' vote campaigns. It is an alienation that is particularly true of the national regions of Britain like Scotland, a separate country until 1707, and Wales, with its own language and culture: although it is a reaction not unknown in parts of England such as Cornwall or Tyneside who feel just as equally distant and alienated from a political culture based in the south-eastern corner of the island. Since alienation of this kind can be a powerful force in the generation of unrest it has been the practice of successive British governments to use devolution as 'a policy instrument ... to assimilate the demands of nationalist movements within the "nations" seeking greater autonomy' (Evans, 1999, p. 47). Vernon Bogdanor puts it rather differently, seeing devolution as being central government's way of avoiding trouble from militant separatists when pressure for regional autonomy becomes intolerable: 'If there are these powerful centrifugal forces at work in Britain today it might well be that the best way to strengthen national unity is to give way to them a little' (1999, p. 297).

A political concept often associated with devolution is subsidiarity which, as a term, has been in use for some time. However, it came to have a specific application in the negotiating sessions leading to the Treaty on European Union (TEU) (Maastricht) when a particular interpretation of subsidiarity was developed in order to counter British fears of what was seen as the pro-federalism of the Maastricht agreement. In Britain popular attitudes concerning federalism were shaped by Eurosceptics both in Conservative, Labour and UKIP parties and elements of printed press. They turned the concept of federalism on its head and instead equated it with 'centralism', giving rise to fears of a powerful 'federal administration' in Brussels imposing its will on the member states, with no regard being paid to the wishes of national parliaments. What was developed at Maastricht therefore was a form of subsidiarity, defined in the treaty as being when, 'decisions are taken as closely as possible to the citizen ... In areas which do not fall within its exclusive competence, the Community should take action, in accordance with the principle of subsidiarity, only in so far as the proposed action cannot sufficiently be achieved by the Member States and can therefore, by reason of the scale or effects of the proposed action, be better achieved by the Community' (TEU, Title II, article 3b, 1992).

Although the term 'subsidiarity' has largely been used in the context of politicians arguing about the relative sovereignty of national governments within the decision-making process of the European Union, hoping thereby to counter the overcentralisation of the EU in Brussels, it is a two-edged sword which can also be invoked when action by national governments may be considered as inappropriate when compared with regional or local action. During the 1997 referendum campaigns in Scotland and Wales the prospect of each nation having greater representation in Europe was a plus point for the 'yes' campaigns. The nationalists also interpreted the concept of subsidiarity with enthusiasm of a concept that would led to independence for their nation states. In the subsequent elections both Plaid Cymru and the Scottish National party used the slogans of 'Scotland in Europe' and 'Wales in Europe', meaning that, in matters of importance to Scotland and Wales, there need be no intervening English body between Brussels and future Scottish and Welsh parliaments. This has been particularly relevant in recent years as the Committee of the Regions (COR) has become a more important institution of the European Union, allowing the regions of EU member countries to have a say in the decision-making and legislative processes of the European communities.

There are, however, two forms of subsidiarity; divided between the 'bottom-up' and 'top-down' versions. Neunreither states that there is religious Calvinism, in which the thoughts of the individual or congregation are more important than the *diktats* of cardinals or bishops and where the individual can communicate directly with God without the use of a priestly intermediary (1993, p. 211). This is the 'bottom-up' version of subsidiarity in which 'a larger unit only assumes functions in so far as the smaller units of which it is composed are unable or less qualified to fulfil their role. Starting from the individual, civil associations, communes, regions to national states and beyond, each larger unit has only a subsidiary role' (Cooper, 1995, p. 179). It is this 'bottom-up' version of subsidiarity that provides the model for devolution from a central government to regional parliaments or assemblies.

Catering for regional autonomy

As has been said, there are two main solutions to the problem of unifying a multinational state under one government and they are broadly defined as the alternatives of either a federal or a unitary constitution. The unitary states are further subdivided according to the degree of devolved autonomy they give their regional components and there is also the additional complication of the union state which accepts diversity of administrative or judicial practices within a unitary system and which usually possesses a degree of administrative devolution for its component parts. In Europe the need for some means of reinforcing unity has been made more urgent by an awareness of what happened to the federal state of Yugoslavia once the influence of President Tito and the Communist party was removed. The complete fragmentation, inter-state warfare and ethnic cleansing which followed set a dreadful example to any government that had minority populations within its borders, particularly when those minorities were asking for some form of autonomy if not outright separatism.

Even in European states that have been democracies for over a hundred years federalism can lead to fragmentation and division of power. Most divisions within so-called nation states are created by either conflict over religion or disputes hinging on language and it was the inherent conflict between linguistic communities that created the federal state of Belgium in 1981. The division of Belgium into the linguistically based provinces of Flanders and Wallonia gave rise to three regional community assemblies each with its own executive council. The Flemish community assembly is responsible for Flanders and the Flemish-speaking population of Brussels, the Walloon regional assembly is responsible for the French-speaking provinces of south-eastern Belgium, while the French community assembly is responsible for the French-speaking population of Brussels and certain matters in Wallonia. Apart from these three there is a German-speaking community assembly based at Eupen, granted autonomy in 1984, and a Brussels regional council with a five-member executive that was created in 1989. The linguistic differences are so great in Belgium that even the political parties are divided into separate Flemish and Walloon organisations so that there is, for example, a division of the Greens into *Ecolo* (the Francophone Ecology party) and *Agalev* (the Flemish Environmental party). In Britain linguistic communities are not an issue of division even in Wales where around a quarter of the population speak the native language of Welsh as well as English. Despite the fact that the main Welsh-speaking areas tend to return Plaid Cymru politicians to Westminster and the Welsh assembly there has never been a demand that these areas cede from the areas of mainly English-speaking Wales and form their own state.

Two countries in Europe may provide a more useful model to Britain of a union state devolving power. They have reformed their constitutions to permit a considerable amount of devolution to their constituent regions and can therefore provide a useful model for any devolution proposed for the United Kingdom since they, like Britain, are also union states and wish to satisfy the demands for self-determination of minority nationalities within their borders before those demands become separatist in nature. Furthermore the two countries in question both apply a system of asymmetrical devolution, in that different regions get different levels of devolved powers and have a differentiated representation in the national parliament, which is explored in more detail in the final chapter. These arrangements might well provide useful guidance for the different versions of devolved government suggested for Scotland, Wales and Northern Ireland as well as providing a possible solution for the so-called West Lothian question. The two countries are Italy and Spain.

In 1970 Italy was divided into fifteen regions with extensive powers of local government but devolution to certain regions has a much longer history. Italy rejected its monarchy in 1946 and a new republican constitution was drawn up, coming into force in 1948. That constitution allowed for the existence of five autonomous regions, each with its own assembly and having primary legislative powers in economic, social and cultural matters. When a new constitution was drawn up for Spain in 1978, after the death of Franco, the country was divided into seventeen autonomous communities, each with its own parliament and government. Seven of these regions – Andalusia, the Canaries, Catalonia, Euskadi (Basque country), Galicia, Navarre and Valencia – have additional powers over health, education and policing. There are several parallels between the situation in Spain and that in the United Kingdom which have a specific relevance for any discussions of devolution in Britain. There are areas that have their own language such as Catalonia, Galicia and the Basque country. And in the Basque country Spain has a province similar to Northern Ireland where a separatist movement has proved ready to use violence and extremist measures in their struggle for full independence. It was very noticeable that, ever since the 1970s, when the British political establishment first acknowledged the possibility of introducing devolution at some future date, the position of Catalonia within Spain became the template for any British proposal for Scottish or Welsh devolution. Spain in general and Catalonia in particular became the chosen destination for a whole series of British parliamentary delegations investigating the possibility of devolution. Tom Nairn wrote about the way in which the experience of Catalonia was a sound indication of the future prospects for a Scottish parliament and something that was also aspired to as a model for Wales (cited in Osmond, 1995, p. 132). In Scotland there was even Catalonian endorsement when 'President Pujol came to Scotland to rub the point in, and shortly thereafter Donald Dewar went out to Barcelona to confirm it. The official message is that there is no reason why the Scots should not follow the Catalan example, as a non-state autonomous region' (Nairn, 2000, p. 291).

Conclusion

The main thrust of the argument in this chapter is that devolution of political power is not by any means a uniquely British phenomenon. Across Europe over the last century all of the nation states with large populations have introduced some forms of devolution. In some instances such as in Belgium, France and Spain devolution has been used in part to evade any threat to its integrity that might be posed by nationalism and separatism; particularly the sort of separatism that is backed by violent action. In other cases such as Germany and Italy federalism or devolution has recognised that these nations are in fact a union of smaller states and that to counteract centralised power some autonomy should return to them. Thus by the time the New Labour government was elected in 1997 Britain had become the only large nation state in Europe that still had its legislative and executive power concentrated in just one parliament. Europe had changed and as the research fellow for the Institute for Public Policy Research (IPPR) Stephen Tindale noted of change in Europe: 'Where there is a strong public demand for Home Rule, and as long as granting it would not conflict with any fundamental human rights, there is a strong case for granting the wishes of the majority' (1996, p. 1).

Three years after Tindale wrote about that the demand for devolution it was tested throughout Britain and was found to be there in sufficient strength to start Britain on a course of what was believed at the time to fundamental constitutional change. When devolution arrived on the policy agenda it was not viewed as yet another political process but instead a major and fundamental shift in the political structure of the British state and the engine by which the uncodified constitution and system of government evolved to match that of the other large European nations. The extent to which this has occurred in practice, and the process and events that led to this state of affairs, will be examined in the following chapters of this book.

2

The making of the United Kingdom

'Happy is a country which has no history' goes a nineteenth-century proverb. In respect of present-day devolution, history, stretching back in some cases millennia, can go a long way in explaining the nature of the current institutions we have. This chapter is therefore needed in order to explain how a nation's history shapes and moulds its current political outlook. It starts two millennia ago.

Before the Romans arrived in Britain there were no nation states or countries as such, merely a collection of warring Celtic tribes. Britain therefore first became a united political entity under the Roman Empire, but Roman Britain never included Ireland, never extended further into Scotland than a line from the Clyde to the Forth, and included no more than one tribal territory in southeast Wales. When the Romans left Britain in AD 410, the abandoned Romano-Britons were left to face Germanic invaders who infiltrated the river valleys of southern and eastern England in a westward expansion that the British were unable to resist, given the inability of Celtic peoples to organise their own defence. Writing about the British in his *Life of Agricola*, Tacitus said that 'nothing has helped us more in war with their strongest nations than their inability to co-operate. It is but seldom that two or three states unite to repel a common danger' (Mattingley, 1948, p. 62).

England

Those Germanic invaders are commonly known as Anglo-Saxons, after the Angles, Saxons and Jutes who inhabited the North Sea coast of Europe between Flanders and Jutland. An interesting insight into the nature of these people is provided by the names by which they are known. In speaking of themselves, they nearly always used the word *Angli* – English – but to their enemies they were Saxons. Even today the Gaelic word for English speakers is *Sassenach*, while the Welsh call them *Saesneg*, both words meaning Saxon.

The English formed themselves into small political units based on the ships in which they came to England. The captains of those ships, having become local chieftains, gave their allegiance to powerful warlords or kings. By the year 600, England had become a patchwork of kingdoms, most prominently Northumbria, Wessex, Mercia, East Anglia, Kent, Sussex and Essex. These seven are customarily known as the Heptarchy.[1] Some 1,400 years later all of these names still exist either in county or regional names.

Of these kingdoms it was Northumbria which began a century of dominance between 600 and 615, when Æthelfrith extended his rule north into the Lothians, and attacked the British in Chester to the west. This latter action drove a wedge between the Celtic peoples of Wales and their cousins elsewhere, helping to create Wales as a separate entity and completing the work begun by the battle of Dyrham near Bath in 577, by means of which west Saxon expansion had cut land communications between Wales and the Celts of Devon and Cornwall.

In 736, the Mercian king Æthelbald was the first to style himself *Rex Britanniae* – King of the British. Murdered in 757 he was succeeded by Offa, who maintained Mercian dominance for almost half a century, annexing the kingdoms of Kent, Sussex and Wessex and acquiring London and Middlesex from Essex, and completing the making of his kingdom with the addition of East Anglia in 794. Offa styled himself both *Rex Anglorum* (King of the English) and *Rex totius Anglorum patriae* (King of all the English lands). Offa's important contribution was the construction of Offa's Dyke to separate Mercia from Powys. This long earthwork, running from near Wrexham to a point on the Wye near Chepstow became accepted as dividing England from Wales.[2]

After 825 England was divided into the four kingdoms of Northumbria, Mercia, Wessex and East Anglia, but only Wessex remained English after the Danes, or Vikings, had established a permanent army on English soil in 865. However, Alfred, who succeeded to the throne of Wessex in 871, forced the Danes back into what became known as the Danelaw, behind a line drawn from London to Chester. In 911 Alfred's son Edward the Elder gained control of Mercia and went on to occupy all Anglo-Danish lands south of the Humber, at the same time receiving homage from Hywel Dda (Howell the Good), prince of western Wales. In the north the Danes of Northumbria were replaced by Norse-Irish from Dublin who set up the Kingdom of York in 919. In a northern campaign Edward enforced submission on the King of Scots, the King of York, the King of Strathclyde and the Northumbrian lordship of Bamburgh.

Athelstan succeeded Edward and, in 927, received the homage of Scotland, Strathclyde and Bamburgh as well as occupying York. He also dealt with his western borders, receiving homage from Hywel Dda and other Welsh princes, fixing the border with Wales on the Wye and the border with Cornwall on the Tamar. Ten years later, in 937, Athelstan and his brother Edmund defeated an allied army of Irish-Norse, Scots and Strathclyde British, setting the seal on the unity of the kingdom. There is no accepted date for the unification of England but there is a good case for regarding 973 as significant. In that year Edmund's son Edgar became the first English king to open his reign with a coronation. Crowned at Bath in 973, he then went by sea to Chester and received the submission of several British princes.[3]

After Edgar the English state remained virtually unchanged, despite an interlude under Danish kings. The most significant change of direction came with the conquest of England by Duke William of Normandy in 1066. It was a unified England that William conquered and, although the Normans contributed a sense of organisation and administration to consolidate English unity, it was a unification already completed. From 1066 onwards the main aim of the English state became the gradual absorption of Wales, Scotland and Ireland.

The unification of England is not just about geography but concerns the union of peoples. First and foremost among those peoples are the so-called Anglo-Saxons who first assumed the name of *Angli*, living in *Angle-land*. However, the English by no means replaced the indigenous Celts. Dismissed slightingly as *weallas* ('Welsh' – meaning 'foreigners'), there was a large-scale Celtic survival in England, as witness the number of Waltons (meaning 'Welshtown') to be found in almost every English county and the frequency with which rivers, hills and other features of the landscape are given Celtic names. Perhaps the most notable examples of this Celtic presence today remains in Cornwall with the words 'Porth' (port), Tre(f) (town) and 'Pen' (head or mouth) appearing in many place names, just as they do in Wales. The Cornish language is also similar to Welsh, albeit with a differing alphabet and spelling of many common words.

The rulers and political institutions were English but most of the ordinary people were of Celtic descent. As the various kingdoms converted to Christianity they found a common bond to unite them against the pagan Vikings. In time, however, even the Vikings became Christian. These Norse and Danish incomers after 800 had no difficulty in integrating with the English, their origins, religion and languages being sufficiently close as to make them almost indistinguishable. In certain parts of the country the use of Scandinavian personal and place names persisted for some centuries, while differences in language created a difference in dialects and accents between the Anglo-Danish north and Anglo-Saxon south which continues to this day. The Norman-French, who followed Duke William in 1066, and further French immigrations under Henry II and Henry III, played an important part in the development of language and administration for the ruling classes but the ordinary people were hardly affected. The Normans came as conquerors, securing lordships for themselves but outnumbered by the people they had conquered: a Norman-French élite ruled, but most people were a mixture of English, Dane and Celt.

The creation of the English state, as we have seen therefore, was the product of conquest and coercion, imposing the rule of one part of the population over the rest, and the actual unity of England was originally secured by the forceful expansion of Wessex. The rule of the king was enforced across England and parts of Wales by the royal 'franchise' of various barons and Lords acting on behalf of the king in virtually any manner they saw fit. They in turn helped promote and foster county and regional identities that persist into the modern day. As the power base of the kings and queens eventually settled in London a greater sense of Englishness began to be associated with the royal court. This meant that later on one of the factors influencing calls for devolution in our own time has been the fact that Englishness has often been associated with arrogance and feelings of superiority, not only of the English over the Scots, Welsh and Irish, but also of the southern English of the Wessex homeland over the northern and western English of the Danelaw. The frequent battles between the English and their Celtic neighbours caused long-lasting resentment across the British Isles. In 1442 a monk of Dunfermline wrote that the military campaigns of the English: 'against the Scots, the Welsh, the French and the Irish proved they were the cruellest nation in the world' (cited in Davies, 1994, p. 201). This military superiority later became a notion of racial superiority, and this nineteenth-century view of Englishness has being defined by the Welsh historian, John Davies, as being the fact that: 'The central myth of British imperialism was the racial superiority of the English. The characteristics of the English were their emotional stability, their political maturity, their courage and their enlightened judgment, characteristics not shared by the Celts ...' (1994, p. 66). Later on in the twentieth century the prejudices that had developed in the nineteenth century and before concerning the superiority of one 'racial group' over others, whether explicit or implicit, were to restrict moves to gain political devolution again and again.

Wales – Cymru

The Welsh people never achieved an early union in the same sense as the English. The propensity of the Celts for arguing among themselves, already noted by Tacitus, allied to the mountainous terrain in the interior of Wales, poor transport communications and the constant integration of Norman and then English lords with Welsh nobility, meant that the territory they called 'Cymru' was geographically and politically fragmented throughout the Middle Ages. From time to time Welsh princes such as Hywel Dda or Llywelyn ap Gruffydd succeeded in uniting the Welsh principalities, only to have the unity fall apart on the prince's death. Unlike England, Wales had no memory of political union in the Roman period. Romans occupied Wales militarily but the only civil settlement was in the south-east, where the Emperor Hadrian decided that the Silures deserved self-government and a new tribal capital was built and named Venta Silurum (now Caerwent), which gave its name in turn to the post-Roman kingdom of Gwent.

Wales only developed separate politico-geographical areas after the English reached the west coast; the men of Wessex reaching the Severn estuary in 577 and the Northumbrians gaining the Irish Sea in 603. After that time the British inhabitants of Wales were isolated and forced to develop separate political and cultural institutions. Within the confines of modern Wales a number of kingdoms developed, with names that were to return in the local government reforms of 1974 and 1995: names like Ceredigion, Gwynedd, Powys and Ynys Môn (Anglesey).

In the immediate post-Roman period a prince named Cunedda was uprooted from the area around Edinburgh and resettled in Caernarfon for defensive reasons, thereby founding the Kingdom of Gwynedd. In the south-west the Kingdom of Dyfed was founded by Irish immigrants, becoming important in the early Middle Ages as the home of the Welsh Church, founded by St David. To the north of Dyfed and separating it from Gwynedd was Seisyllwg, a kingdom formed by the merger of Ceredigion (Cardigan) and Ystrad Tywi (Carmarthen). For much of the first millennium the Brythonic people's of Wales mixed freely with those of Brittany, Cornwall, Devon, Somerset and Strathclyde. Over time the English kingdoms took over Cornwall, Devon and Somerset.

Much of boundary between Wales and England was formalised when the Kingdom of Mercia under King Æthelbald built Wat's Dyke in the North of Wales (around AD 750). This was consolidated by his successor King Offa (AD 757–96). His dyke went from Irish Sea to the Bristol Channel and was twelve kilometres longer than Hadrian's Wall (Davies, 1994, p. 65). Although both dykes often contradicted each other and the Welsh later repossessed large areas beyond them, they represented the first attempt to divide the 'Celtic Welsh' from the 'Saxon English'. Perhaps most importantly for the future of Welsh nation the Brythonic language became the forerunner of Welsh and many of the words developed during this period later became common to the Breton, Cornish and Welsh languages. It was through their own languages that the people of these Celtic nations would later be able most effectively to distinguish themselves from their dominant linguistic English or French neighbours.

After 920, Hywel Dda united Seisyllwg, Dyfed and Brecon to form Deheubarth. Acquiring Gwynedd and Powys Hywel Dda can claim to be the first ruler of a united Wales, albeit excluding Glamorgan and Gwent. In the face of Viking threats he did homage for his lands to claim the protection of the Anglo Saxon rulers Edward the Elder (918) and Athelstan (927). This act ensured that England would later claim such support as proof of its sovereignty over Wales. Hywel was much influenced by English practices; minting silver pennies after the English model and codifying Welsh law. The laws of Hywel Dda remained valid in Welsh courts until 1536.

After the time of Hywel Dda there were essentially four kingdoms in Wales: Gwynedd, Deheubarth, Morgannwg and Powys.[4] Powys was the weakest of the four since it occupied the area between Dee and Severn later known as the Welsh Marches and, unlike Gwynedd or Dyfed, constantly confronted the English through a land border which covered most of the eastern side of Wales.

The Norman conquest marked the beginning of the end for Welsh independence. First the lowland areas were taken. In order to defend his borders William I established the first Marcher lordships in 1067, his most effective followers receiving the lordships of Hereford, Chester and Shrewsbury. Other gifts followed until a line of Anglo-Norman lordships stretched the length of Offa's Dyke, from Denbigh to Chepstow. In 1070 the Marcher lords merged the Kingdom of Gwent with the Lordship of Newport to form Monmouthshire while, in 1090, Robert Fitzhamon moved from Gloucestershire to form the Lordship of Glamorgan in southern Morgannwg, building a castle in Cardiff, and gaining palatine powers. Most prominent of the early Marcher lords was Arnulf of Montgomery who went on to establish the Lordship of Pembroke in the south-west. The Anglo-Norman occupation of southern Pembrokeshire replaced the native Welsh so completely that the area is still known as 'Little England beyond Wales'! As late as the 1930s, 80 per cent of northern Pembrokeshire were Welsh speakers whilst the figure in the south was around 10 per cent (Awbery, 1986, p. 4).

The Marcher lordships were free of royal authority and able to make and administer their own laws. In many cases, former Welsh principalities divided their allegiance between the Marcher lords on the coast and native Welsh princes in the hills. Two systems of law, known as the Englishry and the Welshry, co-existed and reflected the lowland-upland division. The advance of the Normans also ended the independence of the Welsh Church; it now came under the dominance of Canterbury. The expansion of the Marcher lords ended in 1169 when the Anglo-Normans of Pembroke became involved in Ireland, but even before that the Welsh kingdoms of Gwynedd, Powys and Deheubarth had consolidated themselves to resist the Anglo-Normans. The final century of independence within Wales belongs to the supremacy of Gwynedd, under the rule of three men.

Owain Gwynedd became king in 1137 and, during the anarchy created by the struggle for the English throne between Stephen and Matilda, extended his borders to Cardigan in the south and Flint in the east. In 1157 he paid homage to Henry II and survived unchallenged. His grandson, Llywelyn ab Iorwerth (Llywelyn Mawr), succeeded in 1203 and was recognised by King John. Shortly thereafter he argued with John and went on to profit from civil war in England, siding with the rebel barons and earning a number of concessions in the Magna Carta plus acquiring the counties Cardigan, Carmarthen and Powys.

Llywelyn ap Gruffydd, grandson of Llywelyn Mawr, was recognised as prince of Wales by the Welsh lords after he restored their land. Perhaps as importantly he was recognised by the English crown as the first and last native prince of Wales. Like his grandfather he exploited the troubles of the English king, Henry III, by joining the rebel barons under Simon de Montfort. After the death of

Henry III, Llywelyn was accused by Edward I of failing to pay due homage to him not just once but on five opportunities and, in 1276–77, was faced by a massive English invasion. Edward was determined to make an end of an independent Wales and, under the terms of the Statute of Rhuddlan in 1284, a principality of Wales under English rule was established. Edward I's son, the future Edward II, was then proclaimed the first English prince of Wales. The largest military fortification programme of medieval Europe enforced the peace. As a result nearly eight centuries later the Wales Tourist Board could still promote Wales as a 'nation of castles', most dating back to this fortification programme by Edward I. Unable to resist this English military dominance Gwynedd, as it had existed under Llywelyn, was divided into the shire counties of Anglesey, Caernarvon and Merioneth, with Deheubarth becoming the counties of Cardigan and Carmarthen. The counties were now shires in the English sense with each having a sheriff and coroner to represent royal authority. Criminal law was English law but civil cases remained Welsh under the laws of Hywel Dda. From 1301 the heir to the throne became known officially as the Prince of Wales and had a council to advice them on the administration and governance of Wales. Few of these were princes were really Welsh and therefore the governance of Wales was left to officials and nobles within Wales. Their interest in Wales was normally limited to their title and the occasional visit to the principality. From 1301 to the present day no Prince or Princess of Wales has ever had an official residence in Wales.

Wales in the fourteenth century was now divided. The shires of the north and west together with Flintshire were crown lands held by the king and dispensing his justice. The east and south was given over to a patchwork of Marcher lordships, independent of the crown and each other. Ironically it was the half of Wales directly ruled by England that remained most Welsh, while the Marches had an increasingly English character. Seven hundred years later it is interesting to consider the devolution referendum of 1997 when, apart from West Glamorgan and Mid Glamorgan, the former Marcher lordships all voted 'no', while the old crown lands of Gwynedd and Deheubarth voted 'yes'.

The first real bid for Welsh independence or devolution came after a century. There was resentment because English merchants in Welsh towns had commercial privileges denied the Welsh, while Welshmen were said to be excluded from office in church and state. At the same time the lower clergy had become embittered by their lack of opportunity and the pretensions of their superiors (Davies, 1994, p. 196). The dethroning of Richard III and his replacement by Henry IV consolidated this general feeling of unrest as the Welsh nobility no longer felt bound to the English throne. These resentments motivated the actions of Owain Glyn Dwr who was crowned Prince of Wales in the presence of envoys from Acstile, France and Scotland early in the reign of Henry IV. Glyn Dwr's actions helped consolidate an uprising that gathered momentum across Wales. He did not fight alone and made an alliance with English rebels like Hotspur, made famous in Shakespeare's *Henry IV Part I*.

At the same assembly in Machynlleth in which he was crowned, Glyn Dwr demanded an independent principality, a Welsh Church independent of Canterbury, a university and a civil service. Despite some support from France he was defeated at Shrewsbury and fled to the Welsh mountains after Harlech Castle had surrendered in 1409 and his court, wife and children were taken prisoner. Glyn Dwr was not heard of after 1413. He had been defeated in part by the man who some describe as the first 'Welsh' King of England, Henry of Monmouth (Henry V). Henry had been born in Monmouth in 1387 and later became a military genius who used the Welsh archers of Llantrisant to much effect at the battle of Agincourt. But Henry of Monmouth saw himself as no Welshman. He merely saw Wales as a useful source of experienced soldiers for his military campaigns. As proof of his contempt for the Welsh for the next half century the Welsh nation suffered harsh penal laws which restricted any Welshman from public office. The only way around these laws was to petition parliament to become an Englishman. Many nobles did this and from then onwards for the next five hundred years most prominent Welshmen saw that for advancement they must be closely associated with the English (British) state.

Glyn Dwr's rebellion also called into question the autonomy of the Welsh Marches and the Marcher lords. Edward IV countered the independence of the Marches by calling a council for Wales in the Marches, a body that was recalled by Henry VII and later still by Thomas Cromwell during the reign of Henry VIII. It was a wish on the part of Cromwell to cut back the separate jurisdictions of the Marches rather than any desire to curb the independence of the Welsh which motivated the so-called Act of Union. At the time it was not called an Act of Union since it was held that the act merely confirmed an existing state of affairs that had existed ever since Hywel Dda and other Welsh princes had done homage for their lands to the King of England. Wales was said to be 'a very member and joint of the English realm, as it rightfully is and ever hath been' (quoted in Bogdanor, 1999, p. 6). There were two acts: the first, setting out the principles of union, was agreed in 1536, while the administrative details of union were laid out in the second, in 1543. The delay between the two acts enabled Welsh MPs, elected as a result of the former, to be present in the House of Commons to debate the passage of the latter. The main provisions of the acts of 1536 and 1543 were:

- the Marches were abolished and replaced by the shire counties of Monmouth, Brecon, Radnor, Denbigh and Montgomery, together with the palatine counties of Pembroke and Glamorgan;
- English law replaced Welsh law, although it was administered in separate Welsh courts with Welsh justices – a system that lasted until 1830;
- each Welsh county elected one MP (Monmouth had two) and each county town (except Harlech) chose a burgess as MP;

- four judges' circuits were set up, although there was doubt as to whether Monmouth was Welsh or English and that county was attached to the Oxford circuit;
- English administrative practices, including the appointment of justices of the peace, were introduced throughout Wales;
- English became the only recognised language of administration and the law.

The union was accepted by the Welsh without difficulty mainly because it put them on the same legal status as the king's subjects in England with the exception of the Welsh language. The status of the monarchy in Wales also changed. The Prince of Wales no longer ruled (Wales) and required no council to formulate policy. Instead this now came directly from the king. All that remained was his title and his lands, which he owned as a private landlord. The prince's former subjects now became tenants (Deacon and Belzak, 2000, p. 9).' The new kings of England and Wales still called their male heir the Prince of Wales and on occasions, such as with Elizabeth I, even their female heir the Princess of Wales. Wales as a nation, however, was deemed to be so much part of England that between 1746 and 1967 the word England in an Act of Parliament was deemed to include Wales and the Encyclopaedia Britannica in its nineteenth-century editions under the entry for Wales merely stated 'For Wales see England' (Deacon and Belzak, 2000, p. 13).

The English-Welsh union became a model for the expansion of the English state throughout the British Isles and beyond. In 1775 Edmund Burke even used the union with Wales as a good example of how the British government should treat the American colonists, via a process of assimilation. When Wales became so enamoured of its own nationalism in the nineteenth and twentieth century, that nationalism was not so much concerned with political independence as with a desire to reassert a distinctive culture, religious freedom and way of life based on the Welsh language. The Welsh nationalist movement, however, did not forget that in the deep mists of history Wales had once, albeit briefly, been free from the English crown. The historical legacy therefore ensured that although the seeds of national consciousness remained dormant for centuries they would grow again and push for political devolution.

Scotland

Scotland is as much a mixture of peoples as England and just as fragmented politically as Wales, making the union of peoples extremely complex. And, as was the case with Wales, the process of unification with England carried with it the seeds of future disunity. In the aftermath of the Roman occupation the peoples of Scotland could be divided into the pre-Celtic Picts north of the Antonine Wall and the Brythonic Celts between there and Hadrian's Wall. Very little is known about the Picts other than that their name, which was given to them by the Romans, simply means 'painted people'. From the sixth century on they shared the lands north of the Forth with groups of Goidelic Celts known as Scots, who came from Ireland.[5] The Scots settled in Kintyre, Lorne, Argyll and the Western Isles, naming their new homeland Dalriada after the lands in Ulster from whence they had emigrated.

South of the Antonine Wall the north British tribes formed two loose confederations. To the west was Strathclyde, extending from the Clyde to the Mersey, while in the east was Manaw Gododdin, named for the Votadini tribe. These lands as far north as the Forth were infiltrated by Northumbria after 500 AD, putting the Lothians under English control. For nearly 200 years the four peoples – Picts, Scots, Britons and English – coexisted in Scotland, fighting endless wars with each other, and often tied up flimsy temporary alliances.

A fifth people came to Scotland in the ninth century when Norsemen occupied Orkney, Sutherland, the Hebrides and Galloway and attempted to take Moray. In 839, they killed a leader of the Scots, Alpin of Gabhran, at the same time wiping out the Pictish army together with their king. The son of Alpin, Kenneth MacAlpin, used his mother's Pictish ancestry to claim the throne of Pictland and was named High King over all of northern Scotland. Originally the unified kingdom was called Alba, but its ruler was known as the King of Scots. This unified kingdom had dealing with many other nations and even today the Welsh for Scotland is Yr Alban, bearing direct reference to this unified kingdom.

Between 921 and 973, a King of Scots accepted English overlordship at least three times. On the most famous of these occasions Kenneth II did homage to Edgar at Chester. In return Kenneth received the Lothians and was granted suzerainty over Strathclyde, a Brytonic stronghold. In 1040 King Duncan, a descendent of MacAlpin, was beaten in battle by Macbeth, the ruler of Moray, but in 1057 Duncan's son, Malcolm, returned to avenge his father's death, taking the throne as Malcolm III.[6] Malcolm was little more than a barbarian chieftain but during his seventeen years' exile he had married an English princess, Margaret, as his second wife. A very pious woman, recognised in Scotland as a saint, Margaret initiated many changes, overthrowing the independent Celtic Church and subordinating it to Rome. She was also the first to invite Norman knights and churchmen to journey north and become the sixth of Scotland's peoples.

The sons of Malcolm and Margaret were more English than Scots. The court moved from Dunfermline to Edinburgh, the English dialect known as Scots replaced Gaelic as the language spoken at court and the legacy of the sons of Canmore caused southern Scotland to turn its back on its Gaelic-Pictish heritage, forming a nation sharing much of its culture with its southern neighbour. The greatest of Malcolm Canmore's sons, David I, personally invited large numbers of Normans to accept major land holdings in Scotland, resulting in a Scottish nobility more than half made up of Norman families such as Sinclair, Bruce, Seton or Balliol.

Despite a crushing defeat at the Battle of the Standard in 1138, David I received Cumbria and Northumbria from King Stephen during the English anarchy. However, David's grandson, Malcolm IV, known as 'the Maiden' because of a long-standing belief that his life had been strictly chaste, surrendered the two counties to Henry II in return for the Earldom of Huntingdon. This became the cause of many of Scotland's ills since, when the Scottish king was obliged to do homage to the English king, it was never clear as to whether that homage was in respect of Huntingdon or of Scotland.

In 1266 Alexander III defeated Haakon of Norway at Largs and the Treaty of Perth which followed ensured the unification of Scotland by ceding Man and the Western Isles to the King of Scots. In 1286, after the premature accidental death of Alexander III and the subsequent death of his six-year-old granddaughter, the Maid of Norway, the future of the kingdom fell into the hands of Edward I of England who was named Lord Paramount of Scotland in order to arbitrate between rival claimants to the throne.

Edward, who as we saw earlier had crushed the last independent prince of Wales, now felt obliged to consolidate English control of Scotland. He nominated John Balliol as king but repeatedly humbled him by treating him as a vassal. When Balliol rebelled, Edward invaded Scotland and subjugated the kingdom; an act symbolised by removing from Scone the Stone of Destiny, on which Scotland's kings had been crowned since the days of the Picts.

Reaction to Edward's occupation of Scotland most famously came with the action of William Wallace, a Strathclyde Celt who killed the Sheriff of Clydesdale, William Hazelrig, and then took arms in support of a rebellion led by Bishop Wishart of Glasgow and James FitzAlan, the steward. For a time Wallace was successful against the English but his followers were finally beaten by the long-bow wielded so effectively by his newly acquired Welsh subjects and Wallace, captured after a period on the run, was hanged, drawn and quartered by Edward, a punishment for treason which implied that Wallace was not a patriot but a rebellious subject of the English king.

Wallace was a man of the people but he was not part of the establishment. The real contenders were the Anglo-Norman families who formed the aristocracy of both England and Scotland. John Prebble has described the conflict between Robert Bruce and Edward Plantagenet as 'a civil war within the Anglo-Norman state' (Prebble, 1971, p. 57). Bruce's success did no more than ensure that Scotland was ruled by Scots-Normans rather than Anglo-Normans.

In the two centuries that followed Bruce's victory at Bannockburn, Scotland developed as a nation and the royal administration ran ever more smoothly under the system of sheriffdoms that were introduced throughout the lowland east and south. It was largely a time of peace. This was because England was preoccupied first with the Hundred Years War with France and then with the Wars of the Roses. It therefore had no time for 'the problems of conquering and then controlling, from London, a country whose farther reaches were geographically both remote and difficult' (Falkus and Gillingham, 1981, p. 90).

Scotland finally joined England, not by conquest but through dynastic marriages, the two crowns merging on the death of the heirless Elizabeth I in the person of Stuart James VI of Scotland becoming James I of England in 1603. The political centre moved south with the king and for some time Scotland was ruled largely through the Scottish privy council, especially during the reign of Charles I. Yet, despite the accession of a Scottish king the culture of the royal court was essentially English and Charles I attempted to force bishops on to the Church of Scotland, a move resisted by the national covenant in the armed conflicts known as the Bishops' Wars. In the course of these struggles episcopacy was swept away by the covenanters and the Scots parliament became the effective ruler of Scotland.

The covenanting army allied itself with the English parliament during the civil wars and was of decisive assistance at the battle of Marston Moor. But the execution of Charles I was regarded as an insult, since the English had in effect killed a Scottish king without consulting the Scottish people. Charles II was crowned King of Scots and a Scottish army invaded England in 1651, only to be defeated at Worcester. Between 1651 and 1660 Scotland was ruled by the New Model Army under General Monck and the two countries were united in 1654.

After the Restoration the situation reverted to a union of the crowns, with the two countries retaining their own parliaments, laws and institutions. James II and VII then made himself unpopular by his advocating episcopacy for Scotland and, after his flight from England, the Scots parliament declared him deposed on the grounds of his tyranny, although he still retained the loyalty of Highland Scots.

William and Mary who followed him were confirmed on the throne of England by the 1689 bill of rights which created a constitutional monarchy by subordinating the monarch to parliament. However, in north Britain it was hard to see how a monarch subordinated to an English parliament could rule Scotland. In 1701 the Act of Settlement fixed the succession to the English throne on the House of Hanover, the nearest the English could get to a non-Catholic heir, but no provision was made for the Scottish throne to pass to Hanover along with the English throne. This caused much trouble in England as the most obvious successor, the Catholic James Edward Stewart, was also an ally of England's French enemy Louis XIV.

The reign of William II and III saw the start of a process designed to reduce the independence of the Highland clans: a process that included what is popularly known as the Massacre of Glencoe when government soldiers from Clan Campbell turned on their Clan Donald hosts. William was very unpopular in Scotland and, unlike Northern Ireland where he is the heroic 'King Billy', the flower named after him is known to the Scots as 'Stinking Billy'. It began to look as though England and Scotland might drift apart after the death of Queen Anne. The English even passed an act in 1705 declaring that all Scots in England were to be treated as aliens. Yet at the same time the Scottish economy and Scotland's own viability as a nation state had been wrecked by a disastrous colonial expedition to Darien in New Caledonia (Panama). Here the Scottish nation had lost a quarter of its liquid capital in a trading venture which failed in part because of English attempts to wreck the endeavour (Schama, 2001, p. 332).

In the midst of these fears and squabbles negotiations began which led to the 1707 Act of Union. As well as the financial inducement to Scottish MPs and new estates for Scottish gentry the English parliament voted to give some £398,085.10s. This was the exact amount lost by Scottish investors in Darien and was therefore a tremendous spur towards getting the proposed union. The Scottish commissioners agreeing the union managed to obtain recognition for an unaltered Scottish legal system and the Scottish Kirk (church). But, while a strong case was made out for a confederation of the two countries in which the two parliaments would be equal in status and power, this was seen as impractical and the act in its final form suppressed both parliaments, replacing them with a single parliament of Great Britain. In fact the English parliament continued virtually unaltered and, with 45 Scottish members (157 had sat in Holyrood) as against 513 from England, the House of Commons left the Scots under-represented and in a minority.

Under the terms of the treaty:

- Scotland was granted forty-five Commons seats and sixteen elected representative peers;
- Scotland retained the Presbyterian Kirk as the established Church of Scotland;
- Scotland retained its own courts and legal system;
- the royal burghs (urban councils) retained their privileges and self-governing status;
- all hereditary offices and jurisdictions were retained.

Many of the safeguards vouchsafed to the Scots were short-lived. The Scottish Privy Council was abolished in 1708 and, while Scotland's own legal system was independent it was nevertheless subject to the House of Lords in Westminster as a final court of appeal. In 1747, after the '45 rebellion, the Abolition of Heritable Jurisdictions Act did away with the power of Scots lairds and clan chieftains. In the same period the laws against the use of tartans and Highland dress reinforced the view that Englishness was being imposed upon the Scots.

Although the union was favoured by the lowland legal and business establishment as an economic necessity, eased by the payment of bribes and inducements, it was greatly disliked by most of the Scottish people. There was a sense of betrayal that was summarised in the Jacobite ballad 'We are Bought and Sold for English Gold'. As was the case in Wales the Act of Union carried the seeds of discontent with it. At the same time as being spurred forward by the Calvinist tradition, Scottish legends such as David Hume, Adam Ferguson,

James Watt and Adam Smith aided Scotland in this new union to develop into the hub of commerce, science and industry for the expanding British Empire. Two decades after the last Jacobite rebellion, James Thomson laid out the design for the New Town of Edinburgh, viewed as 'a new Rome'. From now onwards, economically at least, the leaders of Scotland saw themselves as best served by the union with England (Schama, 2001).

Ireland

Of the four nations making up the United Kingdom, Ireland was the last to join and the first to leave, at least the southern part was. What is more, the whole concept known as the 'devolution of powers' has its origins in the Home Rule for Ireland movement of the nineteenth century, just as the first example of a devolved parliament in the United Kingdom was to be found at Stormont in Ulster.

Ireland never knew a physical Roman presence other than trade and was never united as one nation except under foreign rule. St Patrick, however, opened up Ireland to 'Latin civilization and the culture of Rome, which, though the Empire died, survived in the Church' (Curtis, 1936, p. 6). In the post-Roman period, Ireland's Celtic art, literature and system of laws mixed with a devout and evangelical Christianity to evolve into a cultural golden age for Ireland in what to the rest of Europe was known as the Dark Ages. Its missionaries went out to convert the rest of Europe, and one St David became the patron saint of Wales. Ireland was united culturally but never politically; rule of the island being divided between literally hundreds of 'kings', of whom there were three classes. By AD 800 each village and its surrounding area had its own king or chieftain, who deferred in turn to a regional over-king. Over regional over-kings came the kings of the four main provinces of Ireland – Ulster, Leinster, Munster and Connaught. There was also a fifth province, Meath, in which Tara, seat of the *Árd Rí* or the High King, was located (Curtis, 1936, p. 2).

The office of *Árd Rí* was most important during the Viking invasions when the duty of the High King was to lead resistance against the invader. The Norsemen almost conquered the island before the best known of the High Kings, Brian Boru, defeated them in 1002. After their defeat the Vikings settled down and were assimilated by the native population, often becoming 'more Irish than the Irish'. Nevertheless, the Norsemen changed the nature of Ireland since, as merchants and traders, they established market towns and ports such as Dublin, Wexford and Cork in what had been a purely pastoral society. The chief Norse town, Dublin, grew to be so important that it replaced Tara as the symbolic capital and the Lord of Dublin effectively became the 'King of Ireland'.

The independent and liberal beliefs of the Irish Celtic Church were in constant conflict with the doctrines of the Roman Church. In 1155 the English Pope, Adrian IV, issued a papal bull for the reform of the Irish Church, known as *Laudabilitur,* and passed it to Henry II of England for execution. Nothing happened for ten years and then, in 1166, the High King, Rory O'Conor, drove out the king of Leinster, Dermot McMurrough. Dermot looked to Henry II for assistance and it was at his wish that Richard de Clare, Earl of Pembroke ('Strongbow') invaded Ireland at the head of a Norman-Welsh force, followed in 1169 by the king himself.

Intermarrying with the Irish nobility and part-assimilated by Irish culture, the Norman lords conquered and brought under English suzerainty something like two-thirds of the island. Henry II was confirmed as 'Lord of Ireland' by the Pope and the island was absorbed into the Angevin Empire. However, English power did not last long and a decline set in with the Scottish invasion by Edward Bruce in 1325. By the end of the fifteenth century, the direct influence of the king was restricted to Dublin and its hinterland, in the territory known as 'the Pale'. Beyond the Pale the great Anglo-Irish lordships of Ormond, Desmond and Kildare were as independent of the English crown as were the Marcher lords in Wales.

Any movement towards separatism by the Irish was halted by Poynings' Law of 1494, when Lord Deputy Sir Edward Poynings ruled that the English Privy Council must approve the summoning of an Irish parliament and any legislation of that parliament. It had the effect of reducing the Lordship of Ireland to 'whole and perfect obedience' to the English crown, the failure for not doing was severe (Curtis, 1936, p. 131). The law was re-affirmed in 1719 and stated, '[Ireland] is and of right ought to be subordinate unto and dependent upon the imperial crown of Great Britain' (Cannon, 1997, p. 767).

This movement against Irish separatism continued under Henry VIII when, after the rebellion of Thomas Fitzgerald in 1534, the English king smashed the power of Kildare and the Geraldines, taking Ireland under direct rule and dividing the country into shires after the English model. At the same time as Henry was bringing Wales into a union with England in 1536 he was also declared to be head of the church in Ireland. Finally, in 1541 Henry became the first English king to be known as 'King' rather than 'Lord' of Ireland.

Throughout the sixteenth century Connaught and Ulster remained outside the Pale and gave rise to a series of anti-English, anti-Protestant revolts. The most serious rebellion was led by Hugh O'Neill, third Earl of Tyrone between 1594 and 1603 which involved an anti-English alliance between Ireland and other Catholic countries and which led to landings at Kinsale by the Spanish. Once the rebellion was put down, the government of James I and VI intensified the policy of imposing Protestant settlers on Catholic areas in what were known as 'plantations'. Between 1603 and 1640, some 30–40,000 Scottish and English Protestants were placed on plantations in Ulster, thus leading to the north–south religious divide which still exists. These memories remain as fresh in some people's minds today as if they happened last year.

The massive plantation programme which dispossessed so many Catholic farmers and peasants led to the 1641 great Irish rebellion in which thousands of Protestants were killed by Catholics, and were then avenged in a number of savage reprisals. The mixture of religious, political and economic factors which fanned the rebellion laid down a heritage of hate and suspicion that is still remembered and can be regarded as the start of 'the Irish question'. The rebellion was viciously put down by Cromwell and Ireton, who massacred the Irish at Wexford and Drogheda. Attempts were then made to imitate the Cromwellian union of England and Scotland with a union of Britain and Ireland. Bills to this effect were introduced in 1654 and 1656 but both failed.

War between the Catholic and Protestant populations resumed in 1689, when Irish Catholics espoused the Jacobite cause of the deposed James II and VII. But James fled from Ireland after the Battle of the Boyne and the whole affair petered out in the following year. The Treaty of Limerick promised religious freedom for Catholics but the promise was never honoured and there was instead a series of anti-Catholic laws. Catholics were excluded from the Irish parliament in 1692 and disenfranchised in 1727. 'In Ireland, the king and the English state were associated with alien Protestant settlers ... in Ireland the political nation was the Protestant nation' (Bogdanor, 1999, p. 16).

During the American War of Independence British troops were withdrawn from Ireland. Fears grew that Ireland might be used as the springboard for a French invasion and moves to pacify the Catholic population were introduced. A pro-independence paramilitary force, the Irish Volunteers, was set up, anti-Catholic laws were relaxed in 1781 and Poynings's Law was repealed in 1782, creating a *de facto* parliamentary independence.

When the war with revolutionary France broke out in 1793, fears grew as to French involvement in Ireland. This fear was aided by the appeal of Wolfe Tone, of the United Irishmen, to France for help, which resulted in two unsuccessful French landings. The French threat led the authorities to a fierce repression of those Irish nationalists suspected of helping the French and in reaction to the brutality of that repression the United Irishmen rose in 1798. The rebellion was easily put down but an Anglo-Irish problem obviously existed. As a solution, the prime minister, William Pitt, proposed to unite the Irish and Westminster parliaments. Originally the proposal failed because of Protestant hostility, but a campaign of persuasion and bribery won over the waivers and the Act of Union was passed in 1800, coming into force on 1 January 1801. The Act of Union was passed in two places, one by the Irish parliament in College Green, the other by the parliament at Westminster.

Article 1 of the Union with Ireland Act 1800 stated that the United Kingdoms of Great Britain and Ireland would, from 1 January 1801, and 'for ever after, be united into one kingdom, by the name of the United Kingdom of Great Britain and Ireland' (Hennessey, 2001, p. 1). The Act of Union also provided for a complete shake-up of Irish political, religious and administrative arrangements. Although some of the mechanisms of the former kingdom or Ireland survived the union (the viceroy, the Irish privy council and the separate Irish judiciary) most did not (De Paor, 1986, p. 46) and therefore:

- the Irish parliament was dissolved;
- twenty-eight Irish peers were elected for life to serve in the Westminster House of Lords;
- 300 members of the Irish lower house were replaced by 100 MPs in the UK House of Commons;
- Irish Westminster seats were divided into sixty-four for the counties, thirty-five for the boroughs and one for Dublin University;
- there was also a union of the Churches of England and Ireland, four bishops of the Church of Ireland serving in the Lords;
- a customs union was formed between Ireland and Great Britain, although it was over fifty years before variable taxes between Ireland and Great Britain were equalised.

In one way the Act of Union can be said to have succeeded in that its provisions remained unaltered for 120 years. Like the Act of Union in Scotland, the Irish act allowed for considerable blessings economically for much of the ruling Irish class, and therefore was popular with them (Kennedy, Liam and Johnson, 1996, p. 34). However, it is also fair to say that the union was flawed from the start. Religion was always at the heart of the 'Irish problem'. In order to encourage the Catholic population to support the union, Pitt had effectively promised that Catholic emancipation would be granted alongside the Act of Union. But this proposal met with strong opposition from the devoutly Protestant George III and, although Pitt resigned and his government fell over the issue, emancipation was not granted until 1829. Unlike Scotland, where the Presbyterian Kirk of the majority population was recognised as the established Church of Scotland, the Catholicism of the majority Irish population was ignored and the Anglican Church of Ireland was imposed on the country. Aided by memories of massacres during the 1641 rebellion the causes of Catholicism and Irish nationalism became inextricably linked. As the distinguished professor of Irish history, Alvin Jackson, said, 'The Union formulated on January 1st 1801 was not (as Pitt had envisaged) between Britain and Ireland but between Britain and the Irish Protestant élite' (Jackson, 2001, p. 21).

In one other way the union with Ireland was vastly different from the situation existing with Wales and Scotland in their relationship to England. It was only the Irish parliament that was suppressed under the act and an Irish administration continued to be run in Dublin under the lord lieutenant and the chief secretary for Ireland, who was a cabinet minister. As we noted earlier Ireland also retained its own Privy Council, complete with judges and law officers. Ireland therefore had an executive and judiciary of its own but no independent legislature. By this measure it was seen as a subordinate country ruled by the British and Irish Protestant élite rather than an integrated part of England, as was Wales. In addition 'Scotland had been treated as a partner after the union, but Ireland seemed a dependency' (Bogdanor, 1999, p. 20).

The Act of Union in Ireland was therefore unable to stifle the troubles there for long, and as we will see in Chapter 3 the issue of Ireland was to trouble politicians of all political parties from now on.

Conclusion

The union of parliaments in 1801 created the last stepping-stone in the creation of the United Kingdom but, in recognising the achievement of melding together what Gladstone called 'a partnership of three kingdoms, a partnership of four nations',[7] it has also to be said that the process of unification carried within itself inherent flaws that would lead to tensions and resentments, which would lead in turn to pressures for fragmentation and political devolution.

- Although the acts of 1707 and 1801 spoke of the union of parliaments as though it were a happy marriage of equals, it was more clearly an English acquisition rather than a merger. Despite the fact that the nations of Scotland and Ireland were still seen to exist as cultural, religious and geographical entities, much more so than Wales, their common good was now linked to that of England's will.
- Similarly, the union was created by the supremacy of an ascendant people's values over those of the rest of the kingdom. In Wales, Scotland and Ireland, if you were to prosper then you had to pay at least lip service to values of the Anglo-Norman élite, and even in England this Norman-Saxon dominance gained the upper hand over the Anglian midlands and north.
- The folk memory of the Celtic nations was scarred by events which occurred during the period covered by this chapter. This can clearly be seen in Ireland but also in Wales with the linguistic divisions caused during this period and in Scotland through events like the theft of the Stone of Destiny by Edward I, and the land clearances following the Jacobite rebellions.
- Attempts to take back power from England have a long history when it comes to the creation of the union. At around the time he was elected first secretary in Wales, Rhodri Morgan wrote an article in which he said that one had to understand Owain Glyn Dwr to understand Welsh aspirations. 'Owain Glyn Dwr wanted a country united in a properly organised society with representation from all parts of Wales. He envisaged a Welsh future in a European context ... Six centuries later we are starting to think in those terms again' (quoted in Hazell, 2000, p. 41).[8]
- The greatest benefit of the union for the ruling classes was the free trade area it created across the British Isles. This in turn enabled each nation to play its part in the commercial expansion of the British Empire. Through industry, agriculture and commerce the capitals or chief towns of the nations of the United Kingdom prospered or declined on the fortunes of Empire and international trade. They provided armies to protect this trade and settlers to

colonise this Empire, the profits of trade encouraged all the ruling élites of
these nation states to keep feeding the economic 'goose that was laying these
golden eggs'.

• The industrialisation of Britain during the eighteenth and nineteenth
  centuries was at its harshest in the Celtic fringes of the union state, where
  the under class was deemed to be surplus to requirements – as was the case
  with the Highland clearances in Scotland or the Irish potato famine – and
  were so mistreated that they were forced to abandon the land and emigrate,
  which in turn fuelled an American and colonial mistrust of Britain based on
  the misdeed done to the citizens of these new lands forbears.

• Religion was a factor of conflict both within the nations and between the
  nations of United Kingdom: in Wales, where the majority were chapel-going
  non-conformists, in Scotland where there was a split between Catholics and
  Protestants and greatest of all in Ireland, where the majority were Catholic
  but the rulers were Protestant. All nations worshipped the same god but this
  did not stop them warring over how they should worship him.

Many of these factors above held the nations of the British Isles together but
failed to suppress their individual identity. Yet the glue of economic wellbeing
became unstuck particularly on the issue of religion in Ireland and later on in
Wales. The problems of the divisions within the Christian religion and the way
the union had papered over them meant that something would have to be done
to let off this growing head of steam. Failure to do so would result in the demise
of the union.

Notes

1 The Heptarchy was not always made up of seven kingdoms, and they were not
   always the same seven.
2 It is interesting to note that the present-day border between England and Wales
   very closely mirrors the line of Offa's Dyke.
3 In a symbolic act, Edgar was rowed on the Dee by rowers who included Kenneth,
   King of Scots, Malcolm, King of the Cumbrians (Strathclyde), Maccus, Lord of the
   Isles, and Iago of Gwynedd (Stenton, 1947, p. 364). The historic reality of this
   event is questionable but the political reality of what it symbolises is very real.
   From that time on English sovereignty was fully recognised and from the submission of the British princes came all later claims for English suzerainty.
4 Morgannwg was situated in the South Wales valleys and occupied an area similar
   to that occupied by Glamorgan today.
5 The words *Gael* or *Goidelic* come from the Welsh word *Gwyddel*, meaning 'Irish'.
6 Malcolm III, King of Scots, is more commonly known as Malcolm Canmore
   ('Canmore' = 'Bighead').
7 Gladstone speaking to the House of Commons in August 1892.
8 The comment by Rhodri Morgan appeared in the *Western Mail*, 17 April 2000,
   and referred to an exhibition in the National Library of Wales where a letter from
   Glyn Dwr seeking a French alliance was exhibited.

3

Home Rule:
precursor of devolution

The last half of the nineteenth century saw the development of nationalism. Not only did this result in the rise of Irish nationalism but also the development of Scottish and Welsh nationalism into its modern-day image. However, the nation-building nationalism that was so admired by the liberal establishment was very different from the Irish nationalism that began to emerge mid-century. Liberal nationalism welcomed the creation of new nations by the liberation of their component parts from an imperial power and the assimilation of those parts within a nation state: the great achievements of the nineteenth-century nationalist movement being the unifications of Italy and Germany. To that kind of nationalist the great achievement of British nationalism would have been the creation of the United Kingdom as outlined in the previous chapter, while the fragmentation of that union into autonomous units was out of sync with the mood of the times.

It is worth noting that, in all his years of negotiating for Irish Home Rule, Mr Gladstone never once mentioned 'Irish nationalism' but instead always referred to Irish 'nationality'. Importantly, he recognised that the nationality of all four nations in the United Kingdom and Ireland were equal with each other (Morgan, 1960). Overall, however, first loyalty was to the United Kingdom not the separate nations. An Irishman, Welshman or Scotsman might have a 'local patriotism' to Ireland, Wales or Scotland but 'it does not follow that because his local patriotism is keen he is incapable of Imperial patriotism' (Bogdanor, 1999, p. 22).[1]

For the most part, those inhabitants of the British Isles that counted (the enfranchised ruling classes) were content with the union as it existed in 1801, or at least they were not particularly excited at the idea of political separatism. The riches that came with the expanding markets of the British Isles and a free trade area suppressed any nationalist demands to break this market up. Any concerns over the union were largely material and involved the fairness or otherwise of the distribution of wealth between the component nations. For Scotland and Wales this meant that the concerns of the people were largely left to the existing British political parties most concerned with social issues: first this meant the Liberal party and later the Labour party.

In Ireland a nationalist answer to social and economic issues began to emerge after the potato famine of 1848, encouraged by the widespread European revolutions of that year. For both Wales and Ireland, however, the main disputes with the union state concerned both the land issue of tenant farmers and various problems of a religious nature. In both countries they suffered with a general lack of rights for tenant farmers, particularly severe in Ireland. Religiously, in Wales an overwhelmingly non-conformist, chapel-going population sought the disestablishment of the Welsh Church. In Ireland, as has already been mentioned, the issue which most detracted from the Act of Union was the failure to include Catholic emancipation in its provisions. Between 1801 and 1842 the repeal movement which, as the name suggests, wanted repeal of the Act of Union but whose primary concern was to gain emancipation for Ireland's predominantly Catholic population, took the initiative.

Catholic emancipation and the Young Ireland movement

After 1800 there was a movement towards Catholic emancipation in Britain as a whole but the English establishment, faced with a mere 60,000 Catholics in 1780, did not view the matter with quite the same urgency as it was seen in Ireland, with its majority Catholic population running into millions (Steinberg and Evans, 1970, p. 63). Prior to the union from 1750 onwards there were limited changes which enabled the poor position of Catholics in Ireland to be improved. George III sent Lord Townsend in 1767 to become the new Lord Lieutenant of Ireland. Townsend was instructed to be based in Ireland, unlike his predecessors. George III was taking Ireland seriously. Dublin prospered and became the second city of the Empire. Townsend then set about ending the corruption and 'jobbery' encouraged by the Anglo-Irish ruling class that was rife in Ireland (Curtis, 1936). It was a slow process and for the first thirty years of the union the main issues in Irish politics were those of tenancy, divides between Protestant and Catholic and tenant farmers and Catholic emancipation. Although Irish Catholic wealth was increasing towards the end of the eighteenth century some five thousand Protestant landlords still owned nearly the whole of Ireland (Nowlan, 1986, p. 95).

Ireland was the only nation within the British Empire with a Roman Catholic majority in the population. Yet this majority had very little voice in determining its own affairs. Edmund Burke was one of the great orators and advocates of Irish Catholic rights. Initially it was felt that Catholic emancipation would impact only to a limited degree upon the new union due to the fact that the Catholics would always remain the smallest group within it. The limited political reforms reassured the Protestant landlords that there was no real threat to their position. One man, an upper-class Catholic lawyer called

Daniel O'Connell, was to challenge this view and galvanise the Catholic majority into a political force. The decline of Irish Gaelic as the main language of
Ireland incidentally passed with no real political repercussions during this
period (Walsh, 1986). Politics would now shift its centre to Westminster and
therefore the language of politics became English; in that sense England left a
legacy upon Ireland that would last forever more.

In 1823 O'Connell, whose later success was such that he became known as
'the liberator', formed the Catholic Association in order to bring pressure to
bear on the government by such acts as electing Catholic MPs. Organised
among the ordinary population through a network of parish priests, the association was immensely popular.[2] It was dissolved in 1825 before it could be
suppressed by the government, but was instantly reformed. In 1828 O'Connell
was elected as MP for County Clare, although he was unable to take his seat
because of the Test Act of 1673 which prevented him from taking the oath as a
Catholic.[3] At the same time the British government was becoming disturbed by
the level of disaffection in Ireland and both Wellington (himself an Irishman by
birth) and Peel feared an outbreak of civil war that the government would not
have the military resources to subdue. In that light the government moved,
despite intense opposition from the Conservatives and George IV, first to repeal
the Test Act in 1828 and then to pass the Catholic Emancipation Act of 1829.
The act made it possible for Catholics to serve as MPs and to accept any public
office with the exceptions of becoming lord chancellor or lord lieutenant of
Ireland.

The Catholic Association was dissolved for the second time in 1829 since it
was felt that it had achieved its aim in having secured Catholic emancipation.
But the attention of the people had turned from the question of religion towards
those social and economic concerns that now became more important, especially as regards questions of land tenure. As unrest grew, agitation for repeal of
the Act of Union resumed after 1829. O'Connell founded the National Repeal
Association in 1841 and started the journal *The Nation* a year later in order to
promote Irish nationalism. The British government did not welcome his work
and as a result of this he was imprisoned in 1843 for conspiracy. Despite his
imprisonment many in the association deplored the willingness O'Connell had
shown during the 1830s to work with the Whig government in London and he
lost much of his influence as a result. With O'Connell's demise the leadership of
Irish nationalism passed to two Protestants, Smith O'Brien and John Mitchel.
They formed a Young Ireland movement in imitation of Mazzini's nationalist
'Young Italy' and, in 1846, the more militant members of Young Ireland finally
split with O'Connell on the issue of how willing the movement should be to use
force and violence to achieve its ends, forming the Irish Confederation. After
O'Connell's death in 1847 the militants gained in influence and in 1848,
inspired by the spate of revolutions that were sweeping Europe, promoted a
peasant's revolt in Tipperary that was easily put down in a few days. O'Brien
and Mitchel were both arrested and transported to Australia.

It is a mistake to imagine that the only pressure in Ireland during the nine-teenth century came from Catholics desiring emancipation or Protestants seeking a united Ireland. Other Protestants were also seeking to exert their claims to Ireland. In part this was brought about by frequent confrontations between the Protestant Orangemen and Catholic Ribbonmen throughout the century. This trouble did not just occur in the Irish rural counties. In urban Belfast there were nine serious years of sectarian rioting between 1835 and 1922. In just one of these years, 1886, eighty-six deaths occurred in Ulster due to rioting. The Orange Order was increasingly seen as a threat to the union rather than a disorderly ally. In 1825 it was banned and between 1832 and 1844 there were various attempts to prevent provocative Orange leaders emerging in Irish politics. In addition, whilst it was true that the Orangemen always tended to be better armed and supported and as a result came off the best in most confrontations with Catholics, they faired little better in the 'Great Potato Famine' of 1845–50, where some 210,000 Ulster protestants died. When it came to death through starvation the grim reaper did not distinguish between Protestants and Catholics.

In 1867 William Johnson of Ballykillbeg led an illegal 'Twelfth of July' Orange demonstration (commemorating William's victory of James) in Bangor, County Down. He was fined, refused to pay and subsequently impris-oned for non-payment of fines, but became a Protestant hero who was elected to Westminster in 1868 and who succeeded in getting the Party Processions Act repealed in 1872, allowing Orangemen to hold their marches unimpeded (Mulholland, 2003). As Catholic Irish nationalism increased so the Protestants began to realise that to avoid domination by the Catholics they must defend the union by all possible measures. The scene for future large-scale conflict between Irish Protestants and Catholics was now set.

The growth of nationalism

The critical event of the nineteenth century, an event that is crucial in under-standing Irish alienation from British rule, was the potato famine of the 1840s. Traditional Irish laws of inheritance meant that land was not passed as a whole to the eldest son but was divided between all a man's sons. Over the generations a small farm was divided time and time again until the average Irish cotter's family possessed about as much land as would make a large garden. At the same time the Protestant landlords, highlighted by the 1843 Devon Commission, kept Irish agriculture in a dangerously impoverished state by 'letting land rather than farms and robbing the small farmer of all tenant rights' (Curtis, 1936, p. 315). The people depended almost entirely on the land with outlets for industry having been reduced by the competition from the British mainland that had resulted from the union. Needing a crop that could feed a family with the highest possible yield from a small area the Irish became almost totally dependent on the potato: so dependent that, if the potato crop failed, the family starved. In 1845 about half the total crop became diseased and rotted in the fields. In 1846 there was a total crop failure. There was a partial recovery in 1847 with a fair harvest but in 1848 there was a total failure again. As an immediate effect of the famine about one million people died in Ireland and three million emigrated to Britain – many to Wales and Scotland – a further million of whom went on to the United States. It was the worst recorded famine in Europe to occur during peace time until the agricultural collectivisation of the Soviet Union in the 1920s and 1930s (Curtis, 1936, p. 316).

Initially the crisis was handled well by Peel's Conservative government, but they lost the election in 1846 to a doctrinaire Whig administration. After initial aid the partial recovery of 1847 persuaded the government that the crisis was over and aid was suspended. The British government continued to export meat and grain from Northern Ireland to Great Britain while millions were starving in the south and west of the island. This fanned considerable anger in Ireland. The combined lack of sensitivity, complacency and maladministration shown by Britain had no immediate consequence but the famine and consequent emigration was of lasting importance to Irish nationalism. The reason why support for Irish nationalism has always been so strong in the United States is because from 1701 onwards around 40 per cent of British emigrants to the US were Irish. At first they were attracted by the 'prospect of happier climes and less arbitrary government', but latterly by the sheer necessity for survival (Ferguson, 2004, p.71). After 1848, over two million people went there, each of them handing on bitter and resentful memories of British treatment. These emigrants paid for their own passage and weren't even provided with the smallest Imperial passage. They sent back money at first to their relatives but in time they would also send money to support the anti-English political cause groups of Irish republicanism that fought against those they held responsible for their own 'expulsion' from their homeland.

Many American Irish, including those who had fought in the American civil war, supported a secret society called the Irish Republican Brotherhood (IRB), better known as the Fenian movement (named after the legendary Fianna, a band of armoured warriors who protected the ancient High Kingdom of Ireland), which emerged in the years after the famine. The IRB encouraged rebellion and in 1867 succeeded in promoting a Fenian rising, although the authorities fairly easily put it down. Many of the Fenians taken prisoner during the uprising were defended by Isaac Butt who, despite coming from a Protestant and Orange background, had become interested in the nationalist movement when he defended a number of Young Ireland members after the 1848 rising. Claiming to believe that Ireland's problems could be mitigated by the existence of a subordinate parliament in Dublin, Butt went on to found the Home Government Association in 1870, renamed as the Home Rule Association in 1873. The aim of the movement was not separatist, but wanted a return to the

1783 constitution, having both a legislature in Dublin and a token Irish presence at Westminster.

Charles Parnell and the first Home Rule bill

Some 80 per cent of Ireland's population were Catholic; even the nine counties of Ulster only had a slim Protestant majority. Britain could not continue to define Ireland as a Protestant nation when the evidence pointed to it being a Catholic one (Mulholland, 2003, p. 14). This was evident to the Liberal leader, William Ewart Gladstone, and it was also apparent to the Irish Nationalist party leader Charles Parnell. Coming from County Wicklow, Parnell was an Anglo-Irish Protestant, like so many in the Irish national movement, whom after centuries of oppression had an inferiority complex about electing Catholics. His views were so radical, however, that he alienated most Protestants but not Catholics, and he was elected as MP for Meath in 1875. He was associated with the Home Rule Association group in parliament but was one of those who were disenchanted with Butt's moderate policies. In 1878 he split with Butt and formed a group known as the New Departure, in alliance with former Fenians, Irish American sympathisers and land reformers.

In 1879 when the socialist Michael Davitt formed the Irish Land League to fight against the worst offences of landlordism, Parnell became its president. Under his guidance Parnellite MPs began their disruptive tactics in parliament and this, allied to agrarian unrest in the countryside and the rent 'Boycott' campaign of 1880, forced Gladstone to concede a revised Land Act in 1881.[4] The act did not go far enough since it did not deal with the question of rent arrears and the agitation continued, as a result of which Parnell and two other MPs were arrested in October 1881 and sent to Kilmainham prison. They were released in May 1882 by the terms of the so-called Treaty of Kilmainham. Agreed between Parnell and Gladstone and brokered by Joseph Chamberlain, the treaty required Parnell to renounce violence and restrict himself to parliamentary action in return for Gladstone's promise to introduce a new Arrears Act. The new act did little to help restore the role of the smallholder in Irish agriculture. They continued to head for the boat to America or elsewhere as soon as opportunity allowed. In the thirty years between 1880 and 1910 the number of Irish labourers fell by a quarter from 400,000 to 300,000 (Lee, 1986, p. 115).

In 1882 the new Irish chief secretary, Lord Frederick Cavendish, and his under-secretary Thomas Burke were murdered by a repubican terrorist gang, 'The Invincibles', in Dublin's Phoenix Park in a protest against coercion. In reaction the government clamped down on nationalist supporters in an exceptionally severe Coercion Act.[5] Refusing to be provoked into violent action, Parnell obeyed the Kilmainham terms and devoted himself to political action, organising his Irish Nationalist party in parliament and beginning his campaign for Home Rule.

In the 1885 election a total of eighty-six Irish Nationalist MPs were returned, while the number of Liberal MPs was so reduced that Gladstone could only form a government with the assistance of Irish members. Parnell used a combination of the Nationalist party's strength in parliament together with this Liberal alliance to persuade Gladstone that Ireland had spoken and to accept the necessity of Irish Home Rule – a bill to bring that about being placed before parliament in 1886. Unfortunately, both Parnell and Gladstone had underestimated the extent of hostility to Home Rule on the part of Ulster Protestants and a significant number of Liberal MPs. Sufficient dissident Liberals, the most prominent of whom was Joseph Chamberlain, voted to defeat the bill on its second reading in the Commons. The same dissidents, by leaving the Liberal party to form the Liberal Unionists and ultimately making common cause with the Conservatives, caused the Liberal administration to collapse, replaced by a pro-union Conservative-Liberal Unionist government. Notably, few of these Liberal Unionists came from Scotland or Wales or other parts of the Celtic fringe. Despite widespread victories for the Conservatives in England, in Wales, Scotland and Ireland there was an overwhelming rejection of the Conservatives. Radical Liberal nationalists saw this rejection of the Conservatives as an alliance of the Celtic people who would unite to push forwards nationalist issues such as Home Rule and disestablishment of the church. It could soon be a case of 'Home-Rule-All-Round'. Soon, however, Liberal nationalists were to discover that the first battle to be won was not between Liberals and Conservatives and their allies the Liberal Unionists but instead between Liberal radicals and Liberal traditionalists (Masterman, 1972, p. 85). It also provided a clear indication to Celtic nationalists that their desires of Home Rule would only arise from a Liberal government.

In the light of that failure the Irish Nationalist party languished and Parnell's career went into decline. In 1887 he was accused of complicity in the 1882 Phoenix Park murders. A parliamentary commission investigated the accusation but although Parnell was cleared of the charge in 1889 he was then plunged into another scandal. Cited as co-respondent in the O'Shea divorce case, his affair with Kitty O'Shea became public property, offending both the non-conformist conscience of the Liberal party and the sensitivities of Catholic Ireland. Two years later Parnell was dead and without him the Irish party split and was totally eclipsed between 1890 and 1900.

The nature of, and problems posed by, Home Rule

The Liberal government under Gladstone was pushed into considering the option of Home Rule by the parliamentary tactics of the Irish MPs and increasingly nationalist aspirations of his MPs in Scotland and Wales. Quite apart from that pressure Gladstone had himself become convinced that repressive coercion acts from the centre to bind the union together had had their day and could well become counter-productive. There was also the purely pragmatic point to be made that a continued denial of legitimate demands for self-government might well lead the protesters to attempt taking that self-government for themselves by means of armed rebellion, as had happened to the American colonies. If Burke's solution to American complaints had been adopted would the revolutionary war have happened and would the colonies have been lost?

Once the decision had been made to grant some form of Home Rule the central dilemma facing the government was how to reconcile the legitimate demands of the Irish for self-government with the overriding importance of maintaining the sovereignty of the Westminster parliament. To resolve this dilemma Gladstone turned again to the writings of Edmund Burke as they related to the Irish and the American colonists.

Burke had claimed that the Westminster parliament had two functions:

1 as a national legislature for Great Britain and Ireland;
2 as an imperial legislature for the constituent countries of the British Empire.

He believed that the two functions should be separated with the power to legislate on national issues being devolved from the imperial parliament to national state parliaments. In this way two political structures could coexist, both dominant in their own areas of legislature.

Gladstone was able to cite the union of Norway and Sweden and the formation of Austria-Hungary as examples of supranational polities currently existing that had a centralised executive but twin legislatures. Moreover, Gladstone was able to point to the more recent example of the British North America Act of 1867 which set up the confederation of Canada. Under that act *all* the legislative powers of the imperial parliament in Westminster had been devolved to the Canadian federal government, under the control of the governor-general and the judicial committee of the privy council.

However, Canada had to make many decisions for itself simply because distance made it difficult if not impossible for London to deal with them. Ireland on the other hand was closer geographically to the London parliament and therefore neither needed nor wanted its own foreign or defence policy. It was proposed that only domestic matters would be devolved to Dublin and for that reason all matters for legislation were divided between the **devolved powers** that a Dublin parliament would deal with and **reserved powers** that would remain the responsibility of the Westminster parliament. Here too Gladstone found a precedent in the Canadian set-up because, although virtually total power had been devolved to the federal government by London, that government reserved certain powers for itself when devolving national matters to the governments of Canada's constituent provinces.

The first Home Rule bill of 1886 was modelled directly on the British North America Act, even to the extent of using the same wording. The reserved powers of the imperial parliament were said to be:

- matters relating to the crown, the armed forces and defence;
- foreign and colonial relations;
- trade protection and customs dues.

With the central dilemma resolved, the framing of the three Home Rule bills of 1886, 1893 and 1912 posed two further major problems, which proved very difficult to resolve and which are both relevant today since much the same questions faced those responsible for framing the devolution legislation of 1997. The questions arise over:

- **Representation**: how were Ireland and the other nation states to be represented in the Westminster parliament after devolved parliaments had been established in those states? What status should their representatives have?
- **Taxation**: how should taxation be raised in the devolved states in such a way as to produce equity between the UK and Irish/Scottish/Welsh taxpayers?

With regard to representation, the first Home Rule bill of 1886 dealt specifically with Ireland and excluded Irish members from Westminster in the first of three possible solutions that were proposed:

1 There should be no Irish representation at Westminster once an Irish parliament had been established. This was a solution that appealed to non-Irish members since the disruption caused by Parnell's tactics after 1880 left many English, Welsh and Scottish MPs feeling that the sooner they were rid of the Irish members the better. The proposal was unpopular with the Irish, however, and many others were less than enthusiastic. The point was that the exclusion of Irish MPs meant that the Irish would have no say whatsoever in the raising and spending of taxation. Everyone was very aware that the clarion call of the American colonists had been 'no taxation without representation'!
2 The so-called 'in-and-out' option, under which Irish MPs would attend Westminster when Irish or United Kingdom matters were in dispute but would not participate in English, Scottish or Welsh matters. Apart from the obvious practical difficulties the in-and-out solution had the ability of creating a constitutional crisis. The British constitution provides that the leader of the party who can command majority support in the House of Commons should be nominated as prime minister and asked to form a government. Yet, in the light of voting patterns in the late nineteenth century, it was easy to envisage the situation where Irish Nationalist MPs held the balance of power so that, with their presence, the government would be in the hands of a Liberal-Irish Nationalist coalition, while the absence of Irish members would automatically hand over government to the Conservatives.
3 There should be continued Irish representation at Westminster but in reduced numbers to compensate for so much Irish political business law-

making now being done in Dublin. In many ways this seemed to be the obvious solution but it still raised the question as to whether it was right for Irish members to discuss English, Scottish or Welsh affairs when English, Scottish or Welsh MPs were unable to vote on matters affecting Ireland. Indeed, ninety years later Tam Dalyell asked in a similar context why the member for West Lothian should be able to discuss the affairs of West Bromwich when the MP for West Bromwich was prevented from discussing much of the affairs of West Lothian. It was during the debates on Irish Home Rule that the original anomaly – that later became known as the 'West Lothian question' and which still exists as the 'English question' – was presented.

In the first Home Rule bill, Gladstone chose the first of these options and if the bill had been passed Irish members would have been excluded from the Commons. This aspect of the proposal met with such objections that the prime minister recognised that changes would have to be made before the second bill was submitted in 1893. Gladstone briefly toyed with the in-and-out option but met with sufficient opposition as to force a change of plan. The 1893 bill, repeated in 1912, included proposals for a continued Irish presence at Westminster but with the number of Irish members reduced by 20 per cent to 80 MPs instead of 103; a similar situation to that which occurred in Scotland a century later.

The question of finance was equally as difficult and controversial. The main point is that there were some heavy expenditures that were an imperial responsibility, the most obvious of them being defence. Since the Irish would 'benefit' from the role of the army in defending the whole United Kingdom then it was thought only right that Ireland should contribute towards the cost of that army. The amount of money needed to pay for the army and all such similar responsibilities was known as the Imperial Contribution. Out of the total amount of money going into the Irish exchequer, a substantial proportion would represent the Imperial Contribution, with the remainder set aside for the day-to-day expense of running Ireland. The question was whether the Imperial Contribution ought to be the first charge on the exchequer, running the risk of not having enough resources left to run Ireland. Or should the money to govern Ireland be paid first with the Imperial Contribution taking whatever was left?

In 1886 it was proposed that the Imperial Contribution should be a fixed sum representing one-fifteenth of the total imperial expenditure. One of the main complaints raised to this arrangement was that it made the Imperial Contribution seem too much like a levy by an imperial power on a subject people. This was then changed and in 1893 it was proposed that one-third of Irish customs dues should go to the Imperial Contribution, with Ireland taking the remainder. But by 1912 everything had changed, thanks to the reforms of the Liberal government elected in 1906. In what is seen as the origin of the welfare state the government had introduced national insurance, unemployment benefit and old-age pensions. This massive increase in public spending on welfare meant that the Irish budget was operating in deficit, the Imperial Contribution could not be afforded and a totally separate Ireland would not be viable unless it gave up the welfare benefits. It began to look as though Ireland could only continue to be governed with the benefits it was now obtaining with a British subsidy.

The Home Rule issue, 1890–1914

The Liberals regained power in 1892 and Gladstone made it evident that even without Parnell's persuasion he was committed to Home Rule. A second Home Rule bill was introduced, differing from the first in that it allowed for the retention of Irish members at Westminster. The Liberals were now forever to be wedded to the concept of Home Rule and, later on, federalism. This time the bill was passed by the Commons but thrown out by the Lords. Home Rule as an issue faded from view; particularly after the Conservatives returned to power in 1895. They were now and for much of the coming century against Home Rule or devolution of virtually any type except when it was politically unavoidable. For the next ten years the Conservatives continued a policy begun by Arthur Balfour when he had been Irish chief secretary in 1891. Balfour had been so severe in his application of the Coercion Acts that he was known as 'Bloody Balfour', but he mitigated the harshness by a generous and enlightened social policy. However, he would soon show some of the political astuteness that would make him prime minister in a few years time. The Conservative administration between 1895 and 1905 pursued Balfour's generous social policy, permitting tenants to buy land and investing in schemes intended to benefit rural communities: schemes that ranged from light railways to new strains of seed potatoes, in a campaign that was said to be 'killing Home Rule with kindness'.

With Parnell now dead the Irish parliamentary party made something of a comeback in the 1900 'khaki' election under the leadership of John Redmond, but it did not have the popular support it had enjoyed in Parnell's heyday. The younger and more radical elements were not enthused by Redmond's cautious policies and tended to go for far more extreme solutions such as those advocated by Sinn Fein (Ourselves Alone).

In 1905 the unionists in Ireland took advantage of the enlargement of the electoral franchise and moved to overtly politicise itself. It moved out from its covert support of Ireland's landlord élite and now stood as the Ulster Unionist Council (UUC). In 1910 Edward Carson, a noted Dublin lawyer, became its leader, and set about galvanising the Protestants of Ireland against Home Rule. On 23 September 1911, 100,000 unionists met at Craigavon of the shores of Belfast Lough to hear and support Carson in denouncing Home Rule; what's more they strove to fight against it. In September 1912, 250,000 unionists signed their names to a declaration called the Solemn League and Covenant which declared them to use 'all means which may be found to be necessary to defeat the present conspiracy to a set up a Home Rule Parliament'. Unionists wanted to remain under a Protestant London and not a Catholic Dublin government. To confirm this viewpoint in January 1912 the Ulster Volunteer Force (UVF) was formed by military-experienced gentry to support the unionist cause. In April 1914 they imported 25,000 rifles and three million rounds of ammunition. By May 23,000 men were in a position to mobilise in order to defend a provisional unionist government in the nine counties of Ulster (Mulholland, 2003, pp. 18–21).

For the Irish Nationalists, Redmond's main hope came after 1910. In that year the Liberals under Herbert Asquith were campaigning on the issue of reforming the House of Lords in response to the Lords' rejection of the 1909 budget. They were returned as a minority government in the first general election of 1910. A second general election that year only produced two more Liberal MPs and the government needed the support of Irish Nationalist MPs in order to pass the Parliament Act of 1911 which limited the power of the Lords. In return the Irish party expected and received a third Home Rule bill which this time passed both houses, even though its main provisions were badly mauled. The opposition from Edward Carson and the Orange Order in Ulster and a mutiny by British army officers at the Curragh Camp meant that implementation of Home Rule was shelved for two years. At the end of those two years Britain was now embroiled in World War I and it became understood that nothing would be done in Ireland until the war was over. Redmond had already acquiesced to allowing the Ulster counties to opt out of Home Rule for a period of six years. But the unionists rejected that as merely a 'stay of execution'. The Liberal cabinet, including Churchill and Lloyd George, supported this exclusion as a way of overcoming the impasse. The 'Irish problem' remained unsolved but it did appear that at least the imminent civil war in Ireland had also been put off.

Redmond supported Irish involvement in the war and also the widespread recruitment of Irishmen for the British army, moves that cost him popularity which increased as the war itself became unpopular. When the IRB and Sinn Fein promoted the Easter Rising in 1916 Redmond failed to condemn the harsh treatment of the republican leaders by the British. The threat of bringing conscription to the Irish in 1918 also added more fuel to the nationalist fire. Compared with Sinn Fein's preparedness to take direct action against the British, Redmond and the Irish Nationalist party lost all credibility with the mass of the people. In the last general election for the whole British Isles the Irish Nationalists gained just under a quarter of the votes and just 7 per cent of the seats. The Ulster Unionists picked up 29 per cent of the vote and just under a quarter of the Irish Westminster seats. It was Sinn Fein, however, who became the big winner at the 1918 (coupon) election, gaining 48 per cent of the vote, which gave them 70 per cent of the Irish seats. Sinn Fein boycotted Westminster and, instead, convened in early 1919 as the *de facto* new Irish parliament (Dáil Eireann) at the Mansion House in Dublin (Mulhollan, 2003, p. 23) A period of civil insurrection and disobedience then occurred through Southern Ireland. When the new coalition government of Prime Minister Lloyd George tried to resume negotiations on Home Rule the mood had changed and the British were faced with an armed insurrection and had to negotiate with persons very different from the moderate, constitutional party founded by Charles Parnell. In the north the UUC was rewarded, to a degree, for its loyal war service to the British Empire and for its continued loyalty with a parliament of their own. The 1920 Government of Ireland Act awarded six counties – Antrim, Down, Armagh, Fermanagh, Derry and Tyrone – a parliament in Belfast. Only a few years before it looked as though the most the UUC would gain as a solution to the Irish problem was a four county opt-out (Antrim, Down, Armagh and Derry) for a limited period, from being run by the Dublin parliament. This new deal was a disaster for all Irish nationalists who wanted a united Ireland. In the north it looked very much as though the southern nationalists' intransigence had resulted in the Ulster Unionists salvation. Ireland would now be partitioned.

Home Rule for Scotland and elsewhere

We have concentrated in this chapter mainly on the question of Home Rule in an Irish context. This is in a nineteenth-century political sense when 'Home Rule' was the term used to apply to the series of confrontations between the British Conservative – Liberal Unionist governments and the Liberals and Irish Nationalist Party between 1880 and 1914. Nevertheless we need to acknowledge that the agitation in Ireland did amplify the echoes of nationalist leanings in Scotland and Wales, both countries becoming involved with thoughts of Home Rule after 1880. In time therefore the notion of Home Rule came to apply to the political aspirations of Scottish and Welsh nationalists as well as Irish ones.

The 1707 Act of Union was initially unpopular in some quarters in Scotland and there was widespread criticism that consent had only been obtained through widespread bribery of the ruling classes by compensating them for their losses made in the Darian scheme. For generations following the union there was unrest, culminating in the Jacobite rising of 1745, which was followed by the Highland clearances. The clearances were compounded by the suppressing of the Highland way of life, with the banning of tartan and Highland dress. In some ways it was as harsh as the Coercion Acts in Ireland, and the enforced evictions and mass emigrations to Canada involved in the Highland clearances carried echoes of the injustices practised a century later during the Irish potato famine. But in Scotland it was not the English who were responsible for the destruction of the Highland clans but rather lowland Scots, while those enforcing the clearances were the clansmen's own Anglicised lairds. Whilst these same Highland Scots left Scotland for overseas a mass of Catholic and Protestant Irish emigrated to the Scottish lowlands. They created new areas of religious diversity with the Irish areas settlement areas leaving a lasting sectarian divide in Glasgow's Celtic (Catholic) and Rangers (Protestant) football clubs.

For the ruling Scottish elite there was a sense that they had gained a great deal from the union and, although a certain amount of resentment was felt at what was seen as English arrogance and a sense of superiority there was not the anger of general suppression and frustration that was felt in Ireland. This lack of resentment was aided by the fact that Scotland still retained its own institutions in the Kirk (church) and the law, which were not regarded as inferior or treated as second rate by the Westminster government. Yet below the ruling élite all was not well. It was not just the Jacobites that resisted change. At the time of the French Revolution there was unrest among the Scottish lower-middle and working classes and revolutionary clubs known as the United Scotsmen were founded in an attempt to emulate Wolfe Tone's United Irishmen. The riots and demonstrations, however, were not the result of any anti-English or anti-union feeling but were much more a class matter, with anger directed at the prosperous middle classes, the factory owners and the landlords, who in most cases were themselves Scottish. When political reform did come it started with the Scottish burghs (urban councils), which were so corrupt and mismanaged that a number were going bankrupt. The 1817 Police Act in Edinburgh and those acts that followed brought about the first elements of elected representation onto local government (Mitchison, 2002, p. 372). In 1833 the Scottish Burgh Reform Act put control of the towns into the hands of the £10 ratepayers, some two years before this occurred in England. Not for the last time would Scotland be the prototype of local government reform.

During the first half of the nineteenth century, early English tourism and the new genre of Scottish historical novels generated by Sir Walter Scott, a regular steam ship between Edinburgh and London, together with the enthusiasm of Queen Victoria and Prince Albert for all things Scottish, led to a complete transformation of the English view of Scotland. The English might patronise the Scots and romanticise the Scottish way of life into a culture of tartan and bagpipes but they grew to respect the Scots in a way that they never did the Irish. Amongst the ruling classes inter-marrying was far more frequent between Scots and English than between the English and Irish, which helped mix the culture of the two nations.

Scotland became tied very much into the British Empire, its soldiers in the fighting Scottish regiments defended it, whilst Scottish architects and marine and rail engineers designed and built the Empire. During this period the Kirk also sent out missionaries across the Empire. Scotland moved away from cotton as its staple industry to the heavy industries of shipbuilding and steel. The

Clyde built the ships, Glasgow became the showpiece of Empire and set the world price for 'pig iron' through its Glasgow Exchange, and Dundee was tied to the Empire through jute and its foreign investments. Edinburgh and Aberdeen became regional centres developing Scottish culture in a distinct way from that developing in England. Scotland invested heavily in the development of the Empire, and through Scottish businesses such as the African Lakes Trading Company a successful replay of Darien occurred. This time with imperial support Nyasaland developed as an affective Scots colony. In many parts of the Empire British colonisation in affect became mainly Scottish. In Australia, New Zealand, South Africa and particularly Canada, Scottish migrants made up as much as a third of the settlers (Harvie, 1994, p. 67).

Unsurprisingly with so much personally invested in the economic might and running of the British Empire Scots looked to the wider world picture in issues of politics. Therefore when Scotland came to consider calls for Home Rule it was a movement without a true figurehead and great popular momentum. There was no Scottish Charles Parnell, David Lloyd George or Tom Ellis. Although Gladstone had Scottish parents and at the end of his career held an Edinburgh seat he never sought to exploit his Scottish ancestry or appear too nationalistic. As if to prove this lack of nationalism an attempt by forty Scottish MPs in 1869 to revive the post of Scottish secretary of state abolished in 1746, and another 1872 motion to set up a select committee on Scottish affairs, were both rejected by Gladstone (Harvie and Jones, 2000, p. 20). The aim of those Scottish MPs who did support devolution was not to separate Scotland and England but to give Scotland equality with England in constitutional law, and it was pointed out that while Scotland had retained its own legal system in the union, it was now in the unusual situation of having an independent judiciary with no legislature to support it.

In 1886 Joseph Chamberlain led some seventy-eight Liberal Unionists to join the Conservatives in 1886, in opposition to Gladstone's Home Rule to Ireland. As the nineteenth century progressed the Liberal Unionists and Conservatives increased their position electorally in Scotland after 1886; by 1900 they had a majority of the seats there (Harvie, 1994, p. 18). A number of these Liberal Unionists were Scottish MPs and they displaced the Liberals from large parts of west central Scotland, where they drew on the newly enfranchised skilled Protestant working class. When the Liberal Unionist and Conservative parties joined formally in 1912 it meant that the party in Scotland was effectively taken over by the Liberal Unionists and therefore took the title of Unionist party in Scotland up until 1965 (Brown *et al.*, 1998, p. 14). In the future this Liberal Unionist legacy would help explain why the Conservatives (Scottish Unionists) where able to do so well in working-class Scottish constituencies which had traditionally been the Liberals' domain.

At the time of the first Irish Home Rule bill, in 1886, the Scottish Home Rule Association was formed and under its auspices no fewer than thirteen Home Rule proposals were placed before the House of Commons between 1890 and

1914, gaining the support of a majority of Scottish MPs on eleven of these occasions. The nature of these proposals can be seen from the text of a resolution passed by 180 votes to 170 in 1894, saying 'it is desirable, while retaining intact the power and supremacy of the Imperial Parliament, to establish a legislature in Scotland for dealing with purely Scottish affairs' (Mackie, 1964, p. 368). Devolution, if only administrative, had arrived the year before in 1885. In that year Lord Rosebery created the post of Scottish secretary supported by the Scottish Office. The new post enjoyed the support of Liberals and even some Scottish Tories. Not all Scottish Tories supported the post, however. The Conservative Duke of Richmond and Gordon, who personally thought the post 'quite unnecessary', ironically became the first Scottish secretary (Harvie and Jones, 2000). The duke was, however, correct in his pessimism concerning the post. At first the Scottish secretary had very little to do, but most importantly he was always a cabinet minister and after 1892 the job began to grow in importance and stature. In his short term as prime minister Rosebery followed up his institution of the Scottish Office and Scottish secretary with the formation in the Commons of the Scottish Grand Committee, formed of all Scottish MPs and expected to give special attention to legislation affecting Scotland. Scotland was gaining a stronger voice in London but still it was not able to shift any substantial power back to Scotland. This was mainly because there was no real passion underlying these Home Rule proposals, merely a feeling that, if Ireland could have Home Rule, so too should Scotland. Despite the sympathy of the Liberal party and support from future Labour leaders like Keir Hardie and Ramsay MacDonald, none of the proposed measures for increasing devolution in Scotland got past the committee stage in the Commons.

In 1900 a Liberal party left-wing group of Home Rulers founded the Young Scots' Society, which spoke out against 'English MPs' and in favour of a 'new Liberal agenda'. They were in the minority, however, and therefore Scottish Home Rule was only likely to come about when Westminster sought to solve effectively the 'Irish problem'. In 1906 Scottish Liberal MP Winston Churchill (Dundee), as home secretary, put forward a scheme for parliaments for Ireland, Scotland and Wales and seven English regions. This failed and then a most determined effort came in 1910 with twenty MPs forming a Scottish National Committee, under whose auspices the Commons voted in 1912 to treat Scotland like Ireland, proposing a separate Scottish parliament of 140 members. A Scottish Government Bill was prepared and presented but no room in the parliamentary timetable was found before 1913 and in 1914 the outbreak of World War I ensured that any such bill was postponed indefinitely.

During this pre-Great War period, perhaps the best example of a successful drive for Scottish independence from England, that had lasting repercussions, concerned the split between the Football Association (FA) and the Scottish Football Association (SFA). On 30 October 1886 a third-round FA Cup match between Preston North End and Queen's Park resulted in a Scottish player with Preston, Jimmy Ross, having to be smuggled out of the ground after his foul resulted a pitch invasion by Queen's Park fans. The incident brought to a head differences between the FA and the SFA and on 10 May 1887: the FA declared that 'clubs belonging to this Association shall not be members of any other National Association'. Scottish teams then withdrew from the FA Cup. The British Football league was dead and one hundred and thirty years later it remains no closer to life (Harvie, 1994, p. 19).

Outside of football, however, Scottish nationalism was slowly building itself up. It had yet to be linked clearly to demands for political Home Rule. It would take almost another century to do this.

Wales

Nationalism in Wales reached a new high during the late nineteenth and early twentieth centuries. The years from 1886 to 1906 saw the Welsh Liberal MPs at their most 'radical'. In parliament they even began to refer to themselves as the Welsh National party in a parallel to the Irish National party. The Welsh Nationalist Liberals played little part in the Gladstone-Rosebery government of 1892–95. With the exception of rising Welsh radical Tom Ellis, who served as chief whip, the other Welsh Nationalist Liberal MPs such as David Lloyd George were too junior to play an active part in government. In opposition the radicalism was therefore channelled into political crusades against what the Welsh Liberal demonology referred to as the 'unholy trinity' (Morgan, 1973, p. 13). This trinity referred to the familiar enemies of the 'brewers' (temperance), the 'bishops' (disestablishment of the church) and the 'squires' (tenant land reform). Added to these causes was also a substantial political sympathy to events that occurred in Ireland. On many issues such as Home Rule and the need for religious reform the events occurring in Ireland were felt to parallel those occurring in Wales. This meant the Welsh Liberal non-conformists MPs such as Ellis and Lloyd George often united with the Irish Roman Catholic MPs in and outside of Westminster because their grievances on religion, the land and Home Rule were so similar in many respects (Morgan, 1960, p. 71).

As was the case in Scotland, the English establishment, in particular the church, was disliked in Wales but without any of the real animosity felt in Ireland. Wales had been a part of England since 1536 and had never been united as a separate state before that time so that there were certainly no separate specifically Welsh institutions, as was the case in Scotland where the Scots were clearly seen to have their own particular legal system. The last distinction between England and Wales administratively and legally, the Great Sessions and the chanceries of Wales, were abolished in 1830 causing Wales to be totally integrated into England (Davies, 1994, p. 364). Another factor distinguishing the Welsh situation was that, unlike Ireland, across much of Wales there was no substantial class of absentee and alien landlords. Although aristocrats like the Marquis of Bute (for a time the world's richest man) and Earl of Plymouth owned large areas of South Wales they personally contributed hugely to the development of Welsh society and culture. Elsewhere in Wales the landlords and squirearchy were often themselves Welsh-speaking and for the most part of the same community as their tenants.

Not all landlords were benign. This was seen quickly with the opening up of the franchise and the Liberal victory in the general election of 1868 that saw an end of Conservative political domination in Wales. From then on it would on the whole remain one of the least successful parts of the United Kingdom for the Conservatives. There was, however, initially a period of revenge by the defeated Tory squires who had been displaced as Welsh parliamentarians, often by the votes of their own tenants. In Caernarfonshire, a Liberal defeated the son of the slate magnate Lord Penrhyn, one of the most staunchly Tory aristocrats in Wales. Many tenant farmers were subsequently evicted by their Tory landlords for 'voting the wrong way' (Grigg, 1997, p. 41). Lord Willoughby d'Eresby on the Gwydir Estate in Caernarfonshire did likewise. The action caused outrage amongst Welsh Nationalist Liberals for generations, becoming part of the folk law of Liberal Wales. Donald McCormick, in his biography of Lloyd George, described the practice (McCormick, 1963, pp. 34–5):

> The election ballots were not secret in those days and many tenants who had not voted for Tory candidates were evicted from their land and cottages. This happened at Llanystumdwy, and Lloyd George's earliest memories must have been of neighbours – often mothers in the last stages of childbirth – thrown out into the street with their few belongings and driven to the fields to find what shelter they could in some distant hayrick. Even they might be charged as vagrants and hounded out of the district. Other landlords were more subtle. They merely raised the rents of those who had voted Tory and reduced those of the faithful Tories. Liberals who owned shops were boycotted; their children were brought before the courts on some trumped up charges of poaching.

The action of the Tory squires understandably caused such outrage amongst Liberal MPs that in 1869 parliament set up a commission under Lord Hartington, the former member for the Radnor district (1868–69), to examine these cases of electoral persecution (Morgan, 1980, p. 26). Almost a hundred cases were proven in Wales. This led to the introduction of Secret Ballot Act, bringing in secret voting, in 1872. Thus electoral events in Wales had led to the reshaping of elections everywhere in Britain. Then nine years later in 1881 Liberals and non-conformists, closely allied to the temperance cause, were able get the Sunday Closing (Wales) Act passed, which made much of Wales 'dry' on Sundays and closed public houses across the principality on the Sabbath. This was the first parliamentary act that applied only to Wales and acknowledged that Wales was a separate nation for legislative purposes. Despite this Welsh act, however, until 1967 all English legislation was deemed automatically to apply to Wales.

When the movement for Irish Home Rule began to gain strength there was a similar feeling in Wales, as in Scotland, that if Ireland could have Home Rule, so too should it. In 1886 a society calling itself Cymru Fydd (Future Wales) was founded in London and soon spread to Wales, but its aims and interests were initially as much cultural as political. As a result much was done to improve the distinctiveness of Wales in an educational context. Measures included founding the University of Wales, and efforts were made to stem the decline in the use of the Welsh language in schools.

Lloyd George's scheme through Cymru Fydd was to organise a highly disciplined Welsh party that could link up with the Irish parliamentary party in challenging Westminster's view of Wales and forcing the Liberal party to endorse Home Rule. He made unsuccessful overtures to this effect through the Irish Nationalist Charles Parnell's mistress Kitty O'Shea. There was no real enthusiasm for Parnell amongst most Victorian non-conformist Welsh Liberal MPs, who were well aware of his adulterous liaisons. Lloyd George's South Wales Liberal rival and MP for Merthyr Tydfil, D. A. Thomas, was furious with the fact that overtures had been made through a mistress. It was made worse by the fact that Lloyd George was himself also being cited in a divorce petition at the time. When Lloyd George put his plan to a small group of prominent Liberals concerning a united Welsh political party it was treated in some quarters with outright hostility. Thomas angrily asked him:

Do you want to repeat Parnell's blunders by ruining everything for Wales' future? You seem to think that the Irish have everything to teach us. It would be better to learn from the lesson of where Mrs. O'Shea will lead Parnell – to Home Rule or the Divorce Court! (McCormick, 1963, p. 46)

As far as Welsh nationality was concerned the members of Cymru Fydd did not look for separation from England. They looked instead for equality, refusing to accept that Wales might be regarded as being in the second rank and somehow inferior or subordinate to England. On the other hand they had difficulty with the notion of a Welsh nation because Wales was rife with inequalities and divisions. The north distrusted the south; the former principality distrusted the former Welsh Marches; rural north and mid-Wales distrusted the industrial south; Welsh-speakers distrusted English-speakers and vice versa while the large counties claimed a greater say in Welsh affairs than the smaller counties were willing to grant them.[6] Apart from the divisive nature of these rivalries and suspicions rooted in the past history of Wales, there were communications problems created by the Welsh mountains, which in essence cut off the north from the south and made it easier for many Welsh people to travel to London for a meeting rather than to make their way somewhere else in the principality. There was no capital city at the time and as if to reflect this even the University of Wales was founded on three separate campuses at Bangor, Aberystwyth and Cardiff.

Cymru Fydd collapsed in the mid-1890s in Newport when the South Wales Liberal Federation refused to be combined with the North Wales Liberal Federation. A few prominent Liberals, including Lloyd George and Ellis, maintained the Home Rule fight but the real concern for Welsh Liberals was not Home Rule but the disestablishment of the Welsh Church and the non implementation of the hated Balfour Education Act of 1902. Figures from a survey carried out in 1906 showed that something like 74 per cent of the Welsh people were non-conformist and chapel-going by religion (Steinberg and Evans, 1970, p. 399) and yet the Church of England was the established church in Wales, a church which the Welsh regarded as remote from the concerns of their daily lives. As was the case in Ireland the vast majority of the people belonged to a religion that was not the established church of the state. And, again as was the case in Ireland, people were penalised for not being of the right religion: in the middle of the nineteenth century Welsh tenant farmers were expected to pay a 'tithe' to a church of which they were not members and widespread unrest was caused by the so-called 'tithe wars' when farmers refused to pay up.

The Church of Ireland was disestablished in 1868 and, with a Liberal landslide occurring in the same year, it might have been expected that the Liberal government would take up the cause of Welsh disestablishmentarianism with equal enthusiasm for acknowledgement of an existing form of religious devolution. Gladstone did not approve initially, however, after the North and South Wales Liberal Federations and then the National Liberal Federation meeting in Newcastle reiterated the call for the disestablishment of the church in Wales in its comprehensive declaration of the policy intentions (the so-called 'Newcastle Programme'), he changed his mind. In 1892 Gladstone put disestablishment for the Welsh Church second on the political agenda only behind Irish Home Rule in importance. Gladstone was not good with dealing with issues of a nationalist nature, however. He had failed with Irish Home Rule and subsequently with Welsh disestablishment. The same cause also floundered under his successor, Rosebery, and it was not until twenty years later under Herbert Asquith that a measure to disestablish the church in Wales was finally put before the Commons. Disestablishment was granted in 1914 but was yet another casualty of the outbreak of war and it was 1920 before the church in Wales separated itself from Canterbury. By then the number of chapelgoers had fallen dramatically, as the 'new religion' of socialism began to displace that of Liberalism and chapel in people's hearts.

While efforts were being devoted to disestablishmentarianism the Home Rule issue had been forgotten, and by the time disestablishment was granted in 1920, things had changed so much that it seemed this forgetfulness might last forever. The Labour party had gained its ascendancy in South Wales and the burning issues had become social matters such as poverty, living conditions, education and pay. In 1922 there was a proposed conference on devolution but it failed to advance the cause due to lack of interest.

In the late nineteenth and early twentieth centuries Wales had become part of the industrial powerhouse of the British Empire. Whereas Scotland built the steam ships that connected the Empire, Wales supplied the 'black gold' (steam coal) that kept them sailing. The iron and steel industries dominated North, South and West Wales so that few could escape their grasp. The price of world coal was set on the Cardiff Coal Exchange, the world's first million-pound deal was done in Cardiff Bay and the coal-owning Marquis of Bute became the world's richest man. Unlike Ireland and Scotland, where an existing over-population had been made so much worse by the potato blight and the Highland clearances that it could only be rectified by wholesale emigration abroad to the United States or Canada, the dispossessed of rural Wales could remain in the principality by going to live and work in the valleys. They were joined in turn by the dispossessed of Ireland and the rural migrants from the west country and border counties. In time this caused increasing militancy with the industrial classes in South Wales whose migration from England and Ireland meant that they had little affinity to the Welsh-speaking Wales which had been so supportive of the Liberal party in the nineteenth century. As the century drew on the evils of industrialisation, in working and living conditions, made for a new divide in Wales that had nothing to do with nationality. The Welsh people had always been radical in their political opinions; now they became ardent campaigners in the class conflict between the workers and the forces of industry and capital. Initially encompassed by Liberalism, within time socialism, supported by the trade unions, carried the banner for the Welsh industrial working class. There was no room on this banner for Home Rule, the workers' struggle was to involve all workers from all nations, and Welsh nationalism was therefore seen as peripheral and belonging to a bygone era.

Conclusions – Home Rule-all-round

Alongside the proposals for Home Rule for Ireland, Scotland and Wales there was an alternative advocated by some politicians which envisaged a federal structure under which Scotland and Wales, as well as Ireland, and together with either England or the English regions would each gain their own legislatures, although all these assemblies would subordinate to the federal parliament in Westminster. The main point to remember about the proposed federal structure – or 'Home-Rule-all-round' as it was known – was that it provided an answer to certain difficulties that had emerged in Home Rule legislation and which are still relevant to devolution today. The federal plan would:

- provide for fair and equal treatment for each component part of the UK;
- equalise fiscal matters since each legislature would have its own taxing powers;
- encourage unity, as the devolved legislations combined could bring others into line.

The plan was first put forward by Earl Russell in 1872 and gained sufficient support for the 1912 Irish Home Rule Bill to be renamed as the Government of Ireland and House of Commons (Devolution of Business) Bill since it contained proposals that would have provided for English, Scottish and Welsh grand committees. The federal aspects were dropped from the bill but they were known to have had the support of Asquith and other frontbench spokesmen (Bogdanor, 1999, p. 45).

The inherent problem in any federal solution is that England, Ireland, Scotland and Wales are very different places with very different needs, and could never be fitted into a uniform pattern. Moreover the real sticking point – and this is still very relevant today – is that while Scotland, Wales and Ireland could all produce good reasons why they should have their own distinct legislature the same is not true for England.

Advocates of Home Rule thought that federalism was irrelevant and little more than a trivial diversion. Unionists on the other hand saw federalism as a great threat to the union which would lead inevitably to the break up of the United Kingdom.

Irish unionists were ironically in favour of federalism if it meant a federation of regions rather than of nations. Under such an arrangement it would be possible to have separate legislatures for the Protestant north and the Catholic south. Irish nationalists on the other hand were equally as certain that Ireland was a nation, whole and indivisible, for which only a national solution was acceptable. In this way the federal argument was laying the groundwork for that resolution of the Irish question, which would involve partition. In 1919, after World War I, a speaker's conference was called to consider devolution and the possibility of a federal solution. But the conference failed to resolve the contentious issues and the whole Home Rule project collapsed. Discussion was overtaken by events as the Irish question moved to confrontation and the armed struggle.

David Lloyd George was perhaps the most nationalist politician ever to become prime minister. He was a politician who had made his early reputation in parliament supporting nationalism in Wales, Ireland and Scotland. It was therefore to him that most nationalist MPs looked when wishing to see their Home Rule ambitions fulfilled. In 1920 a small group of Welsh Liberal MPs called on Lloyd George to create the post of Welsh secretary, but he urged them instead urged them to 'go for the big thing', implying that they should pursue a Welsh parliament (Davies, 1983, p. 21). David Matthews' (MP for Swansea East) attempt to present a bill calling for a Welsh secretary in February 1921 therefore came to nothing. In September that year Lloyd George told Welsh MPs that devolution to Wales would be too expensive. He stated that as 'Prime Minister of the Empire, and custodian of the National Resources' he would oppose a Home Rule bill (Madgwick *et al.*, 1973, p. 55). This was disappointing indeed, for those people who could remember the Welsh radical David Lloyd George of the 1890s and early 1900s. This fact didn't stop Sir Robert Thomas,

Liberal MP for Wrexham, together with the Scottish member, Murray MacDonald, introducing political devolution through the government of Scotland and Wales bill on 22 May 1922. The bill was 'talked out' on its first reading. Six months later Lloyd George was out of office and the issue of devolution vanished with him. Many nationalists felt that devolution had now faded into history with the Liberal party that represented it. They would now have to find other means to secure their cherished goal of Home Rule.

Notes

1　This is a quote from a speech made by Gladstone to the House of Commons, 8 April 1886.
2　An indication of the size and popularity of the Catholic Association can be gained from the fact that a membership subscription of only one penny a month (known as the 'Irish Rent') could produce a revenue of £1,000 a week (Steinberg and Evans, 1970, p. 63).
3　The Test Act of 1673 required all holders of public offices to be communicants in the Anglican Church, who were expected to renounce publicly the doctrine of transubstantiation in a way Catholics would find impossible.
4　The favourite weapon of the Irish Nationalist party was the filibuster by which Irish MPs would speak at length, one taking over from another as the first tired, and thereby prolonging debates beyond their designated time, 'talking out' the bill and seriously disrupting government planning. One side-effect of Irish nationalism was to introduce various devices into the Commons such as the guillotine, by which time-wasting debate could be cut short.
5　Coercion Acts, by which the government sought to control unrest and potential revolution, were a permanent feature of life in Ireland during the nineteenth century and half a dozen acts between 1814 and 1891 sought to control the population through measures such as suspending trial by jury, martial law, banning of public meetings, increased powers of search and arrest etc. The Royal Irish Constabulary was founded in 1836 as a semi-military force to enforce the Coercion Acts. Always the target of Irish nationalists the acts continued until recent times, continuing to be used in Northern Ireland under the name of 'emergency powers' after 1969.
6　An idea of the inequalities can be gained from the fact that well over 50 per cent of the Welsh population lived in just the two counties of Glamorgan and Monmouth.

Part II

Preparing for devolution

4

Scotland and Wales: devolution resurgent

In the political heydays of the pre-World War I era Home Rule was at the top of the political agenda, although the weight given to different nations in respect of Home Rule varied considerably. Whilst in Ireland virtually the whole political class had a view on Home Rule, in Scotland and Wales it was a minority cause. The business of trade for ruling classes in Scotland and Wales meant that being the 'workshop of the world' was more important than virtually any other issue, whilst developments in the colonies, particularly the coming of age of the white dominions of Canada, New Zealand and Australia, gave an important inspiration concerning how Home Rule could be shaped in Britain. As interest in developing Home-Rule-all-round as a solution to the Irish problem became more tangible the catastrophe that was the Great War, the Irish rebellion of 1916 and the granting of Home Rule there in 1922 ended the opportunity to look at devolution all-round. It now looked to be slightly insignificant compared with the domestic and European problems left in the legacy of the war, which had left virtually no village or community in Wales or Scotland without scores of its young men now buried in the fields of France and Belgium. The Celtic nations had proved their loyalty to king, country and Empire but devolution now seemed almost to belong to a far gentler era. In addition many who had advocated it amongst the younger and middle-aged ruling and political classes were now dead, scarred physically or mentally by the war, or putting their energies into the reconstruction of Britain and Europe.

In the decade that followed the Great War the British nation soon developed problems of a massive economic and political nature, which in some areas of Wales and Scotland produced unemployment levels of 90 per cent. Dealing with this economic crisis then dominated domestic the political agenda to such an extent that during the 1930s coalition governments were formed primarily to deal with the crisis of unemployment. However, before a solution was found Britain was plunged back into war. The very future of the British nation was in the balance in the 1940s in the fight against Nazi German and as the British nation pulled together to fight the war devolution was sidelined. Nevertheless it did remain an issue and behind the scenes some politicians, particularly in Scotland, continued to develop administrative devolution. In the post-World War II era of the welfare state and state centralisation devolution once again remained in the wilderness, but by the 1960s it once again gathered momentum. This chapter therefore details something of the events and proposes that put political devolution once more on the political agenda of the Scottish and Welsh nations.

The evolution of Scottish devolution

When the Irish question was settled at the end of World War I it looked as though the issue of Home Rule for Scotland had become irrelevant and would shortly be totally forgotten. As late as 1924, during the first Labour government, the Scottish Liberal Federation had proposed that Scotland should have a parliament to deal with Scottish affairs, and George Buchanan, Labour MP for Glasgow-Gorbals, proposed yet another Home Rule bill that was talked out by the opposition. But these were ideas and proposals that belonged to the old Liberal party, albeit with Labour support and, by 1924, the Liberals were already fading from the scene, to be replaced by Labour at a time when Labour was becoming as much of a unionist party as the Conservatives.

Labour, having supported Home Rule in the days of Keir Hardie as a quasi-nationalist party, cooled on the issue to some degree after the formation of the more Westminster-orientated Independent Labour party under Ramsey MacDonald. Labour failed to progress electorally in Scotland until after World War I. In Glasgow the Labour MP for Bridgtown, James Maxton, and the Marxist John Maclean MA among others brought forward the iconic 'Red Clydeside' as a new movement to pursue the interests of the 'workers'. Red Clydeside continued to be at the cutting edge of the ever-expanding Labour party in Scotland. Maclean, however, died in 1923 and others were not always so predisposed to Scottish autonomy.

The Scottish Home Rule Association, financed by Labour's Tom Johnston, was founded in 1918 with the idea of pushing for a Gladstonian model of Scottish Home Rule, with the Scottish parliament having power over domestic matters. Many within the socialist movement, however, saw the problems of Scotland being concerned with issues of class enhanced by the slump and unemployment of the late 1920s. Labour was already cooling on the idea of Home Rule and when a group of twenty-nine MPs, some twenty-eight local authorities and the Convention of Scottish Royal Burghs formed the Scottish National Convention in 1924 to campaign for Home Rule, the idea got nowhere. The Reverend James Barr MP presented the convention scheme to parliament in May 1927, seconded by Tom Johnston. It was talked out, as was the second amended version in 1928. The Scottish Home Rule Association then went into a period of major reassessment of how to achieve its objectives.

In 1928 the Scots National League was formed to agitate for an independent Scotland. It was a cultural as much as a political movement and a fringe party made up of students, romantics and eccentrics, but it had a minor success in 1931 when Compton Mackenzie was elected rector of Glasgow University on a nationalist ticket (Lynch, 2002, p. 27). The remnant of those who had supported Home Rule for Scotland formed themselves into the Scottish party, which advocated devolution rather than separate independence. On 7 April 1934 the National party of Scotland and the Scottish Party merged to form the Scottish National party (SNP) under John MacCormick, who had left the Labour party while still at Glasgow University in order to campaign for Scottish devolution. The new party was 'decidedly non-ideological, vague on Scottish self-government and with few clear policies' (Finlay, 1994, p. 163). The SNP contested local and parliamentary by-elections throughout the 1930s without any significant success. It lost nine deposits in the fourteen parliamentary elections it stood in between 1934–39, although in the 1935 general election it gained 28.1 per cent of the vote in the Western Isles and in the Scottish Universities by-election of 1936 it gained a pre-war record of 31.1 per cent. The SNP's lack of electoral success and MacCormick's tendency to run the party as his own personal fiefdom led to him being ousted as leader in 1942, replaced by Douglas Young, and the SNP becoming more militant and separatist in its aims (Lynch, 2002, p. 50).

In 1941 the Labour MP Thomas Johnston was appointed as secretary of state for Scotland during the wartime coalition government. Johnston was one of Scotland's most able propagandists, administrators and negotiators. He was able to reorganise the health service, provide elements of free health care, start work on prospective new towns, and deal with the slums as well as with the restructure of the Scottish economy. Above all Johnston made administrative devolution work, albeit in a 'expert-knows-best' way rather than through wider public consultation and democracy (Finlay, 2004, p. 31).

Whilst Johnston dealt with a coalition government running Scotland the SNP remained outside of this coalition. The newly assertive party, however, took advantage of the fact that during the war the main parties had declared an electoral truce and did not contest elections while the fighting continued, maintaining the pre-war status quo. The SNP, however, decided that they would fight any by-election in Scotland, always putting up a candidate against whichever party held the seat. As a result a medical officer with the Glasgow corporation, Dr Robert McIntyre became the SNP's first-ever MP in the Motherwell and Wishaw by-election of 1945 with a narrow 617-vote majority over Labour. Three months later when normal political activity resumed in the first post-war general election McIntyre's vote fell from 51.4 per cent to just 17 per cent and Labour regained the seat.

Motherwell and Wishaw was the SNP's only success for some time. In the fifteen elections the party contested between 1945 and 1950 it held its deposit in only two. Britain was in post-war austerity and Scotland was taking its share of this too. As the wartime Scottish Office had proved itself adept at delivering government policy without the need for substantial democratic oversight so in the post-war era it would continue in this role of administrative management of policy rather than that of Scottish government (Finlay, 2004, p. 31). Although all of Britain suffered years of austerity and hardship after 1945, there were still those who believed that Scotland was suffering disproportionately from the neglect of Westminster. The post-war Labour party in Scotland was devoid of prominent Scottish political figures and therefore took little active part in immediate devolutionary campaigning. Despite this John MacCormick was able to get together a Scottish convention in 1947 of all political parties, business, union and church leaders. The convention resolved to pursue 'self-government', the next step behind which was getting two million Scots to sign a Scottish covenant in 1949 calling for a Home Rule Scottish parliament within the United Kingdom. A number of bogus signatures on the covenant allowed both the Labour and Conservative leadership to dismiss it as irrelevant. MacCormick went on to stand in the 1948 by-election in the Labour stronghold of Paisley. He believed that he could unite moderate nationalist, Liberal and unionist opinion and be elected. In fact his attacks on the London government sounded to Labour like direct attacks on them, he lost the election by 6,500 votes and 'ensured lasting Labour enmity for the Convention and Nationalism' within Scottish Labour (Harvie and Jones, 2000, p. 59). Two years later, on Christmas Day 1950, MacCormick and three students stole the Stone of Destiny from under the Coronation Throne in Westminster Abbey. It had been the coronation stone of Scottish monarchs until Edward I took it in 1296. Although its theft attracted great media attention until it reappeared at Arbroath Abbey four months later it did not ignite nationalist feeling in Scotland. Memories of that stunt lingered on over the years and were reflected in Scottish secretary Michael Forsythe's act of 1996 in returning the stone to Edinburgh in an attempt to curry favour with the Scottish people.

Home Rule for Scotland was very much a non-issue for the two main Scottish parties. The Labour government was too concerned with the creation of the welfare state, the nationalisation programme and planning the Festival of Britain to spare any thought for such parochial matters as Scottish devolution, and Attlee even refused to meet MacCormick to discuss the covenant. The Conservatives in Scotland, who styled themselves as the unionist party, were lead by a former Scottish-seated MP, Winston Churchill, who in 1911 had publicly endorsed the notion of a Scottish parliament but who no longer had the Liberal pedigree that had led him to this conclusion. The public mood was one of ambivalence to devolution and therefore the public were not deterred by the unionist failure to endorse Home Rule. As proof of this viewpoint the unionists were riding a high electoral tide in Scotland and in 1955 they became the only party in Scottish political history to achieve both a majority of seats and total percentage of the vote in Scotland. This meant that unionism was now the most popular political creed in Scotland.

Meanwhile in Wales

Wales has always been very different from Scotland in the way that devolution has been perceived. As we have seen, Wales was never united as a fully independent state as Scotland had been and whereas the conflict for united Scotland was with England, for Wales divisions were always internal rather than external. Even after the days of the native Welsh princes had passed, it was still divided between the lands conquered by Edward I and under royal jurisdiction on the one hand and the semi-autonomous Marcher lordships on the other. Equally as important, over the years since the divide over who ruled Wales passed, new divisions arose. These were between the north and south, 'church and chapel', industrial and agricultural, industrial valleys and urban coastal cities, Welsh-speaking and English-speaking. These divisions surfaced during the ill-fated Cymru Fydd attempt to unite the Liberal party across Wales into one Welsh national and cultural party. The south rejected a united movement on the twin reasons of fear of domination by the Welsh-speaking north and fear of alienating links with the English, particularly with Bristol and the surrounding areas.

As we saw in Chapter 3, World War I had put devolution into the background but it had an important affect on developing Welsh nationhood. After the war had ended there was a chance to return to domestic politics once more. During the coalition government's 1918 'coupon' election the Lloyd George Liberals put out a joint general election manifesto with the Conservatives under Bonar Law.[1] It talked mainly of the successes of winning the war and the future of 'our Empire and the nations of which it is composed' (Dale, 2000a, p. 21). Despite his Welsh heritage and numerous warm words towards Wales whilst prime minister, there was no mention by Lloyd George of Welsh aspirations. Herbert Asquith replied with his own manifesto for the non-coalition Liberals, which consisted of just over 300 words and similarly made no mention of Wales or things Welsh (Dale, 2000b, pp. 36–7). Devolution had become a remote issue for those in power.

To the Welsh working classes the struggle was now economic rather than political or religious. Their increasing loyalty to the party was now based on the belief that it was the party that could obtain the best possible economic outcome for the workers of Wales. Over the decades various attempts were made to start a purely Welsh political party, but from Cymru Fydd to the Welsh Nationalist League the attempts fell upon stony ground. A seed which would grow, however, was planted on the Wednesday of the National Eisteddfod week in August 1925 at the Maesgwyn Temperance Hall, Pwllheli in North Wales. This would establish a political movement that in time would eclipse the Welsh Liberals. Six members of two separate nationalist organisations, Byddin Ymreolwyr Cymru (Welsh Home Rule Army) and Mudiad Cymrieg (Welsh Movement) met together to form Plaid Genedlaethol Cymru. This was later to become known as Plaid Cymru – the Party of Wales. The new party was driven by a man called Saunders Lewis, who saw a need because Welsh nationalism 'could not be represented by either the individualism of the Liberals or the socialism of the Labour Party' (McAllister, 2001, p. 28).

Labour might have been expected to be more sympathetic to Welsh aspirations but there was a widespread belief that only the workers united across all nations in socialism could deal with the problems of poverty and unemployment. In Wales this philosophy was led by the radical left-wing rebel Aneurin Bevan (MP for Ebbw Vale), who became the main obstructer of political devolution. Bevan was the senior Labour political heavyweight who was totally opposed to any form of Welsh devolution. His dominance of the Labour party as a whole was enough to block it. In the first 'Welsh Day' debate on St Davids Day (1 March 1944) Bevan sardonically asked 'How are Welsh sheep different from English sheep?' and went on to dismiss the whole idea of a Welsh debate being a waste of time (Deacon, 2002, p. 17). Such views at the highest levels of the Labour party were by no means unique. In 1945 the Labour home secretary, Herbert Morrison, in rejecting the idea of Wales having a Welsh Office on the same lines as the Scots had a Scottish Office, declared: 'The proper remedy for Wales, as for Scotland, is to ensure that they both form part of a single economic plan for the whole country' (quoted in Evans, 1999, p. 51).

During the immediate post-war period Welsh nationalism continued through Liberal MPs such as Clement Davies, Emyr Roberts and Megan Lloyd George. In addition some Labour MPs such as S.O. Davies, Jim Griffiths and Cledwyn Hughes supported the devolutionary cause. In March 1955 Davies even brought forward a Private Members Bill for a Welsh parliament. Only six MPs supported it, five of them from the Labour party in Wales. All were reported to the party's National Executive Committee for opposing the party line against devolution (Deacon, 2002, p. 17).

Whilst Labour rebels and Liberals fought for devolution Plaid Cymru was largely ignored by the majority of the Welsh electorate. In the 1950s, however, the issue of the extent to which Wales was exploited by the English was kept alive by such high-handed actions of the British government as the proposal to flood the Tryweryn Valley in Merionethshire to provide drinking water for Liverpool, drowning the village of Capel Celyn and dispossessing sixty-seven Welsh-speaking families. Nevertheless, until 1959, Plaid Cymru put up candidates in only a few constituencies, mainly in Welsh-speaking areas. In the 1959 general election, however, in the face of growing unease at what was seen as English exploitation, Plaid Cymru put up twenty candidates and polled over 77,000 votes. Although they failed to gain any seats, and lost more electoral deposits than they kept, they contested more seats than the Liberals in Wales, and stood in a large number of non-Welsh-speaking South Wales seats for the first time.

The 1950s had seen the Campaign for a Welsh Parliament, led by former Liberal and from 1957 Labour MP Megan Lloyd George. In late 1956 Megan delivered its petition of 240,602 signatures calling for a parliament for Wales to

Conservative Welsh home secretary (also a former Welsh Liberal MP and Megan's brother) Gwilym Lloyd-George. Gwilym accepted the signature but as expected the Conservatives had no intention of creating a Welsh parliament. The action of these two former Welsh Liberals (and children of David Lloyd George) effectively saw a final curtain drawn on the parliament for Wales campaign until the 1980s; it wound up a few months later exhausted by campaigning, disorganisation and debt (Graham Jones, 1992). In the 1960s there was a growing Welsh-language movement in Cymdeithas yr Iaith Gymraeg (the Welsh Language Society) that showed itself ready to take direct action to support its cause. Most direct action was fairly innocuous and involved vandalising road signs and posters worded in English, but there was a more extreme wing that developed during the agitation surrounding the flooding of Capel Celyn and culminated in the student protest year of 1968. A handful of activists, the most formidable of whom were known as the Free Wales Army, showed that they were prepared to burn down holiday cottages and second homes belonging to English owners, while several English-language radio and television transmitters belonging to the BBC were blown up or threatened. On Saturday 25 May 1968 a bomb blew out the windows in the Welsh Office's Cathays Park building. This was the only bombing of a Welsh government building during peacetime. The investiture of the Prince of Wales at Caernarfon Castle in 1969 was another chance for a number of disruptive acts by extremist groups and it ended with the arrest of a Welsh nationalist accused of planting a bomb. It was true that activists like the Free Wales Army did not have the support of more than a small minority of the population and therefore the situation in Wales was never comparable with the troubles of Northern Ireland, but for a while it looked at though it might develop in that direction. Welsh nationalism, however, was no longer seen as being totally benign. In 1968, Plaid Cymru did not want events of violence to damage its growing political support and therefore sought to distance itself from the more extreme language activists by declaring itself to be bilingual.

In 1901 some 50 per cent of the Welsh population claimed to speak Welsh; by 1971 this had fallen to just over 20 per cent (Foulkes et al., 1983, p. 13). Unlike political devolution the Welsh language did, however, step-by-step gain legal recognition. The Welsh Courts Act 1942 had already made the language equal in the eyes of the courts but this did not cover wider public life. A report on the Legal Status of the Welsh Language was issued in 1965 and the Welsh Language Act was subsequently passed by parliament in 1967, giving equal status to both Welsh and English in many areas of public life. The speaking of Welsh, which had been in rapid decline throughout the century, began to stabilise and in some cases even increase, especially among the young. Welsh-language schools were developed and the ability to speak Welsh became a required qualification for teachers wishing to teach in Welsh-speaking areas, together with broadcasters or public officials in a number of organisations.

In July 1978 the Labour government produced a White Paper on broadcasting which gave its blessing to a Welsh-language fourth television channel. When the Conservatives came into power a year later they stated that they would not honour Labour's commitment. The subsequent political battle included a threat to fast to the death by Plaid Cymru's president and elder statesman Gwynfor Evans. It helped rebuilt the Welsh nationalist movement less than a year after it had been laid low by the failure to gain a 'yes' vote in the Welsh devolution referendum (Deacon, 2002, p. 55). In September 1980 the Conservative home secretary, William Whitelaw, announced a political u-turn and, when Channel 4 was set up in 1982, its Welsh equivalent, Sianel Pedwar Cymru (S4C), was created as a largely Welsh-language television channel. Although it remains one of the most heavily subsidised channels in the world it has also had the affect of greatly reducing Welsh language protests by acting as a conduit for preserving and developing Welsh language culture.

Administrative devolution in Scotland and Wales

We noted earlier in this chapter the events concerning the establishment and then development of the Scottish Office. Brown *et al.* saw the establishment of the Scottish Office as Scotland's own version of the development of the central state (1996, p. 13). This centralisation resulted in the Scottish Office taking over the work of the various Scottish boards that had run much of government business in Scotland in the nineteenth and early twentieth centuries. In the 1920s the Reorganisation of Offices (Scotland) Act 1928 saw the boards of agriculture and health for Scotland coming under the responsibility of the Scottish secretary. With growing responsibility came growing status for the Scottish Office. On 15 July 1926 the Scottish secretary, Conservative MP Sir J. Gilmour, was elevated to principal secretary within the British cabinet. This allowed for there to be greater opportunity 'to lobby for greater public spending, different legislation and welfare policies in Scotland' (Brown *et al.*, 1996, p. 13). Then just before the outbreak of World War II there was another general review of Scottish administration by the Gilmour Committee 1937, which led to the Reorganisation of Offices (Scotland) Act 1939. Then for the first time in over 200 years there was a move to devolve administrative power back to Scotland in a substantial way. The unionist ssecretary of state, Walter Elliot, shifted much of the Scottish Office from London to the newly established St Andrews House in Edinburgh in 1939. This brought into being four departments of the Scottish Office to be run in Scotland: agriculture, education, health and home affairs. All four departments had their own head that in turn worked under a permanent under secretary of state (Butler and Butler, 2000, p. 457).

During World War II the Scottish Office saw further growth when a new parliamentary under secretary was then appointed in 1940. The department further benefited by having at its head the war-time coalition Scottish secretary,

Thomas Johnston, a longstanding 'Home Ruler'. He formed a Scottish Council of State which consisted of all of the previous living Scottish secretaries. If there was consensus within the council then there was no need to take a policy to Westminster, a mechanism through which Johnston laid the foundations for much of Scotland's post-war reconstruction (Hassan, 1999, p. 25).

After 1951 much of the evolution of the Scottish Office occurred under Conservative governments. Churchill expanded the department's junior ministers from two to four. In 1953 he also established a Royal Commission on Scottish Affairs chaired by the Earl of Balfour on the workings of government and the management of the Scottish government. Although its conclusions only brought responsibility for roads and bridges from the Department of Transport to the Scottish Office it highlighted that centralised government in London was damaging to the Scottish economy (Harvie and Jones, 2000, p. 67), Although the Conservatives didn't act on this issue immediately, later on, under the Macmillan government in 1962, the Scottish Development Department was established and under Edward Heath some eleven years later this became the Scottish Development Agency (Butler and Butler, 2000, p. 457).

The Welsh administrative development

In 1890, five years after the Scottish Office was created, an attempt was made to set up a Welsh national body on the same lines. The national institutions (Wales) bill 1890 was brought forward by the radical Liberal MP for Glamorgan East, Alfred Thomas, and aimed to establish a Welsh secretary and a Welsh Office. The bill failed, however, and was subsequently reintroduced in 1891 and 1892. Once again these failed and for the remainder of the Liberals' period in office (1906–22) the pleas for Welsh Home Rule fell on deaf ears.

Despite successive Liberal governments' rejection of the need for a Welsh secretary and Welsh Office, the period between 1906 and 1921 saw something of a Golden Age of Welsh Liberal-inspired administrative devolution to Wales (Deacon, 2002, p. 232). In 1907 a Welsh department was set up in the Board of Education and was responsible for many innovations, not least establishing the place of the Welsh language in the curriculum. In 1911 a Welsh commission was set up to administer the National Insurance Act in the principality and in 1919 the Board of Agriculture, Food and Fisheries acquired a Welsh Office. This process continued under following governments so that by 1950 there were no fewer than seventeen such administrative units in Wales. This didn't result, however, in these devolved units being put under 'one roof' in a Welsh Office headed by a Welsh secretary. This was mainly due to the fact that all Conservative, Labour and coalition governments from 1922 onwards rejected the concept of devolution outright. When Morgan Jones, Labour MP for Caerphilly, led a parliamentary delegation to Neville Chamberlain in 1938 to request that a post of Welsh secretary be established they were also rejected outright. Chamberlain gave the grounds for his rejection as: 'expense', 'the fact that the existing devolved administrative structure was adequate' and the 'lack of a significant distinction existing between Welsh and English public administration' (Deacon, 2002, p. 232). Churchill rejected the same request in 1943 on similar grounds, and the post-war Labour government was no more sympathetic. In the end it was Churchill's Conservative government which in a minor u-turn finally appointed a minister of Welsh affairs in 1951. In 1957, prime minister Harold Macmillan transferred the responsibility for Wales to his minister of housing and local government, Henry Brooke, since it was felt that Welsh affairs were more a matter of local government than a responsibility of the Home Office. Right-winger Brooke began well but destroyed his own credibility by approving the flooding of the Tryweryn Valley by Liverpool Council, an act opposed by twenty-seven of the thirty-six Welsh MPs (Bogdanor, 1999, p. 159).

For the post-war Labour party in Wales, by now the dominant party of Wales for a generation, Welsh devolution was not clear-cut issue. After Morrison's outright rejection in 1945 of the notion, a split developed among Labour's Welsh MPs. It was between those (led by deputy Labour leader and Attlee cabinet member, James Griffiths, and rising Welsh Labour star Cledwyn Hughes) who favoured the appointment of a Welsh secretary and those (led by Labour 'icon' Aneurin Bevan and George Thomas) who were implacably opposed. Unlike Scotland with its own particular legal and education systems, Wales had never been treated as a separate administrative unit and since 1536 had been seen as an integral part of England, leaving 'no justification for a Welsh Secretary' (Deacon, 2002, p. 17). The Conservatives' move to establish a minister for Wales strengthened the hand of Labour's pro-devolutionists. If the Conservatives, as the pro-Unionist party, could give Wales a minister, why not the Labour party? When the Campaign for a Welsh Parliament folded in 1957 the Labour devolutionist activists switched their activities to obtaining a Welsh secretary.

Aneurin Bevan, James Griffiths and the party's leader, Hugh Gaitskell, were the three key figures who eventually established the Welsh Office and Welsh secretary. In July 1959 a Labour tripartite committee containing Bevan, Gaitskell and Griffiths met to discuss devolution. Bevan was against any policy which he felt would 'divorce Welsh political activity from the mainstream of British politics' (Deacon, 2002, p. 19). Griffiths was still passionately for a Welsh secretary and Office and Gaitskell remained neutral. Gaitskell provided three possible options for Welsh devolution:

1 a Royal Commission on Devolution;
2 a Welsh Grand Committee;
3 a minister for Welsh affairs with a seat in the cabinet.

Bevan dismissed the first two options as a mere 'exercise in shadow boxing' (Osmond, 1995, p. 161). He supported option three, but only if the Welsh secretary was granted effective executive power. Bevan was swayed by the emotional commitment of James Griffiths to the concept of a Welsh secretary which eventually persuaded him. Gaitskell then also supported the notion and in the autumn of 1959 the Wales region of the Labour party published *Labour's Policy for Wales*, which gave a firm commitment 'to the appointment of a Secretary of State for Wales with a seat in the Cabinet and with departmental responsibilities, to be exercised through a Welsh Office' (Griffiths, 1968, p. 112). Griffiths's plan for a Welsh Office was now endorsed by the Labour party executive and the party's conference, and was consequently included in the 1959 manifesto (*Forward with Labour: Labour's Plan for Wales*). Although Labour lost the 1959 general election Griffiths ensured that this pledge was also repeated in the 1964 Labour party general election manifesto (*Signposts for a New Wales*). This time Labour won. Harold Wilson's victory meant that Labour was at last able to fulfil its promise and the Welsh Office was created in October 1964, with James Griffiths as the first secretary. The new Welsh Office then fought a gradual and at sometimes fierce battle with other Whitehall departments to gain control over its own affairs and gradually expand the role of the department (Rowlands, 2004). Over the years that followed the powers of the Welsh Office were expanded; health being added to the remit in 1968 and schools in 1970. Ultimately the Welsh Office acquired almost as much power and control as the Scottish Office, growing to ten times its original size in terms of staff and budget, although never reaching parity with the Scottish Office, with law and order being the most notable omission .

It was always intended that, in an ideal world, the secretary of state for Wales should be Welsh and that the Welsh Office should be staffed by Welsh MPs. For twenty years this worked well enough. Even Peter Thomas's appointment as Welsh secretary when he was Conservative MP for Enfield South did not prejudice this position entirely. Thomas had very strong Welsh credentials having previously been the MP for Conwy and was a fluent Welsh speaker. Over time, however, the links between Conservative Welsh secretaries and Wales became more tenuous and then broke altogether. Only Nicholas Edwards (1979–87) of the six Conservative Welsh secretaries actually sat for a Welsh constituency. Edwards became the longest serving Welsh secretary and greatly increased its role, power and status in Whitehall and Westminster during his long tenure. When he left in 1987 there was then a ten-year period of English Welsh secretaries. Of these, Peter Walker (1987–90) was moderately successful, at least in terms of attracting industry to the principality. David Hunt (1990–93) was able to start the process of Welsh local government reorganisation, a minefield for the Welsh Labour party because it meant disbanding so many Labour controlled authorities which would have caused substantial grass-roots rebellion. This ironically enabled a rapid transition to a Welsh assembly later on, which would have required a move towards unitary authority anyway. It was essential to any measure of political devolution to remove one of the layers of local government (city/district councils and county councils formed the two-tier system) Unpopular as the local government reorganisation was with many part of Wales the appointment of the arch Thatcherite free-marketer John Redwood (1993–95), was a political disaster from the Welsh Conservatives' point of view. The Welsh verdict on Redwood is epitomised by an embarrassing television shot, often repeated, which shows the Welsh secretary looking desperate, opening and shutting his mouth in a vain attempt to persuade viewers that he actually knew and was singing the words of '*Hen Wlad fy Nhadau*' ('Land of my Fathers').

The growth of nationalism, moving towards devolution

In Scotland the dominance of unionist and Labour parties in the 1950s and 1960s was all-pervasive – the Liberals had just one Scottish seat, the SNP none – ensuring that this time was known as 'The High Tide of Unionism' (Harvie and Jones, 2000, p. 65). In the 1955 general election the SNP put up just two candidates who gained 0.5 per cent of the Scottish vote between them. A Liberal revival in Scotland during this period undermined nationalist growth in a number of Scottish constituencies (Lynch, 2002, p. 98), By 1966, however, the number of SNP candidates had risen to twenty-three against just five seats in 1959. They were now contesting an almost equal number of seats in Scotland as the Scottish Liberals.

Until 1959 the party that won the majority of seats in Scotland also coincided with the party forming the UK government. In 1959 this situation changed: whereas Conservatives had previously had a majority of seats in Scotland when there was a Conservative government in London, this time Labour became the largest party in Scotland, despite there being a Conservative government nationally. That Labour lead not only continued but increased until the 1997 election, which saw no Conservatives at all elected in Scotland. And it was not just the Labour party that took seats from the Conservatives, both the SNP and Scottish Liberal Democrat party also built much of their parliamentary strength by depriving the Conservatives of theirs. Thus the Conservatives could no longer claim to represent a substantial or (between 1997–2001) any portion of Scottish public opinion at all.

In the mid-1960s a major change took place in the nature of party alignment in Britain, leading to growing successes for the SNP and Plaid Cymru. It was a time when a growing volatility in voting behaviour reflected the fact that voters rapidly became disenchanted with governments and would register their disapproval by delivering a protest vote in mid-term by-elections. The party that received the protest vote varied. In times of Conservative government, disillusioned Tory voters turn to the Liberal Democrats. Faced with a Labour government, however, those Scottish and Welsh Labour voters who wished to protest could vote for the SNP or Plaid Cymru, thus not only delivering a protest but making the point that it was primarily against the English orientation of the government, whichever unionist party was in power. As the psephologist, David Butler, has said: 'The accident of by-elections undoubtedly shaped the pattern of successive Liberal and Nationalist revivals since the 1960s' (Cook and Ramsden, 1997, p. 11).

Unlike in Scotland, Plaid Cymru had not won or even come near to winning any Welsh constituency. Therefore Welsh nationalism was only regarded as a irritant in that it sometimes was believed to take enough votes off one party or another to allow their opponent to win the seat. This all changed in the heart of the 1960s. On 14 May 1966, after a long illness, Megan Lloyd George – now a Labour MP – died. For almost eighty years there had been a Lloyd George amongst the Welsh MPs; now this was to be no more. For the Welsh Liberals this meant a chance to regain the seat that Megan had taken off them in the 1957 by-election. In the general election six weeks earlier D. H. Davies had gained almost 12,000 votes for the Liberals. Although he was still over 9,000 votes off winning the seat he was clearly ahead of those others that had contested it. These included Plaid Cymru's Gwynfor Evans (7,416 votes) and his Conservative rival (5,338 votes). In the whole of the United Kingdom, Carmarthen, was the sixteenth most winnable Liberal seat. To most observers the contest was therefore clearly between Labour and Liberal as it always had been.

Liberal MP and Welsh party leader Emlyn Hooson 'dreamt of doing for Wales what Jo Grimond has done for Scotland', where Liberals now had five seats (*The Liberal News*, 10 June 1966, p. 2). Plaid Cymru's candidate was, as it had been for the general election in March, Gwynfor Evans. He was a seasoned campaigner, president of the party and had been a councillor and alderman of Carmarthenshire county council since 1949. He was an immensely popular Welsh nationalist 'hero'. Evans was able to push himself from third position to first in the largest swing against a government in the post-war period. Plaid Cymru now had a seat in parliament, forty-one years after the party's founding, and the Welsh nationalist star was in the ascendancy. In May 1967, the party came very close to winning a by-election in Rhondda West, cutting the Labour majority to 9.1 per cent in a constituency where the smallest Labour majority previously had been 55 per cent. In July 1968 it went on to fight a by-election at Caerphilly, where it reduced the Labour majority from 59.7 per cent to 5.2 per cent, pushing the Conservatives into third place and costing them their deposit.[2]

Nationalism was also developing at a considerable pace in Scotland. In the March 1967 Pollok by-election the SNP gained 28.2 per cent of the vote in a Labour marginal, letting in the Tories. Eight months later Winnie Ewing won her famous by-election result in Hamilton, until then Labour's ninth safest seat in Scotland, gaining 46 per cent of the vote in a seat not even contested in the general election eighteen months previously (Cook and Ramsden, 1997, p. 185). It was a toe-hold for the SNP that they never really lost thereafter. In 1968 the SNP won nearly a hundred places in local government elections, depriving Labour of an overall majority in Glasgow. During the period of the 1966–70 parliament the average SNP vote in by-elections was 29 per cent while, after 1970, the SNP share in general elections rose from 11 per cent to 30 per cent as the party was able to stand in every Scottish constituency. In October 1974 the SNP won eleven seats, passing the Conservatives in terms of total votes to become the second largest party in Scotland.

In Wales the nationalists continued on their march up the political hill. In the two general elections of 1974 Plaid Cymru picked up a total of three parliamentary seats: Caernarfon and Merioneth were won in the February election, while the party regained Carmarthen, which it had previously lost in the 1970 general election, in the October election. These successes encouraged many people to believe that the nationalist vote was growing as fast in Wales as it was in Scotland but this was not necessarily the case. The first-past-the-post voting system favours political parties that are geographically concentrated. The vote for Plaid Cymru was increasing, but only in Welsh-speaking West Wales where the three seats were won, while the Plaid Cymru vote actually fell back elsewhere with more deposits being lost than saved.

The Kilbrandon report

Up until the mid-1960s nationalist pressure in both Scotland and Wales had done very little to influence of the British political parties on their own political agendas. The evolution of the Scottish Office had occurred independently of nationalist pressure as had the establishment of the Welsh Office in 1964 (Kellas, 1994; Deacon, 2002). In Wales the Welsh Regional Council of Labour had promoted the idea of a Welsh Planning Board as early as the mid-1960s (Jones and Jones, 2001, p. 255). In 1965 the suggestion was made that local government should be reformed in Wales so as to establish a two-tier system of local administration in which district councils would form the lower tier and a single all-Wales council would form the only body in the upper tier. This would not have been a devolved administration with the functions of central government but merely a grandiose sort of county council employing delegated legislation, however it would still have played a useful role in decentralising government. Willie Ross's opposition to Scottish devolution had the same affect on Wales. Welsh secretary Cledwyn Hughes's attempts to get an assembly established in 1967 were blocked in cabinet in part by Ross, who feared that Scotland would want the same deal (Deacon, 2002). Labour would not consider Wales in isolation from Scotland, where the nationalists were seen as a greater threat (Foulkes *et al.*, 1983, p. 22). The Welsh idea was lost to a more orthodox two-tier system of local government but, as from 1968, the question of how to deal with demand for Welsh devolution was firmly fixed on the agenda of the Wilson government.

During the late 1960s and early 1970s the Liberal party, still the third party in British politics, had evolved into a structure that would ideally suit it for political devolution three decades later. The Liberal party in Scotland, aided by Jo Grimond, leader of the British party, had grown to five MPs, representing just under half of the British Liberal parties' total strength (twelve). In Wales the Liberal party was close to extinction, however. Having failed to regain Carmarthen in 1957 and 1966 and having lost Cardiganshire, a seat it had held for over a hundred years, in the 1966 general election it was forced to establish itself as a state party, just as was already the case in Scotland, in order to survive. This meant that the Liberal party in Wales had now developed into a federal structure with there being three state parties: England, Scotland and Wales. This meant that they had their own internal structure, policy-creating mechanisms and rules and procedures separate from the party in England on a series of domestic areas. At the same time the Conservative and Labour parties remained in a structure of regional parties under a dominant unitary system whereby all policy-making, rules and procedures continued go through the central organisation based in London.

At the core of the newly established Welsh Liberal party was devolution. On St David's Day, 1 March 1967, wearing his daffodil, Welsh Liberal leader Emlyn Hooson MP rose to his feet in the House of Commons and declared that: 'leave be given to bring in a Bill to provide a scheme for domestic self government of Wales; and for connected purposes' (Ellis, 1968, p. 164). Hooson outlined the scheme for a single-chamber parliament with seventy-two elected members representing the existing Welsh constituencies. It would be a parliament similar to that in Northern Ireland but in a federal United Kingdom. The wider Liberal party and Plaid Cymru's newly elected Gwynfor Evans supported the bill and the second reading was held on 16 June 1967. This time it was also supported by a Welsh Labour MP, S. O. Davies, member for Merthyr Tydfil. The government refused to grant further facilities for a private members bill on that June day and therefore it was in effect killed off.

Whilst killing off the bill, Harold Wilson did recognise that he had to do something to defuse the nationalist appeal and, as was his practice in those years, he chose to do so by way of a royal commission. In 1968 he instituted the Royal Commission on the Constitution which was supposed to look at the entire field of possible constitutional reforms but which nevertheless concentrated its attentions on the issue of devolution for Scotland, Wales and the English regions. Originally the chairman of the commission was Geoffrey Crowther, a much-respected former editor of the *Economist*, but he died and his place was taken by a Scottish lawyer, Lord Kilbrandon. When the report of the commission was published in 1973 it was therefore known as the Kilbrandon report. Both Scottish secretary Willie Ross and Welsh secretary George Thomas were fiercely opposed to devolution in their respective nations. They were not alone: both the Labour party and Conservative party were openly opposed to devolution in their submissions to the Kilbrandon committee (Foulkes *et al.*, 1983).

The outcome of the Kilbrandon report was perhaps unsurprisingly very confused. Two commissioners were so disillusioned by the commission's concentration on devolution to the exclusion of other constitutional matters, like the reform of parliament and the committee system, that they signed a memorandum of dissent. Of the eleven commissioners who signed the majority report:

- eight recommended legislative devolution for Scotland and six recommended it for Wales;
- three favoured a directly elected Welsh advisory council and one favoured a similar scheme for Scotland;
- two recommended executive devolution for Scotland and Wales.

The two commissioners who signed the minority report desired to see the extension of executive devolution from Scotland and Wales to five designated English regions (Foulkes *et al.*, 1983, p. 25). The remainder of the commissioners agreed on three further recommendations regarding devolution:

- the UK parliament must remain sovereign and any suggestions of separatism or federalism were rejected;
- members of the devolved assemblies must be directly elected, not nominated;
- elections to the devolved assemblies should be by the single transferable vote (STV) form of proportional representation, not first-past-the-post (FPTP).

The Kilbrandon report also stated that Scottish and Welsh devolution should not affect representation in the UK parliament, but it is from this time that we can date what later became known as the 'West Lothian question'. This originated when Scottish Labour anti-devolutionist MP Tam Dalyell asked the question: 'What right does the MP for West Lothian [his own constituency] have to vote in Westminster on matters concerning England when English MPs with arrival of a Scottish parliament had no similar right to influence Scottish matters?' Under Britain's unitary system of government the question could never be properly answered.

The Kilbrandon report was delivered to parliament in 1973, when Edward Heath's Conservative government was far more concerned with Britain's entry into the European Community (EC), striking miners and the reform of local government in England, Scotland and Wales. It did, however, change the attitude of some elements within the Welsh Labour party who found its ideological argument of 'extending democracy' more directly to Wales appealing (Foulkes *et al.*, 1983, p. 24). The Conservatives may well have sidelined the issue, which was of minor significance in promoting its ability to stay in power. The February 1974 general election, however, in which the SNP won six seats and Plaid Cymru two, showed that nationalism was on the rise. For Labour this meant a loss of some of their Welsh and Scottish seats; nationalism's appeal was beginning to gain more resonance. This was particularly helped in Scotland by Scottish claims to North Sea oil. The SNP soon adopted the slogan 'It's

Scotland's oil!', in effect meaning that the party had a cause to fight for which was easily understood by the electorate, although the party's rise had begun before North Sea oil started to flow. 'Oil reinforced electoral support for the SNP, it did not create it' (Bogdanor, 1999, p. 126).

Despite the worries obviously felt at party headquarters in London, Labour's Scottish council voted to reject devolution by six votes to five in June 1974, claiming that devolution was 'irrelevant to the real needs of the people of Scotland' (quoted in Bogdanor, 1999, p. 141). London, however, was very insistent and pressure was applied to the extent that, just two days before the date of the second election of 1974 it was announced that the Labour party had agreed that a commitment to devolution should be written into the party manifesto. Labour by this time had become divided into what can be described as 'hedgers and ditchers'. This term had first come into use in 1911 when the Tory peers had become divided over the future of the House of Lords. Now the Labour ditchers (who would die in the last ditch to preserve the power of the union), consisted of former Scottish secretary Willie Ross and Labour MPs such as Tam Dalyell and Neil Kinnock. The hedgers (creating a hedge over which the devolutionists had to jump) were led by Harold Wilson and James Callaghan. They believed that some gestures had to be made to head off the nationalist threat but the conditions would be such as to minimise any potential threat to the union (Willetts and Forsdyke, 1999; McLean, 2005).

On 17 September 1974, just three weeks before the next general election, the government issued a White Paper called *Democracy and Devolution: Proposals for Scotland and Wales*. This was a move that was widely seen as a cynical bid to save Labour seats from the nationalist threat. The White Paper contained six proposals:

- directly elected assemblies for Scotland and Wales;
- the Scottish assembly should have legislative powers, the Welsh assembly only executive powers;
- the assemblies to be elected by the first-past-the-post system;
- the devolved administrations should be financed by block grant, with no tax-raising powers;
- there should be no reduction in the number of Scottish or Welsh MPs at Westminster;
- the secretaries of state would remain as positions with cabinet rank.

After the election, in November, a new, revised White Paper was issued entitled *Our Changing Democracy: Devolution to Scotland and Wales*. This restricted even further the powers that were to be granted to the devolved assemblies so as not to undermine the supremacy of the UK parliament. Under the proposed arrangements matters relating to the economy, industry, energy and agriculture were not to be devolved.

Although the form of devolution being offered to Wales was very different to that being offered to Scotland, the government decided for various reasons to deal with both Scottish and Welsh devolution in the same piece of legislation. This was done because there was a substantial number of Labour MPs who were bitterly opposed to Welsh devolution and the government felt that they would be less likely to oppose the bill if they ran the risk of damaging the much-desired Scottish devolution. The Welsh Labour party executive backed devolution, if only due to the fact that the 1975 annual Labour party conference backed it by a majority of four to one. In 1975 there was a widespread demand, led by Caerphilly constituency Labour Party for a referendum on the proposals. Initially rejected by the executive at the 1976 May Welsh conference, developing resistance to devolution within the Welsh, Scottish and English elements of the Labour party meant that a referendum was now the only way the party could proceed without dangerous splits occurring within it.

The Scotland and Wales bill secured its second reading on 13 December 1976 by 292 votes to 247, a comfortable majority of forty-five which nevertheless included the votes of forty-seven pro-devolution Tories who were liable to return to their required allegiance and vote 'no' at the committee stage. The Liberals also threatened to withdraw their support unless they were promised proportional representation, which was unacceptable to most Labour members. It was a rebel Welsh Labour MP, Leo Abse, who proposed an amendment to the bill requiring that devolution should be approved by a referendum of the electorate before it could have effect (a hedging tactic). In order to pacify Labour dissidents and build up some sort of coalition grouping, the government agreed that the proposed referendums would be held after the bill had received the royal assent, ensuring that it would never become law without the approval of the electorate. This pleased much of the rebel dissent in Wales. Moreover the referendums would be mandatory rather than advisory as the referendum on EC membership had been.

The rather shaky devolution alliance moved on into the committee stage but there was so much dissension between the groups involved that the discussions showed every sign of running out of time. In order not to lose the bill through having it talked out, the government attempted to impose a guillotine on the discussions. The motion was defeated by 312 votes to 283, on 22 February 1977, and all progress on the Scotland and Wales bill came to an end.

By now the Callaghan government was in a minority and the loss of the devolution bill meant that the nationalist parties withdrew their support. In March the prime minister secured his position by coming to an agreement with the Liberals, known as the Lib-Lab pact. Part of the agreement with David Steel's party was that a new and improved devolution bill was to be presented to parliament. The Liberals argued hard for some of their ideas to be included in the bill and as a result there were to be separate bills for Scotland and Wales this time. But they failed to get agreement on two important points:

• The assemblies were not to have any tax-raising powers but would be reliant on a block grant from London. This was paid according to a formula devised by the chief secretary to the Treasury in the Callaghan government, Joel Barnett. The Barnett formula was supposed to move towards equality of spending per head of population and originally stated that for every £85 by which public expenditure on English services rose, Scotland would receive £10 and Wales would get £5. This Barnett formula, at the time a temporarily measure, would remain at the heart of the finance of devolved government from now on.

- Assembly members would be elected by first-past-the-post and not proportional representation, a stipulation that angered the Liberals and caused many to question the value of the pact.

The proposals were widely unpopular at Westminster but Labour, Liberal and nationalist MPs voted for the bills rather than see the government defeated and forced to resign, only to be replaced by a Conservative government – under the party's newly elected leader, Margaret Thatcher – that was now totally opposed to devolution. There was also the factor that the original rejection of the devolution bill had transformed the SNP into the most popular party in Scotland, something which the snub from London only aided. 'Labour dissidents, worried by the rise of nationalist fervour and anxious to preserve their own seats after the next general election, suddenly warmed to the government's proposals' (Evans, 1999, p. 53). The bills for both Scotland and Wales received their second reading on 14 and 15 November 1977 and received royal assent on 31 July 1978. The government walked a tightrope during the whole process of getting the bill through Westminster. The Conservatives continually drafted motions which undermined the role of both the Scottish parliament and Welsh assembly whilst increasing the power of Whitehall and Westminster over the devolved bodies. Many of these were passed as the government found to its costs that trying to compromise with the opposition often alienated its own supporters to the degree that they abstained on opposition options allowing them to get through (Foulkes *et al.*, 1983). Therefore by the time the bills had cleared parliament they had acquired a number of important amendments, and one of these had serious consequences for the forthcoming referendum. An anti-devolution Labour MP, George Cunningham, had proposed and gained an amendment which said that in considering the mandatory referendum a repeal motion would be laid before the House if fewer than 40 per cent of those Scots entitled to vote had said 'yes'. This was done to ensure that a poor turnout in the referendum did not mean that devolution was granted on a minority vote. The result of the referendum held on 1 March 1979 was highly unsatisfactory for Scotland since, while a majority voted for devolution, a turnout of 62.9 per cent meant that the 'yes' vote did not reach the 40 per cent threshold. Of those voting: 51.6 per cent voted 'yes', representing 32.85 per cent of electorate; 48.5 per cent voted 'no', representing 30.78 per cent of the electorate.

James Callaghan's attempt on 22 March 1979 for further talks on devolution with the SNP came to nothing. The government tried to get parliament to vote down the repeal motion but failed. In the light of that failure the Conservatives laid down a motion of no confidence which was passed by just one vote on 28 March. Callaghan resigned and called a general election that was duly won by the Conservatives under Mrs Thatcher. It was the new Tory government which repealed the Scotland Act in June 1979 with a division of 301 votes to 206. Of the seventy-one MPs for Scottish constituencies forty-three voted against repeal, nineteen voted for and nine abstained.

For Wales, as was the case in Scotland, a quota of 40 per cent of the Welsh electorate was needed to vote 'yes' for devolution to become law. As it happens, unlike Scotland, there was no need for a minimum vote to be imposed on the Welsh electorate. The 'no' vote was comprehensively successful by 956,330 votes (80 per cent) to 243,048 (20 per cent). Not one county in Wales had voted 'yes': in the most pro-devolutionary council, Welsh-speaking Gwynedd, 34.4 per cent had voted 'yes' but at the other end of the scale in Gwent just 12.1 per cent (or just over one in nine) had supported devolution. The issue of devolution in Wales seemed well and truly dead and when the draft order to repeal the Wales Act was debated on 26 June 1979 it was approved by 191 votes to just 8 against.

The Thatcher factor

The Conservatives' position on devolution in Scotland, if not Wales, until the mid-1970s was broadly pro-devolution. In May 1968 at the Scottish party conference Edward Heath in his 'Perth declaration' committed the party to devolution in Scotland, mainly to counteract the appeal of the SNP. Heath set up a draft committee under Alec Douglas-Hume to draft a plan. This was agreed and put into the 1970 general election manifesto. When Heath came to power the devolution committee was quietly dropped while the outcome of the Kilbrandon report was awaited. The February 1974 Conservative general election manifesto only committed the party to study Kilbrandon, but the October one backed devolution and Heath subsequently appointed Alick Buchanan-Smith as shadow Scottish secretary with a brief to support devolution in Scotland. Buchanan-Smith was backed in his support for devolution by future Conservative grandees Malcolm Rifkind and George Younger.

Initially, Margaret Thatcher, elected party leader in 1975, continued to publicly support Scottish devolution, endorsing it at the Scottish party conference in May 1975. Internally however the party was becoming split, with Mrs Thatcher and other anti-devolutionists such as Julian Amery and Maurice Macmillan pitched directly against a host of Scottish Conservatives. By December 1976, however, most Conservative backbenchers and shadow ministers were against devolution, although a substantial number of Scottish Conservatives were not. Mrs Thatcher then ordered a three-line whip (compulsory vote) against the Labour government's devolution proposals. A group of senior Scottish Conservatives, including Malcolm Rifkind, George Younger and Russell Fairgrieve (Scottish party chairman), met Mrs Thatcher and demanded that shadow Scottish secretary Alick Buchanan-Smith be given the opportunity to abstain in the three-line whip against Scottish devolution. She refused. Both Buchanan-Smith and Rifkind then resigned, and four other Conservative frontbenchers tendered their resignation but Mrs Thatcher refused to let them go. The anti-devolutionist Teddy Taylor replaced Buchanan-Smith and then strove to bury the devolution proposals, despite the fact that Francis Pym, the Conservative spokesman on devolution, tried to make them workable (Thatcher, 1995). Whilst some Conservative MPs would continue to support devolution for Scotland (none supported it for Wales), they were heavily outnumbered by those who didn't. Within a short while they would be joined by a number of Labour rebels voting together in the same division lobbies at Westminster to defeat devolution for both Wales and Scotland.

When Margaret Thatcher arrived in Downing Street in 1979 it appeared as though devolution was indeed dead. In respect of Scotland she made vague promises that devolution was not dead because of the referendum result and claimed herself to be closely in touch with Scottish thoughts. 'Tory values,' Mrs Thatcher said, 'are in tune with everything that is finest in the Scottish character' (Young, 1989, p. 528). To add evidence to this view the Conservatives had gained eight Scottish seats, up to twenty-two, reducing the SNP down to just two seats from their eleven. Thatcher herself did not believe in devolution for Scotland or Wales (Thatcher, 1995). When she came to power she did not have things all her own way, however. Her proposed Scottish champion, Teddy Taylor, had been defeated in Glasgow Cathcart and therefore it was the more approachable and amenable George Younger who became Scottish secretary. Younger, like Nicholas Edwards his counterpart in Wales, subsequently kept some of the more Thatcherite policies out of the country.

During the years of Conservative government, support for the Tories in Scotland drained away. The miners' strike in 1984–85 and the decline of the steel and shipping industries left a bitter impression on many Scots' minds. The popular belief was that Scotland was hit disproportionately by the economic slump in wages, employment and the decline of manufacturing industry. That alienation reached its peak when the government reformed the financing of local government and replaced the rates with the community charge or poll tax. It was not only that the poll tax was seen to be unfair and regressive which caused most unrest in Scotland but the fact that the government chose to impose that tax on Scotland in 1989, a full year ahead of its introduction into England and Wales, and to do so without even consulting the Scottish Office. An immediate effect was to spark off a campaign for non-payment, led by the SNP, with Scotland having the highest number of individuals refusing to pay the tax when levied. The irony of the situation was not lost on the Scots when the Tory government ignored Scottish protests over the tax and yet withdrew the tax as soon as English protests began. This insensitivity to Scottish political feelings enabled the Labour party to position itself in Scotland as the defender of valued Scottish social institutions such as those connected with the welfare state. Therefore Labour was able to successfully cast Thatcherism as an 'extreme ideology which had been imposed on a hostile Scottish electorate.' (Hutchinson, 2001, p. 148).

Within parliament, the Scottish Office, to which eleven preferably Scottish MPs/lords were appointed as ministers, handled many of Scotland's domestic affairs. In addition there were two standing committees to handle Scottish legislation and a Scottish affairs select committee on which party membership was proportional to the composition of the Commons as a whole and did not reflect the party balance in Scotland. After Conservative representation in Scotland had dropped to ten in 1987 the Tories did not have sufficient Scottish seats to staff the select committee, once Scottish Office ministers had been appointed. The Scottish affairs committee was therefore suspended between 1987 and 1992 and was only resumed after the 1992 election by being allowed a Labour chairman and having Conservative numbers made up by English MPs (Pilkington, 1997, p. 272).

Pre-devolution groups had started to mobilise support to overturn the referendum decision almost immediately after 1 March 1979 vote was known; these disparate groups forming themselves into the all-party Campaign for a Scottish Assembly (CSA) on 1 March 1980. In 1983 the Labour party committed itself to supporting the idea of a Scottish assembly and Donald Dewar became the acknowledged leader of the campaign for devolution in 1984. In 1987 the Labour manifesto in Scotland once again promised that there would be a Scottish assembly with tax-raising powers created in the first parliamentary session. Labour lost the election but the disastrous slump in Conservative support in Scotland led Labour to claim that the Scottish mandate belonged to them. The years of Tory and in particular Thatcherite dominance of Scotland also had an important impact on the Scottish Labour party's mindset. The fact that the minority party in Scotland could govern the majority party with impunity caused increasing resentment that was channelled by pro-devolutionists into the desire to have a Scottish assembly.

The dissatisfaction with the government began to show in election results. In the 1979 general election the Conservatives won twenty-two out of the seventy-one Scottish seats, exactly half as many as Labour. In 1983, a year when Labour was at its lowest ebb politically since the 1930s, with the Conservatives winning more than 60 per cent of parliamentary seats in the UK as a whole, the Tories slipped back to twenty-one seats in Scotland. By 1987 the unpopularity of the Thatcher government in Scotland was such that six out of every seven constituencies elected an anti-Conservative MP, reducing the government to just ten seats. There was a slight improvement in 1992 when the Tories gained eleven seats but this is partially explained by the fact that the total number of Scottish seats rose to seventy-two for that election. With John Major every bit as much a unionist as Margaret Thatcher, Tory support continued to slip away and Scottish Conservatives began to talk of the 'nightmare scenario' when no Conservatives at all would be elected for Scotland: an event which duly came to pass in 1997.[3]

Er gwaetha 'rhen Fagi a'i chriw – despite Maggie and her crew![4]

The comprehensive defeat of the devolution process in the 1979 referendum might well have been expected to bury the possibility of political devolution in Wales forever. For the next decade it was a non-issue. It would be 1987 before devolution came back onto the Welsh Liberal party's manifesto and 1992 before it crept back onto the Labour party's manifesto; even then it was only in a marginal sense. Plaid Cymru and other nationalists were able to regroup around the cause for a Welsh fourth television channel (S4C). The Wales Labour party's most senior MPs' concerns were around national and international politics. The three Welsh MPs who led the party between 1976 and 1992, James Callaghan, Michael Foot and Neil Kinnock, were more concerned with reforming the British Labour party rather than getting involved with domestic Welsh issues. When it came to Thatcherite policy Welsh Labour MPs were far more concerned with the reform of trade union law than any issues of a devolutionary nature (England, 2004).

The Conservative administration within the Welsh Office between 1979 and 1987 was atypical of any other period of their governance. This was because the Welsh secretary, Nicholas Edwards, was a Conservative MP with a Welsh seat – the first and only time a Conservative Welsh secretary held a Welsh seat. This meant that his legitimacy could not be challenged. Edwards was also formidable politician who had Margaret Thatcher's ear and trust 'to do things his own way in Wales' (Deacon, 2002). Edwards massively improved support for the Welsh language, in part as a means of undermining both the Labour party, who had always refused to do this, and the nationalists who based much of their campaigning around the need to support the Welsh language. He kept the Welsh Development Agency and Land Authority of Wales (introduced by the previous Labour government) in existence as a mechanism for state development of industry despite calls by Welsh Thatcherites to end this state interference in the economy. Yet despite these concessions to the Welsh political climate Thatcherism became loathed. This loathing was most intense in the South Wales valleys and the industrial north of Wales. Here the decline of the staple mining and steel industries and the miners' strike of 1984–85 had left a bitter memory of impact of Thatcherite ideology on the Welsh economy.

What was most evident was the apparent insensitivity of Thatcherism to the human suffering which came with job losses. This insensitivity, after Edwards' departure from the Welsh Office in 1987, seemed to be compounded by the appointment of ever-more English and Thatcherite Welsh secretaries. Whilst the appointment of the Heathite and leftward-leaning Peter Walker was acceptable to some, his successor David Hunt was less so. John Redwood's appointment in 1993 was described by Plaid Cymru's Elfyn Llwyd as 'going down like a rat sandwich' (Deacon, 2002, p. 50) – a colourful simile but not totally inaccurate. Redwood refused to sign documents written in Welsh, pulled the Welsh flag down from public buildings and put the Union Jack up in its place and generally used his post as an opportunity to promote his own notions of Thatcherism on a national platform. He became loathed to such a large degree that his image was used in the 1997 devolution referendum as a method of scaring voters into voting yes 'because Redwood could well be returning' if they voted no.

Despite the general negativity concerning the Conservative period of rule in Wales their legacy wasn't all negative. They established a system of unitary authorities in Wales, thereby enabling a Welsh assembly to be established without the blood-spilling which would have resulted if a Labour government had tried to reorganise a largely Labour-dominated local government establishment. The Conservatives also started reshaping much of the Welsh economy: they were responsible for aiding the massive programme of inward investment, the regreening of the Welsh industrial valleys and the establishment of regeneration in the urban coastal areas such as Cardiff Bay and Swansea marina. Later on, what became known as the 'M4 corridor' in Wales became the heart of the expanding Welsh economy, yet few ever credited the Conservatives for this. In Welsh political folklaw, the Conservatives in Wales were and remain an English party with an 'alien political ideology'. To this affect there was great delight shown when their peak of fourteen MPs in 1984 was reduced to zero some thirteen years later, to create the first 'Tory-free Wales' since 1906.

Preparing the ground

Labour in Scotland was becoming increasingly pro-devolution by the early 1990s, for two main reasons. First, the SNP's contention that voting Labour was not going to prevent the Conservatives, with their large number of English seats, from imposing their will on Scotland was being proved right. A Scottish parliament could help redress this imbalance. Second, pro-devolutionists in the form of John Smith and Gordon Brown were now in the highest levels of the British Labour party and therefore brought the issue higher up the agenda (Hutchinson, 2001, p. 149).

The Labour pro-devolutionists were also involved in the Campaign for a Scottish Parliament (CSP). This grouping had sprung directly from the CSA, which was formed in 1979 as a response to the failure of the referendum. In the early 1980s the CSA had started work on organising a constitutional convention to get all prominent pro-devolutionists together in one campaigning and planning group. Key members of the CSA in 1988 created the constitutional steering committee, containing eminent men, and some women, from the universities, the civil service, the churches and the voluntary sector (Hearn, 2000, p. 60). In 1988 the committee produced a report entitled *A Claim of Right in Scotland* that detailed how a constitutional convention could be organised to design a future assembly and in 1989 the Scottish Constitutional Convention was formed to consider how devolution could be achieved. The Conservatives, from a unionist standpoint, refused to participate, while the SNP took part but then withdrew after internal pressure from fundamentalists who thought that they would compromise their commitment to full independence (Hearn, 2000, p. 61). Despite two of Scotland's main parties refusing to take part in the convention an impressive number of political parties and groups still did.

In the general election of 1992 many within the convention thought that the Conservatives would either be defeated and there would be a Labour government or that they would lose all of their Scottish seats, causing a constitutional crisis in Scotland. Instead the Conservatives won power again and in Scotland they gained one seat to have eleven MPs. Despite their general election defeat in the UK as a whole in 1992, the continuing strong position in Scotland kept Labour in support of devolution. Indeed, as Neil Kinnock was replaced as leader of the party, first by John Smith in 1992, and then by Tony Blair in 1994, and Gordon Brown's political star rose, support for devolution grew even stronger. Smith made it quite clear that establishing a Scottish parliament was 'unfinished business' from the last time he had appeared in the cabinet. The party began to work even more closely with the convention and it was recognised that any proposals made by the convention were likely to be adopted as party policy if Labour were to win the next general election.

All of this campaigning meant that by mid-term, following the election of 1992, the issue of devolution came to occupy an increasing role in the thoughts of all the political parties who set about clarifying what stance they would adopt if they were successful in the forthcoming general election. Generally speaking, there seemed to be three possible solutions for the future governance of Scotland:

1 The status quo could be maintained, but with increased and improved administrative devolution and better representation through committees in Westminster. This was the position adopted by the Conservative party led by Michael Forsyth as the Scottish secretary.
2 There could be executive and legislative devolution, as advocated by the Labour, Scottish Liberal Democrats, Scottish Greens and other minor Scottish parties.
3 There could be full sovereign independence for Scotland within Europe, as desired by the SNP.

The Scottish local election results of 1995, which saw the Conservative party virtually eliminated north of the border and the SNP capturing three councils with 181 councillors, awoke renewed interest in the plans being made by the various parties for the future governance of Scotland. The Scottish Constitutional Convention decided that the time had come to announce their proposals. But other parties and groupings had their own agendas and within the space of just one week three alternative proposals for the future of Scotland were announced.

The first proposal was announced on 28 November 1995. On this day the then Scottish secretary, Michael Forsyth, made a series of declarations to outline government proposals for changes in how Scotland should be governed, concentrating on strengthening the existing Grand Committee of seventy-two Scottish MPs who would be given the right to scrutinise Scottish legislation by having the second and third readings heard in committee rather than the full Commons, while the prime minister, chancellor and other ministers would be asked to debate legislation with the Grand Committee. There would be a strengthening of local government in Scotland but the proposals all related to administrative rather then legislative devolution.

Two days after these declarations, aptly enough on St Andrew's Day, the convention held a special meeting and press conference in Edinburgh. This meeting marked the publication of their findings, which proposed that there should be a Scottish parliament of 129 members, 73 of them elected according to the first-past-the-post system in Westminster-like constituencies, but with 56 top-up members elected proportionately for Euro constituencies. Just over a year after the publication of these proposals Scotland found itself faced with a general election in which the issue of devolution was going to play a leading role, as one commentator said: 'Labour's commitment to a Scottish parliament and Conservative attachment to the status quo ensured that Scotland's governance was going to be a crucial issue in the campaign' (Sell, 1998, p. 204). For the Labour and Liberal Democrat parties there was no problem, as the convention's recommendations were adopted without question as party policy and featured largely unaltered in the parties' election manifestos. Unlike the situation in 1979 the appearance of devolution in the party manifesto meant that when Labour won its landslide victory it could rightfully claim to have received a mandate from the public. The convention had also meant that Labour had abandoned its previous stance of non-cooperation with other political parties. The close work with the Liberal Democrats over the convention would in time make it easier for both parties to form a coalition government in the first Scottish parliament.

The SNP fought the general election on the third devolution solution concerning the issue of separation but, once Labour was elected with a full mandate for devolution, it chose to accept Labour's plans as the best offer they were going to get, at least for the time being. It was certainly an improvement on what the Conservatives had offered them. In the referendum on devolution that Blair had insisted upon, amongst a bitter backlash from Scottish Labour members, the SNP swung alongside Labour and the Liberal Democrats in campaigning for a 'yes-yes' vote on both the establishment of the parliament and on it having tax raising powers. The Conservatives on the other hand remained devoted to the union and as such formed the most vigorous voice in the 'no-no' referendum campaign, insisting that their proposals for the committee system were all that Scotland required, even though the tide of events meant they were no longer relevant.

During the late 1980s the issue of devolution for Scotland had became ever-more central the Labour Party's agenda for constitutional change. There was a greater reluctance to consider devolution for Wales after the failure of such moves in 1979; it was obviously difficult to argue over the democratic deficit in Scotland without considering the matching deficit in Wales. In 1989 the Welsh Labour party issued a policy paper entitled *The Future of Local Government in Wales*, in which it was suggested that any reform should include: 'an elected body for Wales to deal with Welsh Office functions and with functions carried out on an all-Wales basis by nominated bodies' (quoted in Evans, 1999, p. 64). A commission to maintain an overview of the policy was set up in 1992, producing an interim report in 1993 called *The Welsh Assembly, the Way Forward* and culminating in 1995 with the policy document *Shaping the Vision*, which was accepted by the party conference and endorsed by Tony Blair as being legislation that would be introduced during the first year of a Labour government.

On 27 June 1996, George Robertson, as shadow secretary of state for Scotland, and Ron Davies, as shadow secretary of state for Wales, jointly announced that legislation for devolution was promised for the first year of the new parliament and that any such legislation would be preceded by referendums seeking the endorsement of the electorate.

The bitter divisions within the Welsh Labour party, dominated for decades by anti-devolutionists such as George Thomas, Neil Kinnock and Denzil Davies, meant that Welsh devolution was always going to be a more timid affair than that which occurred in Scotland. Pro-devolutionists, however, in reality knew that in the short term only a Labour government could give Wales an assembly. Therefore it was they who would decide on the type of assembly it was to be. Consequently, what Wales lacked was an all-party constitutional talking-shop like the Scottish Constitutional Convention. An independent pressure group, the Parliament for Wales Campaign, attempted to set up a group similar to the convention but the move failed because Welsh Labour refused to take part and the Labour party alone set up a constitutional policy commission in 1994.

The closest Labour came to co-operating with another political party came through the Cook-Maclennan pact of 1996. This agreement between Labour and the Liberal Democrats committed both parties to campaign for a 'yes' vote in the devolution referendums in both Scotland and Wales. In Wales this agreement was consolidated by a further agreement in March 1997 between Welsh Lib Dem leader Alex Carlile and shadow Welsh secretary Ron Davies to commit both to campaign for a 'yes' vote. The stage was not set for a repeat of the 1979 referendum but this time the 'yes' camps would be leaving nothing to chance.

Notes

1   It was called the coupon election because coalition candidates needed a letter from the coalition endorsing their candidate in order to stand for them - the so-called 'coupon'.
2   Figures for the by-elections given in Cook and Ramsden, 1997, pp. 183–90.
3   The figures quoted are from Mark Evans's chapter in *Developments in Politics, Volume 10*, Causeway, Ormskirk, 1999, p. 57.
4   The part played by Margaret Thatcher in the demonology of Welsh nationalism is shown in a song celebrating the survival of the Welsh language despite the efforts of the English, written by Dafydd Iwan in 1983, and called '*Yma O Hyd*' ('We're Still Here'), in which a couplet from the last verse runs:

Er gwaetha 'rhen Fagi a'i chriw,   Despite Maggie and her crew,
Byddwn yma hyd ddiwedd amser.   we will be here to the end of time.

5

Northern Ireland: Stormont, the first devolution and the aftermath

We saw in earlier chapters that there was always a substantial volume of opinion in Scotland and Wales that wished to see political devolution. This was not forthcoming, however, because there was never cross-party consensus on what it should be or that it should even be granted. One area of the United Kingdom did, however, get political devolution due to cross-party consensus – Northern Ireland. Yet ironically this was the one part of the UK in which there was very little political desire for it. Elsewhere in Britain devolution was sought or granted as a product of nationalism but in Northern Ireland the population either wished to be united with another country (Ireland) or was fervently unionist and wished to be governed from Westminster. We therefore have the anomaly that Ulster was given its own parliament because it wished to remain either subject to the Westminster parliament or the Dáil in Dublin. In his memoirs the former Liberal prime minister, Herbert Asquith, said that Northern Ireland was 'to be given a parliament it did not want while the rest of Ireland was to be given a parliament it would not accept'.[1] Some ninety years later the position in Northern Ireland had not changed that that radically.

Events leading to partition

The problems of Ireland had been at the top of nearly every government's agenda in the late nineteenth and early twentieth centuries. It was to this end that the third Home Rule bill had been passed in 1912. Its implementation was so delayed that it was overtaken by events in the form of World War I, causing the act to be suspended for the duration of hostilities. During the war attitudes to Home Rule in Ireland changed considerably. The old moderate irish Nationalist party founded by Charles Parnell was in decline. The constitutional leaders of Irish nationalism like John Redmond and Joe Devlin were sidelined after the Easter Rising of 1916 and its suppression brought forward a new group of more radical nationalists. In the 1918 elections Sinn Fein swept the board, winning 72 of the 103 Irish seats. Having won those seats, however, Sinn Fein members refused to take their place at Westminster. On 21 January 1919 those Sinn Fein MPs who were not in prison formed themselves into Dáil Éireann and proclaimed the republic. The Dáil was immediately declared illegal by the British government and forcibly closed by the army in September. In the north the Protestants were concerned about their own loss of civil and religious liberties, and the Orange Order and Ulster Unionists therefore grew as dominant political forces and counter military forces to those of the Irish Nationalists.

When the Home Rule bill of 1912 was re-submitted in December 1919 it was amended by Lloyd George's government to accept partition and included plans for two devolved parliaments in Dublin and Belfast. They were both to be elected by proportional representation, continuing to send MPs to an imperial parliament in Westminster that would retain 'excepted and reserved powers'. There was also to be a Council of Ireland that would deal with all-Ireland concerns and work for unity. Ulster Unionists accepted the provisions of the act in March 1920, Unionist leader Sir James Craig wrote to Lloyd George that their acceptance of the act would be as a 'final settlement and supreme sacrifice in the interests of peace' (Patterson, 1996, p. 6).

The plan was rejected by the Dáil, the members of which demanded an all-Ireland, independent republic. Open warfare followed between the IRA on one side and the British army, the Royal Irish Constabulary and the specials known as the Black and Tans on the other. Both sides carried out an escalating succession of murders and atrocities and martial law was imposed in counties Cork, Kerry, Limerick and Tipperary. In May 1921 the first elections for the devolved parliaments were held, Sinn Fein winning 124 seats out of 128 in the south and Unionists capturing 40 seats in the north, as against 12 seats for a mixture of Irish Nationalist and Sinn Fein candidates. Éamon de Valera and Sir James Craig were nominated as prime ministers in south and north respectively.

Northern Ireland's politics now evolved according to the settlement, with King George V opening the Northern Ireland parliament on 22 June 1921. In the south a ceasefire was called in July and Lloyd George and de Valera entered into talks, which broke down almost immediately, with de Valera refusing dominion status. An Irish conference was reconvened in October, with Arthur Griffith and Michael Collins representing Ireland. The Anglo-Irish treaty that emerged from these talks was signed on 6 December. Under the terms of the treaty of Ireland:

- twenty-six counties of southern Ireland would become the Irish Free State, with full dominion status within the British Empire;
- six of the nine counties of Ulster were to have the option of withdrawing from the Free State to become the devolved government of Northern Ireland, continuing to send MPs to the imperial parliament in Westminster.

The Dáil reluctantly accepted partition on 7 January 1922 by sixty-four votes to fifty-seven. Despite an attempt by Michael Collins to bring all nationalists together in the new Free State Eamon de Valera refused its presidency, the office passing to Arthur Griffith. The treaty was signed in London on 17 February 1922, with the agreement coming into effect on 6 December 1922. A large section of Sinn Fein refused to accept partition and a bitter and savage civil war broke out between the official Free State government under Collins and Griffith, and the IRA, who supported de Valera's view. The conflict that followed proved the truth of Michael Collins's own prophecy that by signing the treaty he had signed his own death warrant: he was murdered by the IRA almost before the ink on the treaty had dried. Both Northern and Southern Ireland would now follow the path of their most radical religious factions. In the north there was an orgy of violence directed mainly against Catholics in Belfast. In just three months in 1922, the majority of the 232 deaths there were Catholics, 11,000 were made jobless and 23,000 homeless, with some 4,500 Catholic-owned shops and businesses burned, looted or wrecked. Property valued at £3 million was destroyed. Such events were also political ammunition to those who opposed any devolution on the mainland, 'devolution would inevitably lead to the break up of the United Kingdom and events in Ireland were clear evidence of that', they argued.

The nature of partition

At the root of partition was the sectarian ideology and the irredeemable division of Irish society into two communities. Although many leading Irish nationalists, from Wolfe Tone through the leaders of Young Ireland to Charles Parnell, were all Protestant, the overwhelming majority of nationalist sympathisers were Catholic. The politics and religion of Ireland had been inextricably linked since the seventeenth century, with attitudes entrenched by memories of the Rebellion of 1641, when so many Protestants were massacred by Catholics, and of Cromwell's expedition, when the Catholic populations of Drogheda and Wexford were also slaughtered. By the end of the nineteenth century attitudes were so entrenched that the terms 'Catholic' and 'nationalist' were interchangeable, as were 'Protestant' and 'unionist'.

Although there were both Catholics and Protestants throughout Ireland the two communities were polarised to a large extent, with most Protestants existing in the north-east corner of the island around Belfast, where the Scottish plantations had been located. Not entirely coincidentally the north-east was also the industrial and wealth-creating heart of Ireland. This created an interesting by-product of the sectarian division. In Southern Ireland the men and women of the Protestant ascendancy were thinly spread members of the upper-middle class and minor gentry. Around the shipyards of Belfast and the industrial centres of the north there was a substantial Protestant working class. They were, and remain, the footsoldiers of Orange unionism in the north, since the Orange Order was founded as a 'means of mobilising lower-class Protestants for the defence of the institutions of the state, the established Church of Ireland and landed property' (Aughey and Morrow, 1996, p. 3).

It therefore became obvious that there was a substantial section of Northern Irish society which would always refuse to contemplate incorporation within a Catholic-dominated Home Rule Ireland, centred on Dublin. Protestant feeling whipped up by men like the Craig brothers and Edward Carson culminated in outright defiance at the time of the 1912 Home Rule bill. Arms were smuggled into the country and used to set up the paramilitary Ulster Volunteer Force, while hundreds of men were willing to sign the Ulster covenant. They made it clear that if a Home Rule government were set up in Dublin, Ulster would leave that parliament and fight if necessary for the right to rule themselves. As they said, they would: 'vote against Home Rule for Ireland to the end of time, but they would only fight for the exclusion of Ulster' (Bogdanor, 1999, p. 59). If the Protestants did prove to be willing to *fight* for exclusion, there was very little the British government could or would do about it. Certainly they could not adequately suppress such a movement since the so-called Curragh mutiny of 1914 showed that there was a substantial part of the British army that was prepared to desert rather than to take up arms against Ulstermen, while the leaders of that army proved unwilling to treat the mutineers with the severity usually meted out to those guilty of such an act.

The possibility of partition had first been proposed by Lord Macaulay when he criticised Daniel O'Connell by pointing out that Ireland was not all the same and that there should be separate treatment for 'Protestant Ulster and Catholic Munster'. The problem with partition, however, related to where the dividing line was to be drawn. The Protestant presence was only significant in the northern province of Ulster but even there the religious divide was not neat. Of the nine counties of Ulster only four had a clear Protestant majority – Antrim, Armagh, Down and Londonderry. Almost half the population was Protestant in Fermanagh and Tyrone but the proportion was little more than 20 per cent in Cavan, Donegal and Monaghan.

The 1912 Home Rule bill, as amended in the Lords, allowed for the exclusion of all nine counties of Ulster but the matter had not been resolved when the act was suspended in 1914. In 1918 the dilemma facing Lloyd George was that he had a Home Rule bill on the statute book for which he was unable to gain acceptance from the Ulstermen. He was also hamstrung by a government commitment that no agreement on Ireland as a whole would be reached without agreement from the Protestants of the north.

According to unionist thinking, partition did not mean devolution. As they saw it, the south would accept a Home Rule government in Dublin from which Ulster would be excluded, allowing the north to remain under direct rule from Westminster. It was the committee drafting the post-1919 agreement that finally decided that Northern Ireland would have to have its own devolved assembly. It was felt that the Catholic-nationalist community had as their priority the need to escape from British rule. Yet, if Ulster continued to be ruled directly from London that would leave the sizeable Catholic population there still in British hands. A devolved government in Ulster would at least be Irish, albeit Protestant.

It was thought that partition would only be temporary. The government believed that with time the differences between the communities would be ironed out, the Catholics would be reconciled to a less coercive British rule and people from both sides of the divide would see the practical and economic benefits of working together. At some point the mechanism of the Council of Ireland, on which both Belfast and Dublin were represented, would be used to reach agreement on ending partition. In producing its legislation the government stated quite openly that its ultimate aim was: 'a united Ireland with a separate parliament of its own' (Bogdanor, 1999, p. 63).

Over the question as to how many counties should be excluded, the government had wanted to include all the nine traditional counties of Ulster on the grounds that this would give the Protestants such a small majority that it would only require a reasonably short time for demographic changes to alter the balance. The Protestant leaders on the other hand were sufficiently proficient in mathematics as to know that Cavan, Donegal and Monaghan had only 70,000 Protestant inhabitants as against 250,000 Catholics and they realized the threat this posed to the size of the overall Protestant majority in a nine-county Ulster. The unionists therefore forced the government to accept a six-county solution. A move to allow individual counties self-determination was prevented on the grounds that if it had been allowed Fermanagh and Tyrone might well have abandoned exclusion and rejoined the twenty-six counties making up the Free State.

Stormont and the Northern Ireland government

The government of the six counties was established by the Government of Ireland Act of 1920, which was designed to maintain the link established in the Act of Union of 1801 and was part of the Home Rule settlement. The devolved government of Northern Ireland and the partition of Ireland that created it was defined in the Irish Free State Act of 1922, and ultimately underpinned by the Ireland Act of 1949.

In Northern Ireland the bicameral institution was modelled closely on the parliament at Westminster, albeit much smaller. It had a directly elected House of Commons of fifty-two members from which a Speaker, prime minister and cabinet were drawn; these fifty-two members were made up of forty-eight territorial members and four representing the Queen's University of Belfast. The second chamber was known as the Senate and consisted of two ex-officio members and twenty-four members elected by the Commons. The elected senators held office for eight years with half the elected members retiring every four years, the Senate being unaffected by any dissolution of parliament. The Commons had a maximum life of five years, although it could be dissolved before that at the wish of the prime minister. For Northern Ireland the crown in parliament was represented by the lord lieutenant of Ireland while the Home Rule settlement still prevailed, and by a Governor after 1922. The Government of Ireland Act gave Northern Ireland a parliament with extensive powers over a wide range of internal areas that included:

- law and order;
- local government;
- education;
- social services;
- agriculture;
- industry;
- internal trade.

The mechanics of establishing a parliament, however, took some time in coming. In 1932 the parliament of the north was finally given a base at Stormont Castle, a grandiose building on the outskirts of Belfast, set in a park with an impressively long approach driveway. From then on the whole structure of government in Northern Ireland was simply referred to, by enemies and supporters alike, as Stormont, a term that was also used for the ideological ethos which underlay the government of Northern Ireland.

Stormont was made subordinate to the imperial parliament in Westminster, which retained certain powers for itself, the most important of which related to matters affecting the crown, most taxation, the armed forces, foreign relations, external trade and ultimate sovereignty: these were known as **excepted** matters. When the agreement setting up the Northern Ireland parliament was made in 1920 it was still expected that the north and south would be reunited in a few years' time. Therefore there were certain powers, known as **reserved** matters, that were retained by Westminster for the moment, although the ultimate intention was the transfer of these powers to an all-Ireland parliament. The reserved powers consisted of such things as the issue of postage stamps, savings banks, the registration of deeds and land purchase. The reunion of the two parliaments never happened, however, and the reserved powers were retained with the exception of the registration of deeds and land which was transferred to Stormont.

The purpose of the Parliament, according to the declaration establishing its existence, was to 'make laws for the peace, order and good government of Northern Ireland'. The procedure was the same as that of the Westminster parliament, with bills passing through both houses before receiving the royal assent from the governor. Financial legislation had to begin in the Commons and could not be amended by the Senate. If the two houses disagreed over any matter the governor could convene a joint session of both houses. If a bill received a majority vote from a joint session it was judged to have passed both houses.[2]

When Stormont was established in 1920 so many powers were transferred or devolved to it that there seemed to be little need for there to be so many MPs representing the province at Westminster and Northern Ireland. Representation was consequently cut to thirteen, instead of the seventeen that the population of the province would seem to demand.[3] Ambitious politicians in Northern Ireland therefore knew that their best hope for ministerial office lay in service at Stormont. The more able therefore did not bother to contest the Westminster seats and the representatives serving in the imperial parliament always had far less prestige at home than those at Stormont. At Westminster twelve Ulster Unionist MPs were regularly returned, they all took the Conservative whip and, until the 1960s, were treated as an integral part of the Conservative party. It was very seldom that the Ulster members held the balance of power at Westminster as Parnell's Nationalists had in the 1880s, except in the period 1951–55 when the Conservative majority was so small that the government relied on the votes of the Unionists to maintain itself in power; although Labour made no complaint about this at the time. In 1965 Harold Wilson felt it necessary to warn the Unionists that they should not vote against the government on the issue of steel nationalisation because in Northern Ireland regulation of the steel industry was a devolved area of interest. But on the whole there was never the possibility of Irish members holding the government to ransom by the threat of disrupting parliament.

There were two important questions about the form of devolved government established at Stormont, both of which remain important, since they need to be asked of any devolved legislature and administration:

1 How independent was the devolved parliament in Belfast, in relation to the imperial parliament in London, and how far did it retain sovereignty in Northern Ireland?
2 How would the devolved government be financed and would it have primary tax-raising powers itself?

If parliamentary sovereignty means that parliament is the sole body able to legislate by passing laws without referring them to any higher authority, then Stormont was not sovereign. Northern Ireland legislation was open to appeals made to the courts, the House of Lords and the judicial committee of the privy council. There was a clear implication for democracy here in that the unelected law courts retained the power to overturn legislation passed by a democratically elected parliament. Furthermore the UK government could ask the monarch to instruct the governor of Northern Ireland not to give assent to a bill of which London disapproved. Moreover, Westminster still retained the right to pass legislation that would be binding on Northern Ireland – even though the matter in question dealt with devolved powers and should be outside the remit of London.

Despite the Westminster parliament having had the power to intervene in Northern Irish affairs it was nevertheless very non-interventionist and this can be seen to have an important outcome for Northern Ireland in two specific instances:

- Although not laid down in parliamentary procedures, the convention grew that Westminster should not legislate on devolved matters. In 1923 the speaker of the Westminster House of Commons ruled definitively that questions to ministers about Irish devolved issues should be asked at Stormont and not at Westminster. As late as 1967 it was established that there were certain questions in respect of Northern Ireland politics and civil rights that London should not consider under any circumstances. The areas mentioned related to discrimination in housing, education and local government.
- Section 5 of the 1920 act outlawed any form of religious intolerance and discrimination and the London government was supposed to ensure that this was upheld. As it happens, the London government totally ignored the fact that Stormont was quite blatantly intolerant and discriminatory. Sir James Craig (later Viscount Craigavon), the first Northern Ireland prime minister, stated that his intention was to build 'a Protestant parliament in a Protestant state' (Jones, 1989, p. 277) and that is just what he did.[4] Craig used both law and order and government employment policies to ensure Protestant dominance throughout Ulster. The majority of members at Stormont were members of the Unionist party, as were fifteen out of the twenty high court judges in the Northern Ireland courts and the entire command structure of the Royal Ulster Constabulary (RUC). Similarly the Ulster élite's governing the civil service were unionists, to such an extent that by 1927 the minister of agriculture was boasting that his ministry now only employed four Catholics (Patterson, 1996, p. 7). Property qualifications restricted the right to vote and serve on juries, the franchise in local elections only being given to ratepayers. At the same time, the ownership of property and business premises gave the right for the owners of property to have a vote for each of the properties and businesses that they owned, giving some individuals up to six votes in local government elections. As should be obvious, all property qualifications discriminated against the less prosperous 33 per cent of the population who were Catholic and who tended not to own property.

The evolution of devolved economic and fiscal policy: the Stormont case study

We saw in Chapter 3 that a major problem faced by those framing Home Rule legislation concerned the budget and the division of expenditure between the Imperial Contribution that went to London and the amount of money set aside for the day-to-day expense of running Ireland. This problem became even more serious in coping with the budget for Northern Ireland. The evolution of devolved economic and fiscal policy

The 1920 act insisted that the Imperial Contribution would have first charge on Irish revenue and nominated, as taxes reserved for the Imperial Contribution, income tax, customs dues, excise duty and profits tax. Devolved taxation that would go to Stormont after the contribution had been met was limited to:

- motor vehicle licences;
- entertainment duties;
- stamp duty.

In all, the reserved taxes added up to no more than 20 per cent of the taxation income for Northern Ireland. Therefore from the very start Northern Ireland was unable to fund the level of public services required by the UK government out of Irish revenue alone. In 1925 the Northern Ireland arbitration committee, which had been set up under Lord Colwyn to examine the Northern Ireland budget, recommended that the current procedure should be turned on its head. From then on the Imperial Contribution would cease to be a first charge on expenditure and would become a residual charge on what was left when necessary Irish expenditure had been met. It was also proposed that specific needs could be met by agreed subsidies paid directly into the Northern Ireland exchequer by the UK government. Such agreements began with the Unemployment Insurance Agreement of 1926.

Ensuring that Stormont could afford to pay the dole to the unemployed came not a moment too soon because the depression that began in 1929 hit Northern Ireland disproportionately hard. By 1931 the demands on expenditure in the province were such that nearly as much money was received under the Unemployment Insurance Agreement as was paid out in the Imperial Contribution. In 1932 the procedures put in place by the Colwyn committee were scrapped and long and hard negotiations began in order to find a new formula. In 1936 the UK government conceded the principle of parity in the provision of public services between Great Britain and Northern Ireland under which any deficit in the Northern Ireland budget would be made good by the Treasury in order that services could be provided at the same level as applied in Great Britain. The principle was outlined in a speech by the chancellor, Sir John Simon, in which he agreed that the UK government would 'make good any deficit in such a way as to ensure that Northern Ireland should be in a financial situation to continue to enjoy the same social services and have the same standards as Britain'.[5] In 1942 the promise was repeated by the then chancellor, Sir Kingsley Wood, who guaranteed, in the light of the impending Beveridge report, that the UK government would make up any leeway in service provision for Northern Ireland. Over the years, and especially after the 1945 Labour government instituted the welfare state, the list of services for which additional UK funding was required grew ever longer and came to include housing, schools, hospitals, national insurance, family allowances, pensions, regional employment, the health service and supplementary benefit.

The emphasis of the Northern Ireland budget shifted from being revenue-based to being expenditure-based. After 1946 the amount of money to be given to Northern Ireland was decided in talks between the British Treasury and the Stormont minister of finance. Unlike the money that was given to local government in Great Britain there were no block grants available to Stormont since the UK was determined that Northern Ireland should not have more money than it needed: parity meant 'not more than' just as much as it meant 'not less than'. All moneys were therefore given for specific purposes, which had the effect of depriving Stormont of the full powers that should belong to a parliament according to the theory of parliamentary sovereignty. Stormont was totally dependent on UK budgetary decisions over which it had no say, thereby depriving the people of Ulster of one of their democratic rights. It also meant that the Northern Ireland government could not make any plans for the long term because Stormont had no knowledge of the amount of tax revenue that would be made available in future budgets.

By the time Stormont was suspended in 1972 the fiscal situation had become one where 90 per cent of Northern Ireland expenditure was determined by Stormont while 15 per cent of its revenue was provided by Westminster. This meant that Belfast had no fiscal autonomy, given that only spending powers came within Stormont's competence, while taxing powers were retained in London.

Division of responsibilities

The division of responsibilities between London and Belfast and the question of how to determine the differences between devolved and reserved powers was complicated by the fact that the Northern Ireland settlement was drawn up before anyone suspected the extent of the social legislation that would be passed after 1945. A good example is to be seen in the funding and management of the national health service in the province. Health was one of the main areas where responsibilities were devolved to Stormont but where policy decisions were made at Westminster. National standards were laid down for the province in UK legislation but the Northern Ireland constitution demanded that identical legislation had to be passed by Stormont if it were to have effect. This duplication of legislation, which also applied in other areas, was the cause of a considerable waste of time and effort. On the other hand there were great benefits to be gained from devolution in the fields of industry and agriculture. This showed itself particularly in two fields:

- The extent of government aid to industry in Northern Ireland was second to none and, as a result, a significant number of firms was induced to set up operations in Northern Ireland.
- In order to ensure that Northern Ireland agricultural produce could compete with the rest of Britain, despite the cost of shipping that produce across the Irish Sea, quality control agencies were set up that created a particularly high standard for anything produced in the province. Many years later, the legacy of that quality control proved to be justified when Northern Ireland was the one part of the UK said to be free of the BSE problem.

When the Royal Commission on the Constitution, created by the Wilson government in 1968, and led by Lord Kilbrandon, came to consider Northern Ireland they were very enthusiastic over the devolution of legislative, administrative and executive powers in fields such as those of industry and agriculture. The success of devolution according to the Kilbrandon report was due to the easier access to central government provided by the proximity of decision-takers to the public. It was thought by Kilbrandon to be a good argument in favour of regional devolution. It has to be said, however, that part of the benefit to the province came from Stormont's unique status at the time and there is no guarantee that Ulster's performance would have been the same if devolved assemblies for Scotland and Wales had also been in contention as competitors. Northern Irish MPs at Westminster were always fiercely opposed to any proposals that were put forward for Scottish and Welsh devolution; not wanting to see too many snouts in the trough. As an historical footnote in 1984 Lord Kilbrandon returned to Northern Ireland to carry out another independent inquiry which looked at devolution in Northern Ireland which in turn paved the way for the Northern Ireland Agreement.

A somewhat less pleasing aspect of the Stormont version of devolution became apparent under Kilbrandon's first report's gaze. The Northern Ireland government had taken over responsibility for services that were within the remit of local government in Great Britain. These included the police, fire service, housing and education. At the same time local government in Northern Ireland was dominated by sectarianism and services such as the distribution of housing or the appointment of teachers to schools were affected by discrimination on sectarian grounds. It is possible that the situation might have been worse if these services had been in the hands of local councils but their control by Stormont did still leave them open to abuse by Stormont's Protestant unionist agenda. Whilst this abuse was happening, the Westminster government showed little interest in the affairs of Northern Ireland. During the entire thirty-year period that Stormont was in existence between 1922 and 1972, Westminster devoted a mere *two hours a year* to the discussion of Northern Ireland devolved issues (Bogdanor, 1999, p. 79).

A Protestant parliament in a Protestant state

It was Sir James Craig, as first prime minister of Northern Ireland, who defined the nature of Stormont by stating that he wished to create a 'Protestant parliament in a Protestant state'. The partition of Ireland and the Stormont parliament were the product of unionist intransigence in opposing Home Rule and it is only natural that the Unionist party should then dominate that parliament, and have the aim of maintaining that domination. Dominating Ulster and the future of the province was a Protestant triumvirate made up of the Unionist party, the Orange Order and what had been the Royal Irish Constabulary (RIC) but which became the Royal Ulster Constabulary (the RUC).

In 1922 the Protestant establishment used the violence in the north and the excuse of threats from the civil war in the Free State in the south to strengthen the means by which they controlled the province. In that year the Civil Authorities (Special Powers) Act 1922 gave widespread powers of detention and internment to the authorities. It allowed the security forces in Northern Ireland to 'arrest without warrants, detain without trial, search homes without warrants, prohibit meetings and processions, and hang and whip offenders' (Mulholland, 2003, p. 26). These powers were renewed annually but became permanent in 1933. Under the provisions of the act the RUC was formed as a force 3,000 strong, one-third of which was supposed to be Catholic. But, although some Catholics transferred to the RUC from the RIC, the quota was never filled, dwindling from 21 per cent of the strength in 1921 to less than 8 per cent by the 1970s. Also founded in 1922 was the Ulster Special Constabulary, a paramilitary part-time police force in the mould of the infamous Black and Tans and largely recruited from the ranks of the Ulster Volunteer Force. Known as the B Specials they were notorious for their discriminatory use of violence in support of Protestantism.

In every Northern Ireland election, starting with the first in 1921, a Protestant majority was returned. The institutions of the state ensured that the Catholic minority would neither gain power nor achieve parity of representation. The pluralist parliamentary system as exemplified by Westminster envisaged an alternation of parties in government but at Stormont there was never the prospect of anything other than a permanent Unionist party majority and Stormont as a result exhibited all the characteristics of a one-party state, with a variety of mechanisms in place to ensure the continuation of that one-party hegemony.

The 1920 act established that voting in Northern Ireland should be by the single transferable vote (STV) form of proportional representation (PR) so as to ensure cross-community representation. However, in the 1921 local government elections, PR produced nationalist majorities in twenty-one local government districts in the counties of Fermanagh and Tyrone. In both these counties, where the Nationalists had gained control, the councils proceeded to vote that they should decline to recognise Stormont, declare their independence of Ulster and rejoin the Irish Free State. The Craig government thereupon replaced the 'errant councillors' with commissioners who would run the councils until the next election could be held. For that election, and for all local elections after 1922, the STV voting system was abolished and simple majority voting reintroduced. The British government required the lord lieutenant to withhold his consent to this abolition and the bill remained unapproved for two months, but the Craig government threatened to resign if the act were not approved and, faced with the prospect of having to take Ulster into direct rule with a constitutional crisis on their hands, the British government backed down and the bill received the governor's assent.

The reintroduction of first-past-the-post (FPTP) voting led to gerrymandering of local authority ward boundaries on a massive scale so as to ensure Protestant majorities. The favoured situation was where the Catholic population was concentrated centrally in a fairly small geographical area like the Bogside district of Derry, surrounded by more diffuse Protestant areas. The electoral map would divide up the wards like slicing a cake, each slice biting into the Catholic area but with the largest part of the slice located in the Protestant outer sector. By devices such as this the unionists always gained a majority of council seats even in areas like Fermanagh, Tyrone and Derry City where Catholics formed a majority of the population. There was also the point that, although the franchise in all elections had been extended to the entire male adult population in Great Britain, in Northern Ireland only ratepayers could vote in local elections and then they had a vote for each property on which they paid rates. This was of course discriminatory, since most Catholics rented property and were not ratepayers.

In the 1925 election an anti-Unionist mixture of Nationalists and Sinn Fein won twelve seats as they had done in 1921 but the Unionists lost eight seats to a mixture of independent unionists and candidates of the Northern Ireland Labour party, which had been formed in 1924 as a non-sectarian alternative to the Unionist party. In the face of this threat to the Protestant ascendancy Craig proposed the abolition of STV for Stormont elections as well as local elections and this was done in 1929. While there was PR the Protestant working class felt that they could safely vote Labour, but the reintroduction of FPTP reawakened fears that a vote for anyone other than the Unionists would let in the Catholic nationalists. And out of that fear of the Catholics the working-class Protestants remained loyal to unionism, a loyalty that was reinforced by the large working-class membership of the Orange Lodges.

The abolition of PR effectively put the seal on the one-party state. Northern Ireland politics was also notoriously corrupt: the motto of Ulster was said to be, 'Vote early and vote often'. All parties kept a constant watch on the death columns in the local papers so as to get their hands on the dead voter's voting card. Every election saw a proportion of 'dead men voting' and there is a story, possibly apocryphal, which states that there are electoral areas where more people voted than actually lived there. Where corrupt practices did not have effect there was always intimidation. As John Cole, the former BBC correspondent and an Ulsterman himself, said of reporting in the province: 'One of the least reported aspects of the Ulster crisis was the conspiracy of fear ... When Gerry Adams defeated Gerry Fitt in West Belfast it was said that SDLP supporters feared IRA violence against them' (Cole, 1995, p. 135).

Between 1926 and 1969 37.5 per cent of seats at Stormont returned a Unionist member unopposed simply because a Unionist victory in those seats was inevitable. 'Terence O'Neill, for example, entered Stormont in 1946 when he won an unopposed by-election and did not fight his first opponent until 1969' (Aughey and Morrow, 1996, p. 68). In the so-called 'union flag' election of 1949, held after the Republic of Ireland had been established and the Irish government had inaugurated an all-party anti-partition campaign, the Northern Ireland Labour party was attacked in the north for its encroachment on the working-class Protestant vote: unemployed workers being told that, 'you might vote for Labour to get a job but it would mean rule by Dublin and the Pope'. Such a warning was virtually redundant since the FPTP voting system had effectively neutralised the party whose 29 per cent of votes in the 1938 election gained them a mere three seats at Stormont. Despite the bias within the electoral system, after the Boundary Commission had fixed the borders of Northern Ireland in 1925, the Catholic leader in the north and now Irish Nationalist MP in West Belfast, Joe Devlin, entered the Northern Ireland House of Commons. When the Boundary Commission was wound up the following year Mr Devlin appealed to his fellow Nationalist MPs to take their seats as 'the reasons had disappeared why they should remain out of (Parliament). It was their business ... to recognize the Northern Parliament in the interest of democracy.' (Mulholland, 2002, p. 28).

The end of Stormont: 1968–72

The Protestant ascendancy in Ireland before partition, and Northern Ireland thereafter, was maintained by an Anglo-Irish, Church of Ireland hierarchy, with a largely Presbyterian working-class rank and file organised within the lodges of the Orange Order. The working-class Catholic population of Northern Ireland remained permanently oppressed and dispossessed since the influence wielded by the Orange Order ensured that Protestants had preferential treatment in employment and housing. In the 1950s, however, the growing prosperity of what was known as 'the affluent society' touched the province and created an emergent middle class, both Protestant and Catholic, which had entirely different expectations from those of earlier generations.

The working-class Catholic community had grudgingly come to accept the status quo and to acknowledge that the general prosperity, living standards and welfare provision of the north was far better than what was offered in the Republic to the south. An IRA campaign in the late 1950s failed completely and there were those who believed that confrontation had had its day and the end of partition was in sight as extremism on both sides faded away. The growing Catholic middle classes, however, although optimistic, resented their exclusion from the political process, by which they essentially became second-class citizens. They were joined in their concern by a middle class within the Protestant community that was more liberal in its outlook than the hardline members of the Orange Order.

It was a liberal Unionist, Terence O'Neill, who replaced Lord Brookeborough as Ulster prime minister in 1963 and he began to make modest reforms, admittedly under some pressure from London. O'Neill also had a vision of a future united Ireland within a federal system of government in a reunited British Isles, and had a meeting with the Irish taoiseach (prime minister) to this affect (Mulholland, 2002, p. 35). When he resigned O'Neill still predicted that a united Ireland would come, although not in his lifetime. O'Neil was an Anglo-Irishman similar in views to the southern Irish Protestants of the nineteenth century, unsurprisingly therefore he met with opposition from hardline members of his own party, who regarded any concessions to the Catholic community as a betrayal He was also attacked from the opposing point of view by a movement campaigning for civil rights. Thanks to events unfolding in the United States, a great deal of international interest and involvement had been stirred up by Martin Luther King's campaign to gain civil rights for the black community. In the light of the international support given to the American civil rights movement the reaction of Northern Irish Catholics was to point out to the world that they suffered from discrimination every bit as badly as did the blacks of America.

The Westminster government had made a series of half-hearted attempts to examine the discrimination against Catholics in the north. The last attempt had been in 1938 in order to appease de Valera over treaty renegotiations proved to nothing more than a paper exercise. Northern Ireland's sacrifice and support during World War II as opposed to Eire's neutrality meant that both wartime and post-war British governments to become increasingly sympathetic to unionism. In turn, John A. Costello, the Irish Taoiseach declared Ireland a republic and took it out of the Commonwealth in 1948. In 1949 the Ireland Act codified relations with the Irish Republic and clarified the status of Northern Ireland. Although this created a Labour (many in a grouping called 'Friends of Ireland') revolt against Attlee for seeming to endorse unionism, the home secretary, Herbert Morrison, rejected demands to monitor Stormont more closely as being unconstitutional. With a Conservative government following Labour in 1951 for the next thirteen years there was even less of a will to scrutinise discrimination in Northern Ireland. Harold Wilson's Labour victory in 1964 gave some hope to Ulster's Catholics. Wilson was supportive of aspects of Irish nationalism and sent a supportive letter to the Campaign for Social Justice (CSJ), a Northern Ireland pressure group set up to combat discrimination and promote civil rights in the north. In addition the Campaign for Democracy in

Ulster (CDU), a Labour party pressure group of around some hundred MPs, was pushing for Westminster to examine events in the north (Cunningham, 2001, p. 5).

In 1966 the Northern Ireland Civil Rights Association (NICRA) was founded in County Derry and immediately declared that their principal aim was to gain the elementary right of 'one man one vote' in local elections, extending the franchise to the whole adult population and getting rid of the business vote which meant that some people had the right to up to six votes! NICRA was essentially non-violent and moderate in its actions, although parts of the membership were not happy with the campaign's peaceful nature, particularly after a march in Derry during 1968 had been broken up amid accusations of police over-reaction and brutality. One faction of the movement, led by students from Queen's University and a number of Young Socialists, broke away from NICRA and formed a group known as People's Democracy. This group drew up a list of six demands:

- one man, one vote;
- a fairer drawing of ward boundaries;
- houses distributed according to the needs of the people;
- jobs to be awarded on merit;
- free speech;
- abolition of the Special Powers Act.

Although the leaders of NICRA and the founders of the Social Democratic and Labour party (SDLP) like Gerry Fitt and John Hume were advocates of peaceful protest, there were those who wanted direct action and did not mind if the protest became rather less than peaceful. This was especially true of the republican element in the movement.

There was a Protestant backlash against the protest movement led from within the government by the minister for home affairs, William Craig, who directed somewhat heavy-handed police action against the protesters. The Reverend Ian Paisley also began to operate, at this time as a militant unionist, leading counter-demonstrations that often ended in violence. The Wilson government in Westminster, although concerned about the increasing disturbances in Northern Ireland, was split over what to do about it. Direct intervention was ruled out for the time being, instead they hoped for O'Neill to grant the necessary reforms to settle the situation back down (Rose, 2001, p. 118). Thus O'Neil granted a number of reforms in November 1968 that were well received by NICRA but which antagonised members of his own party. Foremost amongst the anti reformers was Ian Paisley, who founded the Protestant Unionist Party, which would later become the Democratic Unionist party (DUP), and William Craig who organised his supporters into the Vanguard Unionist Progressive party.[6] A fragmentation of the unionists had begun that would result in the 1973 election being contested by no fewer than thirteen separate parties each of whom had the word 'unionist' contained in their title.

In February 1969 O'Neill called a general election which he duly won but with the unionist vote seriously split: O'Neill's Official Unionists won thirty-three seats, but eleven went to anti-O'Neill candidates. In April O'Neill was forced to resign and in the subsequent by-election his seat at Stormont was won by Ian Paisley. This left the Labour's government's Northern Ireland strategy in tatters. On the other side of the sectarian divide the success of the agitation for civil rights had the result of finally eclipsing the declining Nationalist party. A prominent leader of NICRA, John Hume, defeated the Nationalist leader Eddie McAteer. Hume and other independents elected in 1969 formed the SDLP in the following year, the party rapidly becoming the party for those Catholic or nationalist supporters who were seeking a peaceful settlement until the end of the century.

Events in Northern Ireland reached their climax in 1969, the flashpoint coming during the summer's marching season. Despite the government imposing a ban on political marches such as those organised by NICRA they permitted the traditional marches of the Orange Order to go ahead, stating that they were religious rather than political. But religion and politics are inseparable in Northern Ireland. In August came the Prentice Boys' march in Derry where the procession's traditional route lies along the city walls in full view of Catholic Bogside beyond the walls, in a provocative display of Protestant triumphalism. Serious rioting in the Bogside followed, suppressed rather more brutally than usual by the RUC. The rioting spread across the province and in Belfast a Protestant mob from the Shankill descended on the Catholic Clonard area, burning and wrecking homes in the process. The most serious aspect of the Belfast trouble was that the Protestant mob was spearheaded by off-duty B Specials. This process of intimidating Catholics and later on Protestants to move out of each other's areas would become know as ethnic cleansing, when applied to other conflicts in the Balkans and beyond.

As we saw earlier in the chapter it was the precedent that Westminster did not interfere directly in the affairs of Northern Ireland. This was a view held in both Belfast and London but during the winter of 1968 the government in London reluctantly started to prepare for direct intervention (Rose, 2001). The Wilson government was horrified and under increasing pressure from its own backbenchers concerning the increasing violence in Northern Ireland. Mr Wilson and home secretary James Callaghan put pressure on prime minister James Chichester-Clark to make him initiate a further round of reforms, including the disbandment of the B Specials and a return to proportional representation in local elections. In return for these reforms Chichester-Clark appealed for help in controlling the situation, asking for and getting the posting of British soldiers to Northern Ireland. As is well known, there is a certain irony in the fact that Catholics, who saw the army as their protection from the B Specials initially, received the soldiers with open arms.

Both sides exploited the army presence. The Northern Ireland government insisted that the army should play a key role in supporting the RUC in its operations but, since those operations were all taken against the Catholic community it was soon perceived as being partisan, losing its original support and alienating the Catholics. The IRA itself had almost ceased to exist by the mid-1960s – its last active campaign had been around a decade before. It was seen as the traditional defender of Catholics but its leadership wanted to take it directly into politics as a socialist organization. Political desires and fear of provoking the Protestant mobs still further kept the IRA well in the background, leading to accusation from Catholics that IRA now stood for 'I Ran Away' (Mulholland, 2003, p. 64). A new breed of IRA now came on the scene, spurred by being joined by activists from the south and an active faction calling itself the Provisional IRA, known as the 'Provos', with a political wing in Provisional Sinn Fein. They took over the Belfast IRA in September 1969 and rest of the military side of the organization by 1972. The Provos now declared that since the army had failed, they themselves would act as defenders of the Catholic, nationalist community. In the months that followed they were involved in a number of confrontations with the RUC and army, leading to an escalation of violence.

The Labour government did not wish, however, to take over control of Northern Ireland, it merely wanted to put the army in to prevent a civil war there (Rose, 2001). The Conservative government that came into power in June 1970 under Edward Heath carried on with this notion, although now it was concentrating on rooting the IRA out of Catholic areas. Curfews were imposed in Catholic areas, thousands of houses were searched and battles with the IRA grew in frequency. In February 1971, Gunner Robert Curtis, became the first British soldier to be killed by the Provisional IRA and Chichester-Clark demanded reinforcements. London was reluctant to be drawn into what was coming to seem like a war and in March, after a long dispute, Chichester-Clark resigned, stating a lack of will by Heath's government to solve the violence in Northern Ireland as the main reason. He was replaced by Brian Faulkner who, within months, had invoked the existing Special Powers Act to reintroduce internment without trial, an alienating measure sometimes referred to as 'the recruiting officer of the IRA' (Coxall and Robins, 1995, p. 433). Alienation set in when the army was called on to support the RUC in making arrests: most of those arrested proved to be innocent civilians while many of the guilty escaped. Thousands of Catholics were interned in an old American air-force base, Long Kesh. Amongst often brutal conditions the camp was run on military lines with the guards recognizing IRA officers for the purpose of all communications. This then enabled the IRA to use the time to provide its recruits with lectures on tactics and arms and even the use of dummy wooden guns. The result of internment, which ended in December 1975, was that the British had helped build up a vastly reinforced republican army rather causing its demise (Mulholland, 2003, p. 79). Political violence also now increased significantly.

On 30 January 1972 (Bloody Sunday) paratroopers opened fire on a civil rights march in Derry, killing thirteen people in circumstances that are still in dispute. This act meant the almost total collapse of Catholic opposition to political violence. It was the final straw for the Conservative government in that it showed that the divided responsibility for security between Stormont and London was not working. Stormont was thoroughly discredited and Edward Heath wanted to be rid of it. On 22 March 1972 Stormont was prorogued and within a week direct rule came into effect with the installation of William Whitelaw as secretary of state for Northern Ireland.

The search for a political solution

In Northern Ireland after 1972 the situation was totally different from that in mainland Great Britain, partly because of the continuing state of emergency and terrorist activity and partly because the province was seeking to regain a devolution they had had and lost rather than gain it for the first time. The whole process was also complicated because the search for a political solution to the troubles of Northern Ireland was inextricably mixed up with the search for a military solution. Throughout all the negotiations that followed the suppression of Stormont, all sides claimed that they wanted peace for the province when in fact what each side wanted was not peace by negotiation but peace by victory for one side and surrender on the other.

That confusion between political and military solutions led to the great paradox in the Ulster situation: the only way to peace was through a political settlement, but it was impossible to achieve a political settlement without first achieving a peaceful solution.

At the beginning of 'the Troubles' the principal concern was to get rid of direct rule, which was an emergency measure forced upon the British government but which was unsatisfactory as a long-term solution. The problem with direct rule was that it was that it did little to help solve the intricate problems associated with politics in Northern Ireland. Instead it became associated with the British government's war against the IRA. As to what could replace direct rule, there were two practicable alternatives as far as British governments were concerned: either the province could revert to a form of devolved government or it could be fully integrated with Great Britain, with a status like Wales or an English region.

The problem inherent in any proposals for integration was that the politics of Northern Ireland were not those of Great Britain. Even the party political system was different and state institutions like education, the law, railways, public utilities and the civil service in Northern Ireland were quite separate and incapable of integration. On the whole these institutions were also in the hands of the unionists and therefore provided little support or co-operation for an integration which would dissolve their own power base. The only possible answer was therefore an agreed renewal of devolved government. But the two main stumbling blocks to this solution were that the nationalist community did not want any devolution that might restore rule by the unionist parties, while the loyalist community refused any form of power-sharing devolution which might permit the Dublin government some say in Northern Irish affairs (Cunningham, 1992, p. 30).

In 1973 the Northern Ireland Constitution Act represented an attempt to restore devolution promoted by secretary of state William Whitelaw. A seventy-eight-seat, multi-party assembly was elected by the STV system of proportional representation in June 1973 and a power-sharing executive composed of the Official Unionists, the Alliance party and the SDLP took office on 1 January 1974. Allied to the new settlement were talks called by Whitelaw at Sunningdale in Berkshire, in which representatives of the IRA took part and which proposed a Council of Ireland made up of seven representatives from Dublin and seven from Belfast.

The Sunningdale Agreement, with its recognition of the role of Dublin in the government of Northern Ireland provoked opposition from the less moderate parties such as Ian Paisley's DUP and such a storm of protest in the north that eleven of the twelve MPs elected for Northern Ireland in the February 1974 general election were candidates opposed to it. The executive was undermined by this and, although members struggled on for a few months, it was finally brought down in May 1974 by a general strike called by the Protestant Ulster Workers' Council. Brian Faulkner resigned from the executive and as leader of the Ulster Unionists. The Northern Ireland Act of 1974 which followed dissolved the assembly and reimposed direct rule.

In May 1975 Labour's Northern Ireland secretary, Merlyn Rees, called a constitutional convention, but it was only a discussion group and in March 1976 it collapsed without achieving anything. The security situation was, however, getting better under the Callaghan government and there were hopes that the IRA was getting weary with the continuing struggle and would seek a peaceful solution. That changed in 1979, however, with the election of Margaret Thatcher, who promised to be more interventionist in her Northern Ireland policy. Constant confrontation created a resurgence of support for the IRA, particularly in 1981 after the death in the Maze prison of the IRA hunger striker, Bobby Sands, who had been elected to Westminster in a parliamentary by-election only a short time previously. Thatcher was always determined to be firm on terrorism, but after Sands' death she became the IRA's number one target (Thatcher, 1993). A tough stance against the IRA did not come cheaply to her: in time she would lose her shadow Northern Ireland secretary Airey Neave MP, personal assistant Ian Gow MP, and in a bomb attack at the 1984 Conservative conference in Brighton she almost lost her own life.

Margaret Thatcher did use the political carrot and stick with Northern Ireland. As well as continuing a direct military war against the IRA her Northern Ireland secretary, James Prior, began a process of what he called 'rolling devolution' in 1982. A Northern Ireland assembly of seventy-eight members was elected in October of that year with the promise that devolution would be granted according to any proposal put forward that had the support of 70 per cent of assembly members. The process was hampered from the start by the refusal of unionist parties to share power with the republicans. As a result it was boycotted by Sinn Fein and the SDLP, the latter entering into talks in Dublin with the separate so-called New Ireland Forum. The unionist parties continued in the assembly for nearly four years as a form of scrutinising committee looking at Northern Ireland legislation coming from London, but a unionist boycott of the assembly in 1985 led to the venture being abandoned in June 1986.

The agreement of 1985 between the London and Dublin governments, signed by Margaret Thatcher and Dr Garrett Fitzgerald and known as the Anglo-Irish or Hillsborough Agreement, was a major advance because Dublin openly recognised for the first time that there could only be change in Northern Ireland with the consent of the majority of people there.[7] The agreement provided for regular meetings between British and Irish ministers and a permanent staff of British and Irish civil servants was based at Stormont to help negotiate agreement on cross-border disputes. The agreement was totally opposed by unionist parties who refused to allow that Dublin had any say in Northern Ireland, and ignored by Sinn Fein who claimed that the point about majority consent was irrelevant because a majority in Northern Ireland is a minority when the whole of Ireland is considered. Support was restricted to the political parties of Britain and the Republic of Ireland together with the SDLP.

The next time London and Dublin acted closely together occurred on 15 December 1993 when John Major and Albert Reynolds set out a joint declaration (also known as the Downing Street Declaration). This stated that:

1 the people of Ireland, north and south, should freely determine their future;
2 this could be expressed in new structures arising out of the three-stranded relationship;
3 there could be no change in Northern Ireland's status without freely given majority consent;
4 this could be withheld;
5 the consent principle should be written into the Irish constitution; and
6 Sinn Fein could enter negotiations once the IRA had renounced violence.

Now both Dublin and London sought to try to win agreement for the declaration not only in Northern Ireland but also in their own respective countries (Cunningham, 2001). However, there was one other party which neither government could ignore in seeking a permanent solution to the problems of Northern Ireland and this was the United States.

There had always been significant interest in the affairs of Northern Ireland in the United States. Some 80 million Americans had ancestry connected to Ireland and the country acted as fundraiser to paramilitary groups of both sides of conflict. The political support in Congress and the Senate included senators

Ted Kennedy and John Kerry (Clinton, 2004, p. 579). In the presidency both John Kennedy's and Ronald Reagan's roots came from Ireland. Many Irish-American activists lobbied the US presidents to help bring an end to the problems in Ulster in one way or another. In turn the presidents often wooed nationalists, unionists and Irish and British prime ministers, particularly during US St Patrick's Day celebrations, to try to help things along (Cochrane, 2001). American intervention was not always welcomed, however, and there was a considerable falling out over the granting of an American visa for Sinn Fein leader Gerry Adams to visit the United States during the Clinton presidency (Major, 1999). Yet it was the Clinton presidency that proved to be so helpful as a broker in the Northern Ireland peace negotiations.

Clinton's granting of a visa to Adams convinced republicans that the United States was now willing to act on behalf of nationalist interests bringing with it the weight of a superpower. Partly as a result of this a serious peace process began in the second half of 1994 with an IRA ceasefire, followed by similar announcements from the loyalist paramilitaries (Mulholland, 2002, p. 132). However, the British government under John Major and the unionist parties refused to take part in talks with parties such as Sinn Fein, as long as paramilitaries kept their weapons and could threaten to restart the violence if talks failed. Adding to this problem was the fact that Major's decreasing parliamentary majority at Westminster meant that he was continually relying on unionist votes to keep him in power. Sinn Fein, for the IRA, stated that they were willing to enter talks as equal partners, but to give up their weapons would be like admitting defeat. They would do nothing that might suggest surrender. In late November 1995, only days before President Clinton was due to arrive in Northern Ireland on a peacemaking visit, a deal was fixed. A twin-track approach would be adopted by which the arms issue should be separated from the question of talks. Negotiations for talks would continue on one track while an international and independent commission under a former US senator, George Mitchell, would examine the arms question separately.

The IRA ceasefire ended in February 1996 with a bomb set off at Canary Wharf in London, Sinn Fein blaming the British government for bad faith and delaying tactics. Other bombs followed in Germany and Manchester and it began to look as though the peace process was irremediably breaking down. During the Protestant marching season in the summer of 1996 there were confrontations and renewed violence between the two communities.

Soon after his election in 1997, Tony Blair, with his Northern Ireland secretary, Mo Mowlam, made serious efforts to get the peace process back on track, taking a middle track that ran the risk of offending both extremes. Both had backed the Downing Street Declaration and now sought to progress from this. For a time during the 1997 marching season it looked as though the whole process could break down yet again in communal violence. On 15 July the entire province was horrified when 'loyalist' gunmen dragged Catholic Bernadette Martin from her Protestant boyfriend's home and shot her dead.

Three days later Gerry Adams and Martin McGuinness for Sinn Fein urged the IRA to call a ceasefire and, on 19 July, that ceasefire was restored. In September, the government accepted that the IRA ceasefire had lasted long enough for Sinn Fein to be admitted to the peace talks, as a result of which Sinn Fein agreed to the Mitchell Principles, foreswore violence and accepted that weapons would have to be surrendered at some future date.

On Good Friday 1998 the renewed peace talks bore fruit when agreement was reached that there was to be an elected Northern Ireland assembly of 108 members, elected by STV in six-member constituencies, the legislative powers of the assembly being weighted to prevent domination by unionists. An executive or 'cabinet' of twelve members was to be appointed, including first minister, deputy first minister and ministers for finance, health, education, agriculture, etc. The assembly was also to set up and supervise a north–south body to deal with cross-border issues. Efforts were to be made to settle outstanding issues such as the decommissioning of arms and the accelerated release of paramilitary prisoners.

Conclusion

John Major wrote in his autobiography that (1999, p. 469): 'Working for a Northern Ireland settlement was the most difficult, frustrating and, from 1993, time-consuming problem of government during my premiership.' Every British and Irish prime minister from the mid-1960s onwards had periods in office dominated and their political agendas determined by events in Northern Ireland, and the continual quest to gain a permanent solution to problems there frustrated them all. Their autobiographies and biographies contain far more reference to issues in Northern Ireland than any area of the United Kingdom. The problems of Northern Ireland often proved more difficult to solve because the complexities of its history meant that not only did the religious divisions of both Protestants and Catholics in the north have to be happy with any settlements, so also did the governments of Dublin and London and, on occasion, the government in Washington. Relations between London and Dublin were often strained to breaking point, which made solutions even more difficult to obtain. Yet the political reward for a solution provided the necessary motivation for all sides to come back and work together again and again. It is ironic, therefore, that 'the Irish question' which so dominated British politics in the nineteenth century should still have such prominence in the twenty-first, thus making it one of the most protracted political conundrums in respect of British politics of all time and indicating the importance of political devolution on the policy agenda.

Notes

1. This is quoted in Bogdanor (p. 66) but was originally said in H. H. Asquith, *Memories and Reflections 1852–1927*, Cassell, 1928.
2. Information on the structure and function of the Stormont parliament is provided in a doctoral thesis on 'The Senate in Northern Ireland 1921–62' (Patrick Francis McGill, PhD Thesis, Queen's University, Belfast, 1965).
3. The thirteen became twelve in 1948 when university seats were abolished, including that of Queen's University, Belfast. When Stormont was suppressed in 1972 and direct rule was introduced, the number of Northern Ireland MPs once more became seventeen.
4. Craigavon made this statement in 1933 when he was responding to a declaration by Eamon de Valera that 'Ireland is a Catholic state'.
5. A statement made to the House of Commons, 12 May 1938.
6. The Vanguard party was fairly short-lived and ceased to exist after 1976 but of course the DUP went on to achieve and maintain a prominent position in the province.
7. The recognition of the north's right to self-determination was in direct contradiction of the Republic's written constitution which committed the Irish government to the abolition of partition.

Part III

The devolution settlement

6

Scotland:
success of a sort

The distinction between New Labour and the Conservatives became blurred on many issues of policy in the mid-1990s. In the May general election of 1997, however, there was still one clear dividing line on policy between the Conservatives and New Labour in respect of Scotland. This concerned the issue of the Scottish parliament, New Labour being for and the Conservatives against. Yet even as the opinion polls indicated that the Labour party was heading for a landslide victory it were uncertain about whether it could effectively bring about a Scottish parliament. In June 1996, eleven months before he won the general election, Tony Blair acknowledged the difficulties he would face in steering such a complex piece of legislation as devolution for Scotland through parliament and laid down certain guide rules in advance. Despite critics from his own and other parties, who said that there was no need for a referendum when the commitment to devolution was so clearly written into the party manifesto, Blair announced that there would indeed be one. The need to gain public approval for his actions was, he said, a necessary by-product of returning the government of Scotland to the Scottish people themselves. Yet in 1979 Scotland had already passed a referendum endorsing a Scottish parliament – would this not suffice? Mr Blair believed it wouldn't and then detailed three ways in which this referendum would differ from the first:

- it would take place before legislation was placed before parliament and not afterwards as was previously the case;
- no minimum level of support was required – instead of a threshold of 40 per cent as in 1979, a simple majority of those voting would suffice to decide the outcome;
- two questions would be asked: 'I agree that there should be a Scottish parliament' and 'I agree that a Scottish parliament should have tax-varying powers'.

Unlike all those previous prime ministers who had introduced Home Rule or devolution measures, from Gladstone onwards, Tony Blair was not under any of the pressures to which they had been subjected. With an overall majority of 177, Labour: (a) did not need to feel threatened by the possibility of a surge in nationalist popularity undermining that majority, and (b) did not require any voting deal with other parties in the Commons to ensure the passage of government legislation, as had been the case when nationalist support had sustained the minority Callaghan government in 1979. Although in respect of winning the devolution referendums Labour still required the support of other parties in gaining victory.

Given the strength of Labour's position the government moved remarkably quickly once the Blair administration took power on 2 May 1997. The Scottish Office, under permanent secretary Sir Russell Hillhouse, had already prepared a detailed briefing on devolution to give to the incoming Scottish secretary Donald Dewar. On the Tuesday following the general election Tony Blair chaired the Constitutional Reform Policy (CRP) committee which was to monitor and push forward constitutional reform of which devolution was to be a central plank. In the same week the DSWR (Devolution to Scotland, Wales and England) committee met under the chairmanship of the lord chancellor, Lord Irving. Events continued to develop at a pace. Before the end of July a White Paper, *Scotland's Parliament*, had been published, setting out the proposed legislation. At the same time the Referendums (Scotland and Wales) Act passed successfully through both Houses of Parliament and received the royal assent. The Scottish referendum itself took place on Thursday 11 September 1997, with two questions on two separate papers, as decided earlier.

The campaign to get agreement to both questions was known as the 'yes-yes' campaign and was very strong, especially when the SNP joined in alongside Labour and the Scottish Liberal Democrats. The 'yes' group had been boosted by the years of cross-party working in the Scottish Constitutional Convention. Both Labour and the Scottish Liberal Democrats had gone into the 1997 general election with a joint platform of working together on the Scottish parliament. Within New Labour ranks, however, there was some resistance nationally in working with other political parties on any issue. After Labour's substantial election victory the desire to work with other parties became more concentrated in Scotland but less so elsewhere within the party, particularly in the cabinet (Taylor, 2002). The Scottish Labour party, however, still had to win a referendum on the Scottish parliament. In respect of the referendum, with the Scottish Liberal Democrats and other smaller political parties on board, the issue for Labour became 'would the SNP join them?'. They had famously declared that they 'wouldn't trust Labour to deliver a pizza – let alone a Parliament' (Taylor, 2002, p. 13). Now for tactical reasons they decided that they would join forces. This meant that every MP in Scotland now belonged to party that was supporting the 'yes-yes' vote in the referendum and the 'yes' camp now therefore appeared to be a unbeatable force. Such was the concern over the size of the 'yes' campaign's support that when Lord Neill's Committee on Standards in Public Life examined the Scottish referendum in 1998 they expressed some concern that the government had substantially overtly supported the 'yes-yes' campaign while the opposition had had to rely on its own resources (1998, p. 168). It was felt that opposition groups had indeed been disadvantaged by this and legislation has since been passed to ensure that public funds will from now on be provided to both sides in referendums.

In Scotland, only the *Daily Mail* backed the 'no' camp, the rest of the press was either neutral or pro-devolution. The Conservatives themselves were split, with some supporting devolution, others supporting the parliament but not tax raising, and others still against both. Therefore the Conservatives were not officially involved in the 'no' camp, instead it was led by a Conservative-Unionist barrister and vice chair of Rangers football club – Donald Findlay. Unlike 1979 there were no key Scottish Conservative MPs to front a 'no' campaign. Their two key players, Michael Forsyth and Malcolm Rifkind, had only recently lost their seats. Lady Thatcher, in Scotland on 9 September to address American travel agents at a conference, came out publicly and advocated a 'no' vote. This led the 'no' camp to say privately that they wish she'd been on the other side so that people would have voted no to spite her (Harvie and Jones, 2000, p. 185). The only hope of the 'no' campaign lay with the fact that opinion polls showed that less than half the Scottish people were in favour of the parliament being granted tax-raising powers. The campaign tried to exploit people's fears with talk of the parliament's proposed 'tartan tax', but their efforts failed. The public were rather less keen on the tax-varying powers than they were on the simple issue of the parliament, but there was still a 2:1 vote in favour of tax-varying. The percentage vote was 44.7 per cent of the Scottish electorate in favour of the parliament and 38.1 per cent in favour of tax-varying powers. This means, of course, that had the 40 per cent threshold been applied, as it was in 1979, there would still have been a vote in favour of the parliament but the question of taxation would have been lost, although in reality only Orkney and Dumfries and Galloway gave majorities against the tax-raising power.[1]

Turnout in Scotland as a whole in the referendum was 60.4 per cent, as against 63.8 per cent in 1979. This was around the same percentage that had appeared in all Scottish referendums. As for most elections in Scotland turnout was higher in middle-class areas. The united strength of the political parties messages on voting 'yes-yes' was beneficial to the 'yes' vote and turnout; in 1979 many in the Labour party had been opposed to devolution (Denver *et al.*, 1998, p. 212). Of those who voted, 74.3 per cent said 'yes' to the basic question, while 60.2 per cent approved of the tax-varying powers. The result was satisfactory enough for Tony Blair to proclaim on 13 September: 'Well done. This is a good day for Scotland, and a good day for Britain and the United Kingdom ... the era of big, centralised government is over!' (quoted in Evans, 1999, p. 68).

The Scotland Act 1998

The Scotland bill to set up the parliament and Scottish executive was introduced to the Westminster parliament on 18 December 1997, at the very start of the 1997–98 session, and had its second reading on 13 January 1998. The Scotland bill contained 40,000 words and had taken 60,000 person hours to produce its 116 clauses. Within it were eight schedules which set out in detail how devolution would work, but the most important was beginning of Clause 1, Part One, which stated simply: 'There shall be a Scottish Parliament' (Taylor, 2002, p. 139).

Donald Dewar stirred the bill through the Commons for the government. Michael Ancram on behalf of the Conservatives gave token resistance, the Scottish Liberal Democrats tried to increase provisions on gender balance in the parliament and the SNP sought to gain further powers such as broadcasting and relations with Europe for the parliament. Apart from these slight disruptions the bill had a relatively easy passage through the Commons with most clauses getting through the committee stage unaltered. This was aided by the by the fact that the referendum decision had given public approval to the measures involved. The Lords, with their unionist sympathies, might have treated the bill more severely but for the Salisbury Convention, which precludes the Lords from querying a bill passed by the Commons if the measure in question was mandated by the public by inclusion in the party manifesto – all the more so when the bill had been approved by the electorate in a referendum. The act received the royal assent in November 1998 with elections to the new parliament scheduled for May 1999.

Provisions of the Scotland Act relating to the parliament's composition and powers

The issues that the political parties were most concerned with initially was how many Members of the Scottish Parliament (MSPs) there would be and how many of these would be theirs. The Scotland Act was quite specific on this:

> The Parliament will have 129 Members, 73 from constituencies elected on the first past the post system and 56 additional members selected on a proportional basis from party lists drawn up for each of the current 8 European Parliament constituencies. Each elector will be able to cast two votes: one for a constituency MSP (Member of the Scottish Parliament) and one for the party of their choice. The Parliament will be kept in order by a Presiding Officer who will be an MSP and will be elected by the Parliament.[1]

The figure for MSPs was again confirmed in 2002 when Scottish secretary Helen Liddell stated that they would not be revised in line with the general reduction of Westminster seats which were taking into account devolution. The seventy-three constituencies for which MSPs are elected consisted of the seventy-two Westminster constituencies but with that of the Orkneys having Shetland separated from Orkney to provide the extra constituency.

The next issue that concerned the political parties after gaining MSPs was with what power the new Scottish parliament would be able to provide them. To this affect the act indicated that 'The Scottish Parliament will be able to make primary legislation (Acts of the Scottish Parliament). Its legislative competence will be limited in a number of ways. It will not be able to legislate about reserved matters. At Schedule 5 the Act specifies all matters which are to be reserved.' Reserved powers are those which the Westminster parliament wishes to retain direct control over. The main reservations are:

- the constitution;
- defence;
- finance and the economy;
- trade and industry;
- transport not particular to Scotland (e.g. railways);
- social security;
- medical ethics – abortion, genetics, surrogacy, medicines, misuse of drugs;
- broadcasting;
- foreign affairs;
- the civil service;
- national security, immigration, nationality;
- electricity, coal, oil, gas, nuclear energy;
- employment;
- equal opportunities.

Apart from these, the main devolved matters are:

- health;
- local government;
- housing;
- planning, economic development, financial assistance to industry;
- transport within Scotland (roads, buses, ports and harbours);
- criminal justice and prosecution system, the courts;
- police and fire service;
- agriculture, food, forestry and fisheries;
- sport;
- statistics, public registers and records;
- education, training and lifelong learning;
- social work;
- tourism;
- environment, natural and built heritage;
- the arts.

During the passing of the Scotland bill, the Scottish Office minister Lord Sewell put forward a statement regarding the boundaries between Scotland and Westminster over legislation. Sewel stated that:

> We envisage that there could be instances where it would be more convenient for devolved matters to be passed by the United Kingdom Parliament. However, as happened in Northern Ireland earlier this century, we would expect a convention to be established that Westminster would not normally legislate with regard to devolved matters in Scotland without the consent of the Scottish Parliament. (House of Lords, Debate, 21 July 1998, col. 791)

In October 1999, a Memorandum of Understanding was signed between the Scottish, Welsh and UK institutions agreeing exactly what Lord Sewell had stated the previous year. Hence forth this principle that Westminster will not legislate on Scottish devolved matters without the consent of the Scottish parliament became known as the 'Sewell Convention'. As soon as the Scottish parliament started operating in June 1999 it gave consent for four bills to continue which had not yet completed their passage but affected devolved matters; the following year consent was given to another ten bills, and so it continued from then onwards (Russell and Hazell, 2000, p. 189).

The structure of the Scottish Executive (government)

From the outset it was envisaged that Scotland would be governed by an executive made up from members of the ruling party(s). In this respect the provisions of the Scotland Act 1998 were that:

> The Scottish Executive (whose members are collectively referred to as 'the Scottish Ministers') will be the Government in Scotland for all devolved matters. The members of the Scottish Executive will be:
> - the First Minister; [the term 'prime minister' was seen as being too close to that of Westminster]
> - the Lord Advocate and the Solicitor General for Scotland (the Law Officers);
> - other Ministers appointed by the First Minister.

The first minister is able to appoint junior ministers (who are not members of the cabinet) to assist the Scottish ministers, who are members of the cabinet. The first minister and law officers all have specific duties assigned to them under the Act, the first minister playing a prime ministerial role in the appointment of ministers while the lord advocate acts as senior law officer within the Scottish executive: the duties of these are known as 'retained functions'. But all the other ministers, once appointed, could be asked to fulfill any one of a variety of governmental functions at the discretion of the first minister, just as UK ministers are appointed to departmental responsibilities by the prime minister.

A presiding officer is also elected to chair the proceedings of parliament in much the same way as the speaker acts at Westminster, although the Scottish post is rather more than simply that. The presiding officer has powers similar to the speaker in the Swedish parliament, with certain monarchical functions and a key role in the direct relationship between parliament and monarch. When a bill has passed through parliament the presiding officer must check very carefully that it is not *ultra vires* by being outside the remit of the parliament, having four weeks to carry out those checks by consulting the Scottish law officers or sending the bill to the judicial committee of the privy council. At the end of those four weeks the presiding officer will pass on the bill directly for royal assent.

Revenue and tax-raising power

The financial provisions of the Scotland Act 1998 are particularly important, given the nature of the second question in the referendum. The Act states very clearly that the parliament's assigned budget (sometimes referred to as the 'block grant') will be determined in much the same way as the old Scottish block was, and that additional expenditure will be allocated using the so-called Barnett formula (see Chapter 4). Through the 1980s and 1990s this formula protected Scotland against any decline in public expenditure.

In Scotland the expenditure is 11 per cent more per head than in the north-east region of England that borders it, despite the fact that Scottish gross domestic product (GDP) per head is some 25 per cent higher (Bristow, 2005, p. 69). In general Scotland enjoys 18 per cent more identifiable expenditure per head than England (Midwinter cited in Scott, 2002). At the 2005 British general election and afterwards there had been continued speculation in Scotland that the Barnett formula would be revised and the Treasury itself has said that it is 'not set in stone' (Scott, 2002). Some of this pressure came in 2001 from the deputy prime minister, John Prescott, and other north-east English MPs who shared widespread anger at the discrepancy between the two nations. The nature of this long-standing Barnett arrangement and its continuance was reaffirmed in July 2004 by the chancellor, Gordon Brown, as being the best method of continuing the funding of the devolved institution without the need for protracted and lengthy negotiations (Treasury, 2004). It is carried on partially because the Labour party fears that a challenge to Scotland's spending advantage would provide an electoral hand to the SNP and threaten its seats there, including a number of prominent cabinet ministers. Despite the 'generosity' of the Barnett formula we should also note that the SNP have always stated that if Scotland were given the revenues from the oil and gas that surrounds it, the country would be even wealthier.

In addition to its central Westminster-derived funding the Scottish parliament has the power to vary upwards or downwards the basic rate of income tax applicable in Scotland by up to three pence in the pound, with proceeds adding to or reducing the parliament's spending power (Section 76 of the Scotland Act 1998). Tax-raising, or the so-called 'tartan tax', has not proved to be a popular policy pledge. In 2003–04 it was estimated to be able to raise or lower some £260 million in a full year, this was some £413 million less than was returned from the previous year's budget unspent and less than 1 per cent of the executive's total budget. The more advantageous funding per head of GDP than in England or Wales has also given the political parties less need to tap into additional sources of revenue. Unsurprisingly therefore the main political parties in Scotland all pledged not to raise taxes in their 2003 Scottish election manifestos and instead to take their resources from the 'central fund'. We should also note that the Scottish parliament's financial role does not end with its tax-varying powers, but that it also controls local government in Scotland giving parliament the further fiscal powers of being able to adjust the size of council tax and fix the business tax rate.

Finance and the budgetary process

By 2005–06 the Scottish executive was responsible for some £27 billion of expenditure. Money and expenditure therefore are at the heart of determining policy and law-making as much for the Scottish executive as any other government. In this respect one of the first major pieces of legislation to go through the Scottish parliament was the Public Finance and Accountability (Scotland) Act 2000 which formalised the process of setting the Scottish parliament's annual budget.

The Scottish parliament's budgetary process is in three stages. The first stage covers March to June in the year previous to the budget being agreed. This is the Annual Expenditure Report (AER), which gives a detailed breakdown of the executive's spending plans and priorities. The relevant Scottish parliamentary subject committees then comment on the relationship between expenditure plans and policy priorities in the spending area. These responses are co-ordinated by the finance committee, which reports to the parliament. Its report is then debated by the full parliament before the summer recess. In the light of this debate the executive then adjusts it plans for Stage 2.

Stage 2 occurs between September and December, and involves the executive's more detailed spending plans, published in September, being scrutinized. Each subject committee reports back to the finance committee on any relevant issues concerned with its own subject area. In the early part of the parliament the committees were reluctant to make proposals, and the extent to which the subject committees have, in the past, been prepared to make changes to the executive's proposed expenditure plans has varied. In 2000, three recommendations were made. In 2001, none was proposed. However, in 2002, a more consistent approach was adopted across committees and twelve recommendations were made (McVicker and Wakefield, 2003, p. 8). Apart from the subject committees the finance committee can also revise the budget as its sees fit as long as it is within the executive draft budget spending limits. Whatever happens during the Stage 2 negotiations and discussion the finance committee produces a report by December, which is then debated before the Christmas recess.

The final stage is undertaken between January and February. The executive then brings forward a budget (Scotland) bill. At this stage in the process only a member of the executive may move amendments. Parliament can then either accept or reject the bill in total. The budget (referred to as Total Managed Expenditure (TME)), is composed of three parts:

1 Departmental Expenditure Limits (DEL), which is the largest part of the budget (the old 'Scottish block');
2 Annually Managed Expenditure (AME) which includes spending that can fluctuate significantly each year such as the Common Agricultural Policy (CAP) spending, housing support grant and NHS and teachers' pensions – this represents about 10 per cent of the TME budget;
3 Non-Domestic Rates Income (NDRI) or business rates, which is one of the main expenditure areas for Scottish local government.

The Scottish Executive also keeps a reserve (contingency fund) for unexpected spending such as natural disasters.

The role of the Secretary of State, Scotland Office and the Civil Service in a devolved Scotland

It became evident that as Scottish devolution developed the role of the pre-1999 Scottish secretary would be very much reduced. The Scottish Office had its staff of 12,000 civil servants transferred to the Scottish parliament; the remaining government department changed its name from the Scottish Office to the Scotland Office. The Scottish secretary was left with three special advisers and 140 civil servants to handle those limited areas where the secretary still has a role. Even its London base, Dover House, no longer belongs just to the Scotland Office; it also provides a London base for the Scottish executive. The Scotland Office does, however, also have an office in Edinburgh, Melville Crescent, from where it can deal directly with the Scottish parliament.

When Helen Liddell was appointed Scottish secretary in 2001, succeeding John Reid, there was widespread media speculation that the post would soon either be scrapped or merged into one post in a new department covering all of the devolved institutions. This did not occur but on 12 June 2003 Tony Blair decided that the role of secretary of state for Scotland would be combined with another post within the cabinet. The Scotland Office, together with the Wales Office, at the same time were moved into the new Department for Constitutional Affairs (DCA). This was headed by Lord Falconer of Thoroton. The announcement was greeted by much confusion in Scotland and elsewhere as the only details people could get were what trickled through the media – the Scotland Office's website remained quiet on the subject. When official news did come out it was revealed that the Scotland Office would be an autonomous unit within the DCA. The DCA was the government department in which everyone of cabinet rank had two jobs. The new Scottish secretary Alistair Darling took on the responsibility of secretary of state for transport and Lord Falconer also became lord chancellor.

There was also continued confusion at the start of the revised Scottish secretary's tenure. This confusion concerned who the Scotland Office would now report to, as it was now part of the DCA. After the dust had settled it was confirmed that ministers at the Scotland Office would report to Alistair Darling and now Lord Falconer. There was also general acceptance of Darling's new role at both Westminster and Holyrood, but with some teasing. Tam Dalyell, Labour MP for Linithgow, asked Darling in a transport committee, 'Are there not situations likely to arise where you may have to go to yourself and tell yourself that you have no case?' Darling replied, 'I have made a habit of not talking to myself for the last forty-nine and a half years. As my mother would say, "if I'm spared, I intend to continue that practice"' (cited in Wright, 2003, p. 24).

The secretary of state for Scotland's main role now is the custodian of the Scotland Act 1998, and the secondary legislation under the act ('Scotland Act Orders'). In addition, the secretary of state retains responsibility for certain limited executive functions, notably in relation to the financial transactions between the UK government and the Scottish executive, elections in Scotland and boundary commission issues, and undertakes certain residual functions for Scotland in reserved areas. The fact that there are so many Scottish Labour MPs would seem to indicate that the post of Scottish secretary would continue whilst Labour hold power. A Conservative government with very few Scottish MPs, however, will feel less of an obligation to keep the post going and there is a general feeling that it will in time wither away.

Scotland's civil service

Before the arrival of the Scottish parliament all civil servants at the Scottish Office simply worked for government in Westminster. After devolution this all changed. The Scotland Office has the power to appoint staff, hold property and enter into contracts in its own right. It is written into the Scotland Act that the Scottish civil service will be part of the home civil service as 'all staff of the Scottish Administration should be regarded as civil servants in the UK Home Civil Service since ... maintaining a unified Civil Service is considered essential for preserving the unity of the UK' (Pilkington, 1999a, p. 153). Although civil servants in the Scottish parliament still remain part of the UK civil service, in reality their direct loyalty lies with the Scottish executive. This new civil service structure is known as the Scottish Parliamentary Corporate Body (SPCB). It took some while for civil servants and MSPs to adjust to each other. The civil servants weren't used to the close scrutiny of the MSPs and the MSPs weren't used to the civil servants working solely to ministers. At the same time the policy formulation of civil servants had to adapt to being outside of the ministerial–departmental set up of the Whitehall civil service apparatus (Keating, 2004, p. 103).

The Scottish parliamentary elections

Unlike Westminster the Scottish parliament is elected for a fixed term of four years. It can only be dissolved earlier than that, and an extraordinary general election called, under two circumstances:

- if two-thirds of the parliament vote that the presiding officer should ask the Queen to dissolve parliament;
- if the parliament fails to elect a first minister within twenty-eight days of the election.

Both devices were introduced to prevent the first minister and the majority party from exploiting the election date for electoral advantage, as is so often done by the prime minister in the UK. The first minister was elected one week after the 6 May 1999 election, a measure that was repeated after the 2003 Scottish elections meaning there was no threat of an election being called again. The devolution settlement had been worked out before Labour's 1997 victory by the Scottish Constitutional Convention. As the elections were to be proportional Labour had recognised that they would probably need the Scottish Liberal Democrats to resist the growing popularity of the SNP and proportional representation was the price that Labour had to be prepared to pay for the Liberal Democrats' support. Many Labour politicians disliked PR and would have liked to have stuck with the FPTP system that had given Labour its landslide victory in 1997. However, even supporters of FPTP knew that it could give a majority of seats on a minority vote and the possibility did exist that with FPTP the SNP could become the largest party in Scotland with a mere 35 per cent of the vote. What Labour feared was that the SNP might claim a mandate for Scottish independence when only a third of the electorate had voted for them. PR would mean that the SNP would have to obtain more than 50 per cent of the vote to be able to claim the mandate.

The system chosen was not the single transferable vote (STV) favoured by the Scottish Liberal Democrats and SNP and that which had been used in both north and south Ireland on occasions since 1920. STV encourages voters to choose between members of the same party for the seats available and this can encourage splits and factions in the party such as left and right, Old Labour and New Labour and so on. Instead the system chosen was the additional member system (AMS) roughly similar to that adopted in Germany. Under this system electors' votes count twice, the first time being for a named candidate in a regular constituency, voted for under the familiar FPTP system, and the second

Table 6.1   *Scottish parliament election results*

Party	May 1999		
	Constituency seats	*Regional seats*	*Total seats*
Labour	53	3	56
SNP	7	28	35
Conservative	0	18	18
Liberal Democrat	12	5	17
Greens	0	1	1
Scottish Socialist	0	1	1
Independents	1	0	1

Party	May 2003		
	Constituency seats	*Regional seats*	*Total seats*
Labour	46	4	50
SNP	9	18	27
Conservative	3	15	18
Liberal Democrat	13	4	17
Greens	0	7	7
Scottish Socialist	0	6	6
Independents	2	1	3
Scottish Senior Citizens Unity	0	1	1

being for the party and leading to additional members allocated by region from party lists. In Scotland this was translated into seventy-three constituency MSPs elected by FPTP, topped up on a proportional basis by fifty-six party list candidates, seven chosen for each of the eight Euro-constituencies in Scotland, allocated by means of a formula known as the d'Hondt method.[2] Within the first parliament the work of constituency and list MSPs started to diverge slightly with the constituency MSPs being drawn into more local constituency issues whilst list MSPs were generally freed from these constraints and had a looser agenda to follow (Bennett *et al.*, 2002, p. 44). The election results in May 1999 and then again in May 2003, due to the result of the proportional system, meant that no party had an overall majority (see Table 6.1).

The Lib-Lab coalition gained a majority of twelve seats in the first Scottish election. This election was also notable for the SNP's good showing, making it clearly the second party in Scotland and lifting it from a party of six MPs into a serious political fighting force of forty-one elected parliamentary representatives in both Westminster and Holyrood. In addition to the SNP's success the election marked the re-emergence of the Scottish Conservatives. They had lost all of their Westminster MPs in Scotland in the 1997 general election and now, although they were unable still to win any constituencies, they did gain a number of list seats. Both the Greens (Robin Harper) and the Scottish Socialist party (under the controversial Tommy Sheridan) gained their first parliamentary seats. The former Labour MP Dennis Canavan won the Falkirk West seat, against an official Labour candidate, Canavan having failed to win a place on this official Labour candidate list himself (Fraser, 2004, p. 15). In winning his seat Canavan started a trend of deselected candidates not only challenging their former party at an election but beating them. In time this would also spread to the Greater London assembly and later to the Welsh assembly.

The second campaign was dominated by the fact that most politicians thought that the ongoing war in Iraq would influence voters' opinions. In the event polling indicated that only around 2 per cent put this as their main reason for choosing a candidate; Scottish or wider British issues, the role of the parties' leaders and policy areas such as health, education and crime were seen as being far more important (Curtice, 2003, p. 35). For the incumbent administration the issues of university tuition and care for the elderly were regarded as the Scottish government's most successful policies whilst public transport and the NHS in Scotland were seen as their biggest failings (Curtice, 2003). When the election came the turnout dropped from 58.7 per cent in 1999 to 49.4 per cent in 2003. This fall was out down to a number of factors including that the Scots' high expectations of the parliament had not been fulfilled and for many this election was now seen as a 'second order' one when compared with Westminster (Curtis, 2003, p. 8; Jeffrey, 2004, p. 304). The most notable factors in respect of the 2003 Scottish general elections were threefold.

First, the Labour-Liberal Democrat coalition was returned to power in 2003, albeit with a reduced majority of five MSPs. Both parties had a disappointing election: Labour lost seven constituency seats, whereas the Scottish Liberal Democrats had failed to persuade voters to give them their second preference list vote and had failed to make any real impact on the list seats, again gaining 77 per cent of their seats from the constituencies.

Second, the SNP had a very poor election. Although they gained two constituency seats they lost ten lists seats. For a party hoping to win control of the parliament and use it to lead towards an independent Scotland this was a major set back. The fall-out resulted in the SNP leader John Swinney being unsuccessfully challenged at the party's September 2003 conference by a little-known party activist, Dr Bill Wilson, who was seeking to become a stalking horse. Swinney won by a handsome majority but the infighting concerning his leadership did not die down and when the SNP once again had poor results in the 2004 European election he resigned. Former leader Alex Salmond succeeded him at the party's 2004 conference. As Salmond was an MP, the leadership of the SNP in the Scottish parliament went to his newly elected deputy, Nicola Sturgeon MSP. Sturgeon became the first female leader in the Scottish parliament, however, at the same time, Salmond became the first leader of one of the four main Scottish parties who was not in the Scottish parliament but in the British one; somewhat ironic for a party having an independent Scotland as its main aim.

The third significant factor about the Scottish election of 2003 was the breakout of some of Scotland's other political parties. Labour and the SNP's loss was other parties' gain. Robin Harper, the sole representative of the Greens, was joined by six more MSPs. In a party which does not like to have a leader, Harper became the party's convener. The Scottish Socialist party, represented by the controversial radical socialist Tommy Sheridan, gained five more list seats. Sheridan himself was now able to pass the leadership over to someone else, which Colin Fox duly gained in February 2005. A number of independents won seats, including Denis Canavan once more, and a political party representing pensioners wanting an increase in the state pension, something which is only determined at Westminster. For those who had indicated that PR would result in a fracturing of the political parties in Scotland, this election provided evidence of this. For those that said it would lead to unstable coalition governments this was not the case, at least in its formative years.

The type of MSPs elected

It was hoped initially that the Scottish parliament would enable a new breed of politician into enter political life, those who were untainted by either Westminster or local government. In fact the background of candidates for those first elections was similar to that of Westminster, with many coming from council backgrounds as a political 'second eleven' to their Westminster counterparts (Mitchell and Bradbury, 2004, p. 288). In this first parliament some 30 per cent of MSPs were in their late forties or early fifties and had spent something like twenty-five years each in Scottish politics. However, Labour MSPs were rather less experienced than members of other parties: only 34 per cent were involved in local politics, while a mere 9 per cent had previously fought a Westminster election. As for the gender of the MSPs, some 37 per cent were female, well below the cherished 50-50 male-female balance desired by many of those establishing the parliament. Only in the Labour party which had a strict gender balance, was the split 50-50. Whilst 43 per cent of SNP MSPs were female, this fell to 17 per cent for the Conservatives and just 12 per cent for the Scottish Liberal Democrats (Brown, 1999).

The inexperience of so many Labour MSPs meant that other ministers were not quite as representative of the old school of politics. For example, three cabinet ministers were women – Wendy Alexander, Sarah Boyack and Susan Deacon. Of the men a significant number were under forty years of age, a fact that indicates the number of young candidates who were elected to Holyrood. Of the first bunch of MSPs, no fewer than twenty were less than thirty-five years old and eight were in their twenties (Henderson and Sloat, 1999, p. 245).

These facts were evidence that, for Scottish politicians, Holyrood was now being ranked as equal if not better than Westminster. When it came to the second election most of the incumbent MSPs remained in place, with those on the lists suffering more party competition for their places than those in the constituencies. In one instance SNP activists in Lothian had managed to put Margo MacDonald (somewhat of a loose cannon in the party) from the top of the list to fifth. MacDonald resigned from the SNP, as she had once before in the early 1980s, stood as an independent and won anyway, depriving the SNP of a seat. Also a small number of MSPs stood down, the foremost being Sir David Steel, the failed former first minister Henry McLeish, and the SNP stalwart, former MP and the UK's longest-serving MEP, Winnie Ewing (Mitchell and Bradbury, 2004 p. 291). There were some changes within the general composition of MSPs after the 2003 elections. The number of female MSPs rose to 39.5 per cent helped mainly by the Greens and the Scottish Socialist party putting six female MSPs into the new parliament between them. This influence of new female MSPs in addition to varied political parties now present in the parliament led to a more diversified representation but at the expense lost political experience (Mitchell and Bradbury, 2004, p. 294). Neither parliament contained an MSP from any of Scotland's ethnic minority groups.

Putting the structures in place through coalition-building

Perhaps the party to gain most from the elections was the Scottish Liberal Democrat party. Although the May 1997 general election had seen it emerge with ten MPs, putting it in second position to Labour's fifty-six MPs, the gap of forty-six MPs in Scotland alone meant that at Westminster it would not be forming a government for a long while. In Scotland things would be different, however, as the proportional element in the Scottish elections meant that the Labour party in 1999 was nine seats short of a majority, while in 2003 it was fifteen seats short. The immediate solution to this failure to gain a majority after both elections was to join with their former Constitutional Convention partners in the form of the Scottish Liberal Democrats. Although it was widely predicted that Labour would not gain a majority and that they would go into coalition with the Liberal Democrats the actual fulfillment of this prediction seemed to take the Liberal Democrats by surprise in 1999. Negotiations between Donald Dewar, as leader of the Labour party in Scotland, and Jim Wallace, his Liberal Democrat opposite number, began as soon as the 1999 election results were known, although the fact that a coalition executive would be needed in Scotland had been recognised for some time. The prime minister, Tony Blair, in commenting on the Scottish election results, had acknowledged that the system of proportional representation was always likely to deny any party an overall majority but went on to say 'I have got no doubt at all that we will form a good, strong and stable government in Scotland'.[3]

The key issue in the negotiations between Dewar and Wallace concerned students' tuition fees, which had been imposed on all British students by the UK government but which the Scottish Liberal Democrats and others wanted to see abolished in Scotland. The Liberal Democrats made it clear that they would not settle for anything other than abolition, while Labour was unwilling to make the first act of a Scottish parliament the reversal of a policy introduced by a Labour government in London. The deadlock was broken by the setting up of the Scottish Committee of Inquiry into Student Finance to examine the matter. The prospect of a proper inquiry into the problem, together with a promise of PR in Scottish local government elections, was enough to satisfy the Scottish Liberal Democrats and to allow a deal to be struck between the two parties.

Wednesday 12 May 1999 saw the first meeting of a Scottish parliament in 292 years. Its first task was to choose a presiding officer whose principal role would be to regulate proceedings and act as speaker. On that first day David (Lord) Steel, former leader of the Liberal party, was chosen. In the Scottish parliament Lord Steel was addressed by his knighthood only and became Sir David Steel. Sir David served the first term of the Scottish parliament before being replaced in 2003 by the SNP, regional list MSP, the Rt Hon. George Reid.

On Friday 14 May 1999 *A Partnership for Scotland*, under the joint signatures of Donald Dewar and Jim Wallace, laid out the details of the agreement between Labour and the Scottish Liberal Democrats to set up a joint administration. Dewar could then begin the process of forming the cabinet and team of ministers that would form the Scottish executive. The executive consists of a cabinet with eleven members and a team of eleven junior ministers; the Scottish Liberal Democrats having two cabinet ministers and two junior ministers as part of the coalition agreement. That agreement was confirmed by Dewar appointing Wallace to be deputy first minister. Wallace also acted as the justice minister, covering the same range of responsibilities in Scotland as was administered in the UK by the home secretary. Wallace had a junior minister, Angus Mackay, drawn from the Labour ranks to be deputy minister, with a special responsibility for land reform and drugs policy. Tom McCabe, who became minister for parliament in the cabinet, a position rather like the leader of the house in the UK parliament, also acted as Labour whip, while his deputy, as junior minister, was Iain Smith, the Lib Dem whip. On 14 May 2003 Labour and the Scottish Liberal Democrats once more joined together in coalition. This time there was a new Labour leader, the Rt Hon. Jack McConnell MSP, and a new partnership document entitled unimaginatively *A Partnership for a Better Scotland*. This time, there were no substantive issues between them that required the setting up of a commission; indeed the parties had sought to ensure that this would not be the case post-election (Mitchell, 2004, p. 34).

In the first parliament the ministers appointed were a mixture of the old and experienced together with the young and enterprising advocates of what has become known as the 'new politics'. Two important members of the cabinet, Henry McLeish (enterprise and lifelong learning) and Sam Galbraith (children

and education), had established a solid political reputation since they were
formerly senior ministers within the Scottish Office. Jack McConnell's appointment as minister for finance would also be significant later on in the parliament
when he went for the position of first minister. The law officers also had to be
experienced politicians: Lord Hardie, who became lord advocate, had a cabinet
seat as the senior law officer, while Colin Boyd became solicitor general, acting
as deputy to the lord advocate but responsible for prosecutions under Scottish
criminal law.

The responsibilities of cabinet ministers mirrored the changes that had been
made to the government departments that had been transferred from the
Scottish Office to the Scotland Office, subordinate to the Scottish parliament. In
1999, as well as these government departments, the Scottish executive also
assumed responsibility for a number of quangos and agencies such as Historic
Scotland and the Scottish prison service. The Scottish Office had had five ministerial departments – education and industry, agriculture and fisheries, health,
home affairs and development and central services. The list was expanded,
partly by dividing existing departments and partly by creating new ones, to
create a total of nine departments, by 2005 this had risen to ten departments.
The cabinet posts (although it must be remembered that not all cabinet ministers were given a departmental portfolio) in 2005 were:

- first minister;
- deputy first minister and minister for enterprise and lifelong learning;
- minister for justice;
- minister for health and community care;
- minister for education and young people;
- minister for finance and public service reform;
- minister for environment and rural development;
- minister for communities;
- minister for parliamentary business;
- minister for tourism, culture and sport;
- minister for transport;
- lord advocate;
- solicitor general.

Changes of the 'keeper of the seal'

In part, although it sought to break away from the traditions of Westminster,
the Scottish parliament in a number of ways has established its own traditions
with the trappings of Scottish history thrown in. On Thursday 13 May 1999
the parliament elected its first minister, the post in effect being that of a prime
minister for Scotland. The post is also referred to as the official 'Keeper of the

Scottish Seal' (the seal is the means of crown approval for 'Letters Patent and Proclamations' under the Scotland Act 1998). In another parallel to Westminster government, just as the British prime minister has an official residence in the form of 10 Downing Street, so the first minister has an official residence at 6 Charlotte Square, Edinburgh which is known as Bute House, formerly the residence of the Scottish secretaries of state. The building formerly belonged to the fourth Marquis of Bute, a prominent Conservative, who coincidentally was responsible for establishing much of the civic architecture in the Welsh capital, Cardiff. The elegant Georgian house also holds the cabinet room in which the Scottish executive meets.

Unlike the UK system where a general election produces a clear majority party in the House of Commons, and where the leader of that party then becomes prime minister, the set-up in Scotland called for a different solution. A leadership election was held in which there were four candidates: Donald Dewar as Labour leader, Alex Salmond as SNP leader, David McLetchie, newly chosen Tory leader in Scotland, and Dennis Canavan the independent. All thirty-five SNP MSPs voted for Salmond, eighteen Conservatives voted for McLetchie, Canavan picked up three votes but seventy-one Labour and Lib Dem members voted together for Donald Dewar and he was duly declared to be first minister. As soon he was elected Dewar (as subsequent first ministers would do) went to meet the Queen in order to gain the royal warrant confirming them as Her Minister. After gaining the royal warrant Dewar was officially sworn by the lord president of the Court of Session, the country's most senior judge, in a six-minute ceremony watched by thirteen of the country's next most senior judges in number one court at the Court of Session.

Dewar was to be in post just over a year. In mid-October 2000 the Scottish parliament, the Labour party and indeed the whole of Scotland were devastated by his death from a brain haemorrhage, the man who had led Labour's devolution campaign for so many years and the man who had done so much to establish the devolved parliament as Scotland's initial first minister. There was an immediate problem for the Labour party in replacing Dewar, since he had been both leader of the Labour party in Scotland and Scottish first minister. As the largest party in the parliament and with support from its Lib Dem coalition allies, Labour would expect the party leader to be chosen as first minister. But the procedures and complex electoral college created by the Labour party for electing its party leader needed weeks to organise and the position laid down in the Scotland Act was that a new first minister had to be elected within twenty-eight days of the death, retirement or resignation of his predecessor.

The solution was to hold an emergency meeting of a Labour party electoral college in Stirling on 21 October 2000 at which a temporary party leader was elected in the person of Henry McLeish, who received forty-four votes against thirty-six for Jack McConnell. The constitutional position in the party required a formal endorsement of McLeish's leadership from a meeting of the full electoral college later in the year, but it was unlikely that McConnell would stand again at this time. His standing had been no more than a token protest against a London nominee getting the leader's position unopposed. Having made their protest the Labour MSPs were quite happy to vote for McLeish in the election for first minister held on 26 October 2000. In that election McLeish got more than twice as many votes as his nearest challenger, thanks to Lib Dem support:

Henry McLeish – Labour–Lib Dem coalition	68 votes
John Swinney – new SNP leader	33 votes
David McLetchie – Conservative	19 votes
Dennis Canavan – Independent	3 votes

It was seen as a watershed in the life of the Scottish parliament. Shortly before Donald Dewar's death Alex Salmond had chosen to stand down as leader of the SNP and the moderate gradualist, John Swinney, had been elected leader in his place. Neither McLeish nor Swinney had the standing in Scotland of Dewar and Salmond but at least the former two were figures who had risen to prominence in the Holyrood parliament, whereas the latter two had made their reputations at Westminster. It was thought at the time that Holyrood had come of age with these two appointments. Within a few years, however, both leaders would be gone.

In April 2001 reports started to appear in the media that when he was MP for central Fife McLeish had been subletting part of his constituency office to a law firm and had received £36,122 since 1987. This money should have been deducted from his office allowances. The issue was reported to Elizabeth Filkin, the House of Commons standards commissioner, and on 22 April 2001 she wrote to McLeish. She then dropped the investigation in June 2001 because McLeish had stepped down as an MP at that June's general election. The subsequent development of the story was dubbed by the Scottish media as 'the Officegate scandal', and it continued to develop even though the Scottish parliament's presiding officer, Sir David Steel, ruled that the issue could not be discussed in the Scottish parliament due to the fact that it did not concern issues there. Despite Sir David Steel's ruling the opposition continued to press the issue. Despite the fact that McLeish paid back £9,000 of the money, committed himself to repay the rest and was backed by the prime minister, his own party and the coalition partners, he felt obliged to resign on 8 November 2001. The combined weight of the continued attacks by the opposition on the tenability of his position and a forthcoming investigation by the Fife Constabulary had helped persuade McLeish that continuing in office would only cause further problems for his party and the reputation of the Scottish executive and parliament. The Scottish Labour party was now put into another selection process, which thankfully – both for them and the reputation of the new Scottish parliament – went smoothly. Jack McConnell stood once again but this time there was no opponent. With his party's backing, and that of the coalition partners (whose leader Jim Wallace was once again acting as Scotland's first minister), the result when it came on 22 November 2001 gave a resounding endorsement for McConnell.

Jack McConnell – Labour–Lib Dem coalition	70 votes
John Swinney – new SNP leader	34 votes
David McLetchie – Conservative	19 votes
Dennis Canavan – Independent	3 votes

McConnell not only served out the remaining period in office as the first minister but was also able to get his party into government in Scotland for the second Scottish parliament. His continued period of tenure in the second parliament helped restore something of the reputation of the first ministers' short office tenures and created a feeling of stability around the Scottish executive.

Legislation and policy-making

The Scottish executive has a number of mechanisms for determining policy. The main ones are (Keating, 2004):

- ideas from within the executive, policy advisers, civil service and other internal processes;
- the political parties themselves and their election manifestos;
- the Scottish policy communities ranging from trade unions and business groups to the professions, academics and the churches;
- commissions of inquiry;
- the work of the Scottish parliamentary committees;
- the media.

Once policy notions have been fashioned, if they require legislation to enact them then they must go through the Scottish parliament's legislative process. Scotland had always had a different legal system from the rest of the United Kingdom and after the first Scottish parliament had been dissolved the distinctive legal system continued to develop in Scotland through specific legislation passed through Westminster. The main problem with passing Scottish legislation through Westminster was that it had to compete for space with UK-wide legislation and therefore parliamentary time was limited. The opportunity to scrutinise secondary legislation was almost non-existent. Therefore the new Scottish parliament was given responsibility for three distinctive types of legislation.

1 **Primary legislation** – as is the case at Westminster the proposed legislation is debated at length both in committee and the parliament chamber. Legislation can be amended by either the executive or the non-executive members of the parliament. Between 1999–2003 virtually all executive amendments were passed, as were around a quarter of the government's

backbench members' amendments. As would be expected, opposition amendments often fell onto stony ground: some 96 per cent of the SNP's amendments and 89.7 per cent of Conservative amendments were rejected (Shephard and Cairney, 2005, p. 311).

2 **Secondary legislation** – this concerns all the subordinate legislation that might well arise as a result of primary legislation passed either in Westminster or Holyrood. Most importantly it legitimises those statutory instruments issued by the Scottish executive.

3 **European legislation** – community law takes the form of regulations and directives which are issued by the European Commission but which are scrutinised and implemented in each member country by the legislature of that country. In the UK prior to 1999 scrutiny of European legal instruments was carried out at Westminster but, since devolution, any European matter bearing upon Scotland must be scrutinised in Scotland. The Scottish parliament has set up a European committee to carry out this task although its findings will be passed on to London since any response to Brussels must be made by the UK government.

With the arrival of a Scottish parliament it was anticipated that Scottish legislation would be able to flourish in a way it couldn't within the restriction of Westminster. Initially, however, a timid approach was taken on 1 July 1999 as the Scottish executive announced a very modest legislative programme of just eight bills. This was criticised as being too thin a programme and a revised programme was issued in September (Scottish Executive, 1999). After this Scottish legislation began to flow apace. By the end of the first parliament in 2003 some sixty-two bills in total had been passed. Of these, fifty were executive bills (including four budget bills), eight were member's bills, three were committee bills and one was a private bill.

The tally of bills makes it clear that Scottish primary legislation is usually proposed by the executive. The progress of a bill passing through the parliament is very slow because the principles laid down by the consultative steering group mean that the greatest possible opportunity is given for the participation of public and pressure groups in the process. Not only is there prolonged consultation in the form of pre-legislative scrutiny but the legislation itself is submitted to scrutiny by the whole parliament in plenary session, by committee, and by the law officers who check the legal validity of the legislation, ensuring that it is *intra vires*.

The legislative process consists of a number of stages, as follows.

1 A proposal is announced by the executive who may then issue a White Paper or other consultative document.

2 Pre-legislative consultation involves MSPs through committees, the public and pressure groups. A bill is drafted and the outcome of the consultation published.

3 The draft bill is scrutinised by the presiding officer and the subordinate legislation committee for its suitability for submission to parliament.

4 The bill is introduced into parliament together with a written memorandum from the executive setting out the main details of the proposed legislation.

5 The principle of the bill is debated in committee.

6 The measure is debated in a plenary session of the full parliament and a vote is taken.

7 The details of the bill are discussed in committee in a process similar to the Westminster committee stage, amendments are made and a final report on the measure written.

8 A final plenary session of the full parliament debates the report stage of the bill.

9 There is a four-week period in which the measure is examined by the law officers to ensure that the legislation lies within the competence of the Scottish parliament. The secretary of state for Scotland also has the right to veto any legislation infringing the UK government's reserved powers or if it is incompatible with Britain's defence or foreign policy.

10 Having passed all these stages the bill is presented to the monarch by the presiding officer for royal assent.

Each MSP is allowed to introduce two private members' bills during the term of a parliament. For this purpose the MSP must secure the support of 10 per cent of MSPs for the proposal to be accepted; after which it goes through the same legislative process as an executive bill. Originally very few members chose to promote legislation but as the parliament settled down into a routine, more and more MSPs chose to do so. In the second year, over fifteen such bills were proposed, most notably the protection of wild mammals Bill, co-sponsored by a Labour MSP, Mike Watson, and SNP member, Tricia Marwick, and intended to ban fox-hunting in Scotland. Even more significant was the success of Tommy Sheriden, sole representative of the Scottish Socialist party, who succeeded in promoting a bill to forbid the forced sale of debtors' property.

Legislation can also be initiated by committees, although this is a rare occurrence. To do this the committee would submit a proposal to a plenary session of the parliament. It may well be that the executive would approve the measure and take it over as an executive bill. If the parliament likes the idea of the bill but it is not adopted by the executive the committee concerned could then draw up a draft bill; after which it would follow the same legislative route from point two onward. In the first eighteen months of the parliament's life, however, no committee felt it necessary to initiate legislation, leaving initiation very largely in the hands of the executive.

The first piece of legislation to be passed by the Scottish parliament did not appear in the initial list of legislative proposals and it was not passed by any of the three processes described above. In August 1999 a mentally ill patient who was regarded as a danger to the public was released from Carstairs hospital because the law did not permit his further detention. There was an outcry in the press and Jim Wallace, as justice minister, came under severe pressure to plug the loophole in the law. Wallace used a form of emergency legislative procedure which enabled a bill to be fast-tracked through parliament. The Mental Health (Public Safety and Appeals) (Scotland) Act 1999 was passed on 8 September 1999 and received the royal assent five days later. This rapid legislation was then the result of the first legal challenge to the Scottish parliament's right to make laws effectively.

Any Scottish legislation can be challenged in the courts but a question mark was raised as to where the final responsibility for any appeal would lie. If the UK were a federal state and had a written constitution there would be a supreme court to rule on matters in dispute between administrations. The House of Lords is supreme court for the UK as a whole but:

- the House of Lords has only a marginal role in the separate Scottish legal system;
- the House of Lords is part of the UK parliament and would find it difficult to sustain a neutral position if there was conflict between the UK and Scottish legislatures.

The role of the constitutional court for Scotland is taken by the judicial committee of the privy council which already acts as a supreme court and court of appeal for a number of British dependencies, crown territories and some Commonwealth countries. The Judicial Committee (Devolution Issues) Rules Order 1999 (S.I. 1999 No. 665) set out the procedures governing any cases that may arise under the Scotland Act 1998. In the first term of the Scottish parliament there were only a few cases that got as far as the privy council. As we stated earlier the first and most notable case involved the Mental Health (Public Safety and Appeals) (Scotland) Act 1999. It was entitled *Anderson and others v Scottish Ministers and another 2001*. The first section of the act was challenged. The Act had stated that 'a person made a restricted patient of a mental hospital following his conviction for serious criminal offences should remain detained in the hospital in circumstances where his mental disorder meant such detention was necessary on grounds of public safety, regardless of whether the mental disorder was treatable'. The appeal concerned the patient's rights under article 5(1) of the European Convention for the Protection of Human Rights and Fundamental Freedoms. The privy council upheld the provision of the act and dismissed the appeal (Privy Council, 2001).

Parliamentary committees

The Scottish parliament was designed 'as a committee-centred institution' (Deacon *et al.*, 2000, p. 48). The committee system devised for Holyrood is considerably stronger than that obtaining at Westminster. It is not just that

Scottish committees combine the characteristics of both standing and select committees at Westminster but the committees have been given much wider powers from the start, including the ability to initiate legislation, even though this last has not as yet been used. These committees are divided into two types. The first are departmental and deal with the subject areas of the various departments of the executive, while the second type are (mandatory) business and procedural committees concerned with the functioning of parliament in such areas as finance, standards and procedures. The membership of the committees, and the allocation of convenors to chair each committee, is decided proportionally by the d'Hondt method to reflect the numerical representation of the parties in parliament. One committee out of seventeen does not fit this pattern and that is the business committee which can be compared with the 'usual channels', the meeting of party whips, speaker and leader of the House at Westminster which rules on parliamentary business. The business committee has one member each for the five parties represented in parliament and has the presiding officer as its convenor. At the end of the first Scottish parliament it was possible to determine what the committee's regular work had become (Sandford and Maer, 2003):

1 scrutiny of annual department budgets;
2 scrutiny of non-departmental public bodies (annual report and accounts);
3 scrutiny of primary/secondary legislation;
4 reponses to topical issues (often one or two hearings, with no report produced);
5 annual or legacy reports.

Initially every MSP had to be a member of at least one committee and, with almost 170 committee places to fill, most of them sat on two committees and some on three or more. In 2001 the number of MSPs on each committee was reduced from eleven to seven MSPs to try to end the problem of multi-committee membership. The Executive, however, still retained a majority of four to three on all committees (Keating, 2004, p. 115). The conveners of all of the committees are determined by the political parties themselves, which tends to mean that those more independent-minded MSPs are not chosen for those posts. There are also a number of all-party groups in a parliament whose way of working has brought about a far less partisan approach than is to be found in other political bodies. Despite the requirement that a group must have members from all four main Scottish parties before it can be registered, no fewer than twenty such cross-party groups were registered in the first year of the parliament.

A number of these procedural committees were a result of the report, *Shaping Scotland's Parliament*, which was published in January 1999 and which laid down the principles that should characterise the devolved parliament and administration. Those principles included the need to share power with the people, acknowledged the accountability of the executive to the people of Scotland and made the point that parliament should be accessible, open and responsive to public participation. Out of these principles was born the public petitions committee, a unique feature of the Scottish system.

Commissions

The Scottish Executive is able to establish commissions of inquiry on a variety of subjects which are normally of a controversial nature or will have far-reaching implications. Indeed, the executive owes its very existence to its ability to set and use Andrew Cubie's Commission on Student Finance to solve the issues of the Scottish Labour and Liberal Democrat parties being split on the issues of whether to introduce student fees.

The first and perhaps most significant commission to impact on the executive's policy determination had actually been set up by Donald Dewar in his role as Scottish secretary before the parliament had come into existence. It was the Commission on Local Government and the Scottish Parliament headed by Neil McIntosh, and therefore known as the McIntosh Commission. This commission set up the new working relationship for the Scottish parliament and local government, suggested various reforms to Scottish local government and recommended a new system of proportional representation to local government elections.

It was an indication of the strength of the Scottish Liberal Democrats within the Scottish executive that enabled the commissions to get most of their recommendations implemented. In Wales, where a number of commissions had also been called to look into controversial issues, the Labour executive simply ignored the recommendations once their coalition partners the Welsh Liberal Democrats had left the government. It was therefore unsurprising that backbench pressure from the Scottish Liberal Democrats once again led to implementation of the findings of a further royal commission which had been set up by Tony Blair in 1997 under Sir Stewart Sutherland to examine funding of personal care in Scotland. In November 2000 the Sutherland Commission proposed free care for the elderly, and this was backed up by the parliament's health and community care committee. A leak of the committee's report to the BBC, however, led to a leak inquiry and a rather sour ending to the commission's report. The majority in the parliament supported the proposals, as did the new first minister, Henry McLeish, who was eager to make his own mark on the executive policy front. The Department of Health in England, however, was opposed to free personal care, fearing that it would start demands for equal treatment in Scotland. The Scottish minister of health, Susan Deacon, was also opposed to the proposals. In the end the funding came from within the existing Scottish budget and marked, just as the other commissions had done, a differing policy path to England for Scotland (Keating, 2004, p. 177). There have been other inquiries since Sutherland reported back; some of these such as Lord Fraser's inquiry into the costs of building the Scottish parliament are dealt with later. The commission remains the best way for the Scottish executive to deal with complex or politically sensitive issues.

Not all commissions that affect the Scottish parliament are created by the Scottish executive. In July 2004 the Scottish secretary, Alistair Darling, set up the Commission on Boundary Differences and Voting Systems under the chairmanship of Professor Sir John Arbuthnott. The Arbuthnott Commission is examining the whole process of elections to the Scottish parliament and how the elected members interact with each other and the general public. It is also examining whether the system of STV, which is to be used on Scottish local government, can be also used on the Scottish parliament.

Doing one's own thing

As one the leading experts of Scottish politic, Professor James Mitchell, noted in 2003:

> A new orthodoxy has emerged in British politics. Scotland is different and the United Kingdom is no longer a uniform, unitary state. Media attention now focuses on the differences which exist within the United Kingdom and in particular how the Scottish Parliament, elected for the first time in 1999, has given rise to these differences. (p.161)

From the start, the Scottish parliament and executive, together with Labour as the largest party, showed itself to be far less confrontational than Westminster and perfectly ready to pursue a Scottish rather than a British line on policy decisions, whether those decisions refer to the UK parliament or the national party organisation. This difference in attitude was largely a result of the proportional electoral system denying any one party an overall majority in the parliament. The Scottish executive had to be formed as a coalition and there were bound to be occasions when the necessary compromise with another party such as the Scottish Liberal Democrats would conflict with a UK-wide policy decision made by a party with a massive overall majority. That members of the Scottish parliament need to show themselves as working in the best interests of Scotland rather for England or Wales results in Holyrood taking a different line on certain issues from that dictated by Westminster.

During the first Scottish parliament the executive differed from England on many issues of policy. The most notable ones were (ESRC, 2003a):

- free long-term personal care for the elderly;
- abolition of up-front tuition fees for students in higher education;
- three-year settlement for teachers' pay and conditions;

- a less restrictive Freedom of Information Act;
- abolition of fox hunting;
- 'one-stop shop' for public sector ombudsmen;
- abolition of the ban on 'promoting homosexuality' in schools by repeal of Section 2A of the Local Government Act (known as 'Section 28' in England).

Not all of these changes were welcomed by everyone in Scotland. The abolition of Section 28 was opposed in January 2000 by an unlikely alliance of the *Daily Record* newspaper, Cardinal Winning, head of the Roman Catholic Church in Scotland, and Brian Souter, the Thatcherite head of the Stagecoach bus and rail company. A 'Keep Section 28' campaign followed in the press and a series of opinion polls suggested that the public was very strongly opposed to abolition. An opinion poll organised by Souter claimed that 86.5 per cent of those who had replied were in favour of retaining the regulation. Despite opposition the bill continued through parliament with the support of most MSPs and became law on 21 June 2000. The passing of the bill coincided with a massive collapse of public support for the parliament and executive and was held to be a typical example of the Scottish parliament's lack of responsiveness to public opinion.

Scottish local government and the Scottish Executive

The other level of democratic government in Scotland, local government, also had to adjust to the difference that a Scottish parliament would make to its own operations. Scottish local government spends around £8 billion a year, employs some 290,000 staff and is responsible for implementing Scottish executive policy in a wide range of areas ranging from education and social work to housing and recycling (Clark, 2004, p. 42). Having a Scottish parliament means that there has been the time to develop specific pieces of legislation such as the Education and Training (Scotland) Act 2000 and the Housing (Scotland) Act 2001, which would have been unlikely to have had the space on the Westminster timetable (Bennett *et al.*, 2002, p. 44).

The arrival of the new parliament meant that there was a new relationship to be established between central and local government. The relationship is based around the local government side by the Convention of Scottish Local Authorities (COSLA), founded in 1975 and which since then has represented the bulk of local government. Between 1979 and 1997 most of the thirty-two local authorities in Scotland were not controlled by the Conservatives, then in power. The Labour party and independents tend to control most Scottish local authorities with the Scottish Liberal Democrats and SNP controlling the occasional council or leading a coalition arrangement in those authorities with no overall control. This meant that COSLA's main objective was in opposing central (Westminster, Scottish Office) government policy. With the arrival of the Scottish parliament COSLA was thrown into something of an identity crisis, a number of its prominent members, including Glasgow city council, left claiming that the organisation was too close the Scottish executive and that it didn't represent value for money. Since then they have mainly all drifted back and COSLA has restructured around core aims and now represents both an employers' organisation and a campaigning body. As well as COSLA and a number of professional bodies representing Scottish local government individual councils also deal with the Scottish executive on a daily basis. In a 2002 Joseph Rowntree Foundation study on Scottish local government is was revealed that many Scottish authorities welcomed the closer working relationships with the Scottish executive as opposed to the old Scottish Office. At the same time they also felt that the centralisation of power to central government had slowed but had not been reversed and that there was often pressure to determine policy differently in Scotland mainly because they had the opportunity to do so (Bennett *et al.*, 2002).

The biggest change to Scottish local government and also perhaps the plainest example of the Scottish executive doing something differently on local government from elsewhere in the United Kingdom came from the McIntosh Commission, mentioned earlier. In response to the revised electoral methods suggested in McIntosh, in 2004 the Scottish executive passed the Local Government (Scotland) Act. This act introduces, from 2007, a new system of election to Scottish local authorities. From then on three to four Scottish councillors will be elected in wards of 10,000 using the single transferable vote. It has meant that every councillor in Scotland has been put in a new ward and introduced to a whole new method of campaigning in which candidates from the same party have to compete against each other as well as the opposition for the council seat. The forecast of results is that most councils will not be controlled by one party but instead by a coalition arrangement, a factor that will have a radical effect on representation in a local government system that is used to being dominated mainly by the Labour party (Curtice and Herbert, 2005). The era of the one-party Labour-dominated councils of central Scotland would appear to be at an end.

Lord Fraser's inquiry into Holyrood

After the devolution referendum had been won and it was decided that a new parliament for Scotland was needed, in September 1997 the cost of constructing a new Scottish parliament building, prior to the identification of a location or a design, was estimated at between £10m and £40m. The following January Scottish secretary Donald Dewar announced that Holyrood would be the site of the new parliament. When the government announced in July 1998 that a Spanish architectural practice led by Enric Miralles would design the new parliament, estimates as to constructions costs had risen to £55m plus VAT, fees and extras. By April 2000 costs had risen to £195m and in July of that year the architect died. In December 2000 the parliament's audit committee published a highly critical report on the management of the Holyrood project. By December 2002 due to delays costs had risen to £325m and in May 2003 the Scottish executive announced that an independent inquiry into the building of the parliament was to be held by Lord Peter Fraser of Carmyllie QC. As the Fraser inquiry was hearing evidence the following March it was announced that costs had risen to £430m, or ten times the original estimate. The building of the parliament had become a national scandal.

After forty-nine days of hearings from anybody and everybody connected with the Holyrood project Lord Fraser reported back to the executive. There were two important exceptions, the two key people responsible for starting the project, the first minister, Donald Dewar, and the principle architect, Enric Miralles, were now dead and had been unable to give evidence. Lord Fraser stated plainly that: 'So far as the Holyrood Project was concerned, if it could go wrong, it did go wrong.' The report detailed the problems (Fraser, 2004):

* Donald Dewar's desire to have a Scottish parliament as soon as possible and thereby using the high-risk fast-track procurement procedure;
* trying to cope with the architect's complex design;
* design changes made by the parliament constantly adding to costs;
* the fact that the initial costs were simply too low;
* that often the key MSPs who were monitoring the project were kept in the dark as its costs escalated;
* the fact that quality of construction brought up the cost.

All of these factors led to the massive rise in the cost of the parliament. Lord Fraser, noted however that 'It is difficult to be precise but something in excess of £150m has been wasted in the cost of prolongation flowing from design delays, over-optimistic programming and uncertain authority'. The Scottish parliament was now housed in a first-class public building and one that most people in Scotland would in time come to love (Fraser, 2004). Within a short time of its opening the Holyrood building was winning numerous architectural awards and also the heart of many of those Scots that visited. Nevertheless the project remains one the most significant areas of 'Scottish policy failure' to test the reputation of the new parliament.

Conclusion

The first Scottish parliament was blessed with some successes and it bedded in quickly. It was able to form a coalition government smoothly and soon got into the business of legislating and governing. There were tragedies, Donald Dewar's untimely death being the foremost. There was also scandal aplenty in the form of 'Lobbygate', which concerned allegations of privileged access to ministers, the resignation of Henry McLeish and the rising costs of the Holyrood parliament building. Despite a decidedly shaky start it is clear that it clear that most Scots would not wish to see a return to the *status quo*. Although most feel that devolution hasn't altered their lives that radically, at the end of the first Scottish parliament, in 2003 some 77 per cent supported a Scottish parliament (ESRC, 2003b).[4] Yet the parliament is not a fixed institution, but is constantly evolving. Committee structures have changed, as have ministerial portfolios. The Arbuthnott Commission is examining the future role of MSPs and in particular the way that they are elected. At the same time the Scottish Liberal Democrats' 2005 general election manifesto committed them to reforming the constitutional convention in 2009 to discuss the future shape of any Scottish parliament.

The 'West Lothian question' has been partially redressed by the dropping of a number of Westminster seats to end Scotland's historic over-representation. Whilst the West Lothian question can never be fully answered without ending Scottish MPs voting on devolved matters in English or Welsh legislation it has been quietened slightly by the decrease in Westminster seats. For the 2005 Westminster general election the number of Scottish MP dropped from seventy-two to fifty-seven. This meant that all Scottish Westminster constituencies have had their boundaries redrawn and none now share them with the MSP constituencies. This led to some enormous rural constituencies being created, with Charles Kennedy, the Liberal Democrat federal leader's constituency of Ross, Skye and Lochaber being some 12,000 square miles, making it larger than Northern Ireland. Scottish Labour took forty of these new seats, the Scottish Liberal Democrats took eleven and at the same time had the second highest amount of votes in Scotland, for the first time since World War I (Herbert *et al.*, 2005). The SNP took six seats on a declining share of the votes and the Conservatives came fourth with the lowest vote of the four main parties and just one seat. It has become a supreme irony in Scotland that on the electoral system they advocate, first past the post, the Scottish Conservatives barely exist: just one MP and three constituency MSPs. Its two MEPs and fifteen regional MSPs are elected by proportional representation and represent the bulk of their Scottish representation. Such an anomaly only indicates further that Scotland has developed its political system differently from England, in which the Conservatives play only a marginal role.

Notes

1 The details quoted are from a simplified version of the Scotland Act 1998. The full text of the Act is available from HMSO, either in the printed version or it can be downloaded from the internet at www.hmso.gov.uk/acts1998/19980046.htm.

2 For details of the allocation of seats to regional MSPs by means of the d'Hondt method, see Appendix 2.

3 As reported in the *Guardian*, 7 May 1999.

4 In 2003 some 52 per cent supported a Scottish parliament in a devolved UK, 22 per cent would have supported an independent Scotland (ESRC 2003b).

7

Wales:
county council or parliament?

The National Assembly for Wales (commonly known as the Welsh assembly) arrived on the political stage around the same time as the Scottish parliament. The Welsh assembly, however, was no 'parliament'. Its power and status, whilst a considerable political improvement on the Welsh Office that existed in the Thatcher and Major period, was still seen as being of second order compared with Scottish and Northern Irish devolution. It was to have none of the primary law-making or tax-raising powers of Scotland, an issue which over time was to cause great resentment amongst many politicians at the assembly. In the 1997 devolution campaign the cry of the 'no' campaign was that the Welsh assembly would only be 'Mid Glamorgan county council on stilts'. The 'Yes' campaign retorted that it would be no mere county council. Yet the assembly was established as a corporate body with no divide between executive and legislature and underpinned by a committee system, similar in many aspects to local government. This was ironically because at the same time as the Westminster government was moving to abolish the committee structure on local councils. The following decade, however, would see the Welsh assembly trying to get away from this 'county council' label and strive towards being more like the vision of a Welsh parliament that many of its members now aspired to being in.

Partly due to Welsh working-class tradition and partly due a non-proportional electoral system the Labour party dominated Welsh politics from 1922 onwards (Tanner *et al.*, 2000). As the Conservatives remained opposed to political devolution for Wales, any devolution proposals would only be delivered through 'Wales Labour's way or no way' at all. The tradition of Labour dominance at local government and Westminster in Wales, with only the occasional political blip, meant the party there never felt the need to consult with other political parties over any of its plans. It felt it had been given a political mandate by the people of Wales to act on their behalf. Therefore, Wales did not have a cross-party, multi-organisational group like the Scottish Constitutional Convention. Labour refused to be associated in any way with pro-devolution pressure groups, especially if those groups were associated with Plaid Cymru. In June 1992 the Welsh Labour executive committee established the Constitutional Policy Commission to work out the form to be taken by the assembly, how it would be run and the system of election to it. The commission refused to hear oral evidence from the other political parties or discuss in any way with them their devolution proposals. Ron Davies, the shadow Welsh secretary, then fought a balancing act within the Labour party between those who did not wish to see any political devolution and those that wanted something on the Scottish model (a group known as Wales Labour Action). When the proposals went before the Wales Labour party conference in 1995 the party dismissed the need for a Scottish-style parliament stating:

> Our proposals are not therefore a carbon copy of the proposals for a Scottish parliament as the Nationalists have advocated ... Our plans provide a Welsh solution to a Welsh problem whilst being compatible with our continued commitment to the United Kingdom. (Labour Wales, 1995, p. 4)

This 'Welsh solution' involved the establishment of a politically devolved body for Wales with executive and some secondary legislative powers over the work currently being undertaken by the Welsh secretary and Welsh Office. It would involve the election of eighty assembly members by the first-past-the-post electoral system. Such a system would mean that Labour would run the assembly on an almost permanent basis, even if they received as low as 35 per cent of the total Welsh vote. Whilst the Labour party could have gone ahead with this proposal regardless of what the other political parties thought, the fact was that Tony Blair was set on referendums for new devolved institutions. This was mainly to ensure that the bodies were established with the clear mandate of the people of each nation and therefore to avoid Conservative plans to scrap any bodies which did not have such a mandate. Therefore, despite Ron Davies and the rest of Wales Labour stating whenever challenged that there was no need for a referendum because the winning of a general election would be their mandate, in July 1996 Davies announced that a referendum would indeed be held. Such a referendum would need cross-party support if it was to succeed, but neither Plaid Cymru nor the Welsh Liberal Democrats would give it unless the electoral system were altered to encompass an element of PR. Therefore on the 15 July 1996 it was announced that both Tony Blair and Ron Davies had asked the Wales Labour executive committee to re-examine the system of election to the Welsh assembly. The following year it was announced that a system of proportional election (the additional member system (AMS)) similar to Scotland's would be introduced for Wales. This was enough to ensure that Plaid Cymru and the Welsh Liberal Democrats would join Labour in supporting a 'yes' vote in any referendum.

Within two months of winning the general election the Labour government was ready to announce its plans for Wales and the White Paper *A Voice for Wales* appeared in July 1997. As had already become quite apparent in comparison with what had been announced for Scotland there was a very significant difference. According to the White Paper, Wales was to have an assembly rather than a parliament, which would be restricted to secondary legislation only. Wales would have executive devolution rather than the legislative devolution granted to Scotland but Labour believed that this important difference between the two countries was justified by Scotland's separate legal system. As Vernon Bogdanor said, Scottish devolution represented a semi-federal relationship, while Welsh devolution was more a form of regionalism: legislative devolution represents the transfer of powers while executive devolution concerns the division of powers (Bogdanor, 1999, p. 255).

The 'little yes' referendum

The referendum in Wales was held on 18 September 1997, deliberately one week after the Scottish referendum. This was because the government expected a 'yes' result in Scotland and hoped that this would produce a momentum for a 'me too' attitude in Wales (Bradbury, 1998, p. 8). Events had, however, been overshadowed by the death of Princess Diana, which had suspended campaigning for a while. There was certainly a wide variety of supporters who would campaign for a 'yes' vote. To the forefront was Wales Labour, led by Ron Davies, the secretary of state for Wales, and Peter Hain, his junior minister at the Welsh Office. Among the political parties there was support from the Welsh Liberal Democrats led by Richard Livsey and Plaid Cymru led by Dafydd Wigley, while a non-party pressure group called 'Yes for Wales' under the leadership of academics Professor Kevin Morgan and Mari James gave strong support, as did the Cardiff-based newspaper, the *Western Mail*. Undoubtedly apart from a desire to see Wales develop its own political systems and bring government decision-making directly to Wales some of the motivation campaign for the 'yes' camp's members came in part from their own frustration with the lack of opportunity in Wales for up-and-coming professional politicians, outside of the few vacancies that occurred at each four/five-yearly Westminster general election. As result there were few in the Yes for Wales Campaign, at its senior and regional levels, that did not have some personal ambition to benefit by the assembly's establishment. Therefore after the victory, within the space of a few years, most of the 'yes' camp's senior supporters were either assembly members themselves, lobbyists at the assembly, consultants, special advisors or members of committees commissioned by the assembly or MPs. A new political elite had emerged in Wales almost overnight but with its roots planted in the Yes for Wales campaign.

It was not an easy road, however, for the 'yes' camp. They suffered from certain disadvantages in publicising their activities and ideas. Quite a considerable proportion of the Welsh population received their news and information by way of the English media. All along the border with England the people looked east to English towns like Chester, Liverpool, Shrewsbury or Hereford for the regional news. The most widely read daily regional newspaper in the border region of Wales is the *Shropshire Star* and in North Wales it is the (Liverpool) *Daily Post*. When it comes to television the people in Cardiff and Glamorgan are often likely to watch West of England television and the English Channel 4 and in eastern and north-east Wales televisions are similarly tuned into the English regional stations. The move to digital TV has also increased the opportunity for channel-hopping outside of Wales. At the same time most people in Wales take a daily paper printed and edited in London. To counteract this English media bias to some extent, the Labour party was able to get the *Daily Mirror* to produce Welsh editions and target them to support the 'yes' campaign. Most of the rest of the other national British press continued to treat Wales as of marginal political interest. The government was also able to get the Welsh Office to spend around a million pounds on publicising both what the assembly would do and that there would be a referendum to this affect on 18 September.

The campaign for a 'no' vote was smaller than the pro-devolution lobby and was headed by Robert Hodge, son of millionaire businessman Sir Julian Hodge. It was Hodge's money which started the campaign and his main advantage was that the plans for Welsh devolution were very easily attacked. Professor Nick Bourne, later the leader of the Conservatives in the assembly, was also a leading 'no' campaigner. Without either legislative or tax-varying powers the proposed assembly was seen as no more than a very expensive 'talking shop' without the ability to achieve much and many people remained sceptical of its merits. Although the only political party officially opposed to Welsh devolution was the Conservative party, many Labour party members, including half a dozen MPs, campaigned for a 'no' vote against the party line. Divisions within Wales also acted against devolution since, as always, the Welsh-speaking north and west did not trust Cardiff, while the south was equally as wary of Welsh-speaking nationalism in rural Wales.

With opinion so divided and with both sides running lacklustre campaigns, the real winner was apathy. Only 50 per cent of the electorate voted in the referendum and those who did so voted for negative rather than positive reasons. At the heart of this was the fact that they felt that in the previous eighteen years under the Conservative government they had lost their voice in national politics. Mines and steel works had closed, strikes lost, and a series of English Conservatives had come in to Wales to introduce Thatcherite policies, throughout which Wales had voted in a majority of Labour MPs. This insecurity was exploited as the thrust of the 'yes' campaign's reasoning: 'Vote Yes to Keep the Tories Out.' Just a few months after this had occurred at the Westminster elections when the Conservatives had lost all of their Welsh Westminster seats, it was a message that found considerable resonance. As became apparent, however, most of the Welsh electorate were ambivalent to the arrival of an assembly.

When the results came into the count at the Royal Welsh College of Music and Drama in Cardiff from across Wales on the evening of 18 September 1997 there was much anticipation in both 'yes' and 'no' camps (Andrews, 1999). It was a contest so close that it was only decided when the very last electoral district declared a result. Throughout most of the count the contest had been seen to be very close but the 'no' vote seemed to have the edge on those voting 'yes'. By the time Carmarthen, as the last Welsh county to declare, was ready to announce the final figures, television pundits and politicians were busy discussing the victory for the 'no' vote and debating as to where the government went from there. Then Carmarthen declared their result with a massive 'yes' vote (65.28 per cent), the second largest favourable vote in the entire country. And that vote produced the slenderest of majorities for the 'yes' lobby. From over a million voters throughout Wales 50.3 per cent voted 'yes' giving a majority of 6,721, or 0.6 per cent, of those voting. Coupled with a low turnout of just over 50 per cent, those who voted in favour represented not much more than 25 per cent of the population: hardly a strong mandate for constitutional reform. In Welsh the inconclusive positive vote became known as *yr ie bychan* – 'the little yes'.

In the way it voted, the country divided neatly into two halves, east and west. The largely English-speaking areas – along the Welsh Marches, in the northeast near Liverpool, in Pembrokeshire (West Wales) and around Cardiff and Newport – voted 'no', with Monmouthshire being the most strongly opposed on a 67.9 per cent adverse vote. The largely Welsh-speaking Plaid Cymru heartland of the north and west voted 'yes', with pro-devolution votes ranging from 50.9 per cent in Anglesey to 65.3 per cent in Carmarthen. Also voting 'yes' were the traditionally staunch Labour strongholds of the South Wales valleys, districts located in the coalfields and the former iron and steel areas, with 'yes' votes ranging from 52 per cent in Swansea to 66.6 per cent in Neath/Port Talbot. As has already been noted, the division of Wales into 'yes' and 'no' was made almost precisely along lines that were drawn up in the thirteenth century. The lands of the Marcher lords, together with Pembroke's 'Little England beyond Wales', voted 'no', while the lands conquered by Edward I were leading adherents of the 'yes' vote. A more recent historical explanation could be found by identifying most of the 'no' voting counties both with their normal support for the Conservative party and their reliance on the English media, both of which helped the 'no' camp either through being hostile to the assembly or not covering the referendum at all. In turn the 'yes' counties voted on the whole in alliance with their traditional Labour and Plaid Cymru support, added to by their greater absorption of Welsh media. The Welsh Liberal Democrats despite being enthusiastic supports of devolution however, were unable to persuade their supporters in their stronghold of Powys to endorse their views with county voting (56.5 per cent voted 'no').

When the Committee on Standards in Public Life's Lord Neill examined the funding of the devolution referendums in 1998 it became evident that the poorly funded 'no' campaign may well have succeeded in winning if it had had access to greater funding. This caused Lord Neill to recommend that in future there should be equal state funding given to referendums between the state-recognised 'yes' and 'no' campaigns (Standards in Public Life, 1998). This was accepted by the government and therefore some six years later when the north east held its devolution referendum both official 'no' and 'yes' campaigns were funded in equal measure by the state and this time it was the 'no' campaign that triumphed.

Despite their defeat supporters of the 'no' campaign claimed that the referendum was too close to justify going ahead with plans for devolution. The government, however, was of the opinion that even a majority of one vote was sufficient as a mandate to establish an assembly. The Welsh Office set up the National Assembly Advisory Group (NAAG) in October 1997 to advise on the structure of the future assembly. This also included members of the 'no' campaign in an attempt to heal the wounds for a nation that had been split in half by the referendum result. For a while, however, the wounds left over by the narrow referendum result were open and public. The Welsh capital, Cardiff, had voted against having an assembly, yet that was where the assembly was proposed to be sitting. The Labour leader of Cardiff county borough council, Russell Goodway, refused to sell the former City Hall building as a base for the site of the new assembly at a price which the Welsh Office believed it to be worth. Goodway wanted much more that the £2 million offered. Welsh secretary Ron Davies responded by putting out the site for the assembly for tender across Wales, a measure that also boasted public interest in the assembly's arrival. In reality, however, it could only ever be based in the nation's capital in Cardiff. In the end it was planned to site it down in Crickhowell House in Cardiff Bay, a government building named after the Conservative peer Lord Crickhowell. Before he was ennobled, Crickhowell had been Nicholas Edwards, not only a Conservative Welsh secretary but also the leading Welsh Conservative figure in the successful 'no' campaign of 1979. A sense of irony therefore went before the arrival of the Welsh assembly: not only was it not to be in its desired location, City Hall, but it was to be based in building named after one of its fiercest opponents. At the same time as the complexities of the assembly's eventual location were unravelling, the government of Wales bill was introduced into parliament on 26 November 1997, receiving the royal assent as the Government of Wales Act on 31 July 1998.

The Government of Wales Act 1998

The government of Wales bill as submitted to the Westminster parliament differed from the *A Voice for Wales* White Paper in just one major respect. It was originally intended that the assembly would be divided into a number of subject committees, each of which would choose its own chair as assembly secretary:

the secretaries together forming the assembly executive. This pattern of committees having executive control has traditionally been the way local government has worked in England and Wales. However, at the same time as the government was setting up the Welsh assembly they were proposing that local government should be reformed by replacing the outdated committee system with a more effective cabinet model. Since it would seem anomalous for the government to advocate a system for the Welsh assembly that it was removing from local government, Ron Davies proposed a number of amendments which instituted a cabinet model for Cardiff in which ministerial positions are chosen by the first secretary rather than subject committees. This in turn was backed by NAAG.

The Government of Wales Act 1998 defined the title of the assembly, in English and Welsh, as the National Assembly for Wales or *Cynulliad Cenedlaethol Cymru*. It was called this, rather than the Welsh Assembly, because Lord Elis Thomas (the future presiding officer) suggested that this name would imply an assembly for the people of Wales rather than being a 'Welsh assembly' forming a kind 'Welsh language elite', in a still-divided population's eyes. Nevertheless within a short while it was generally referred to as the 'Welsh assembly'. The assembly was established as a single-chamber corporate body of sixty members, without a legally separate executive, to carry out certain functions on behalf of the crown.

Assembly membership is by elections held in both assembly constituencies and assembly electoral regions. This system is called the additional member system and means that there are both constituency and regional list members. Assembly constituencies are the same as the existing Westminster parliamentary constituencies in Wales and return one member each by the FTPT system. The assembly constituencies are divided between five electoral regions based on the former European parliamentary constituencies. Under AMS, each electoral region returns four members to the assembly from regional lists. Overall, there are sixty assembly members, with forty constituency members and twenty regional members (see Appendix 5 for a breakdown of constituencies and regions). Registered electors have two votes: one for a member to represent the assembly constituency, and the other for either a political party that has submitted a list of candidates or for an individual who is standing as an independent candidate for the assembly electoral region. The list system is not as proportional as that which occurs in Scotland or the Greater London assembly which has seven and ten list members per region. This therefore gives a much greater advantage to the party who is able to secure the most constituency seats (Labour). These Welsh general elections to the assembly take place every four years on the first Thursday in May. Initially, this date could only be altered by up to one month in either direction in order to avoid clashing with a late Easter, or local elections could be delayed by up to three months if they would otherwise coincide with the Welsh elections. Labour's poor electoral performance in the 1999 assembly election was blamed on it being at the same time as the council elections, where in turn some of their unpopular councils were blamed for pulling down their over assembly vote. Happily for the government requests by councils to separate the elections for administrative and electoral reasons enabled them to ensure that neither would occur on the same day or year again. Both are now one year apart. The assembly is elected for a four-year fixed term.

No mechanism exists for the dissolution of the assembly in anything less than four years under the act, but in 2005 the government announced plans to allow the assembly to dissolve early, '*in extremis*', if a two-thirds majority voted for this (Wales Office, 2005, p. 29). This is similar to the powers of the Scottish parliament. What exactly '*in extremis*' means has yet to be clearly defined.

Powers of the assembly

The assembly has been granted a wide range of administrative and secondary legislative powers. Initially this consisted of the power:

- to make rules and regulations for the administration of primary legislation enacted at Westminster: '... there are more than 300 Acts of parliament under which the Welsh assembly has the power to make rules and regulations' (Deacon *et al.*, 2000, p. 97);
- to enact secondary and delegated legislation through such devices as statutory instruments;
- to make appointments to a large number of quangos such as the various NHS Trusts in Wales;
- to allocate and spend funds assigned to Wales under the block grant;
- to acquire land and property and undertake work within the infrastructure such as the construction of new roads.

All decisions made by the assembly can be challenged in the courts and, as with the Scottish parliament, the final court of appeal is the judicial committee of the privy council. Also as in Scotland, governmental powers are divided into reserved powers, which are fully retained with the Westminster parliament, and devolved powers that can be dealt with by the Welsh assembly. It should be noted that in Scotland it was only the reserved powers that were positively identified, devolved matters being defined negatively as those areas that were not reserved. The position is very different for Wales, however, where, in Schedule 2 of the Government of Wales Act, the transferred functions were quite clearly specified:

- agriculture and fisheries;
- culture;
- economic development;

- education and training;
- environment;
- health;
- highways;
- housing;
- industry;
- local government;
- social services;
- sport;
- tourism;
- town and country planning;
- transport;
- water;
- the Welsh language.

The assembly in most areas has executive competence, which means that it must work within the powers it has rather than using primary legislation to obtain new ones. In the time that it has been in existence virtually every area with its functional remit has had secondary legislation dealt with at the assembly. In some areas such as transport the delegation of powers has been considerable (Richard Commission, 2004).

Powers in relation to legislation: secondary legislation

The assembly had no primary legislative powers. It does, however, have powers to make secondary (subordinate) legislation which have arisen from the enabling provisions in acts of parliament, transfer of function orders made under the Government of Wales Act 1998 and orders designated under the European Communities Act 1972 (Navarro and Lambert, 2005). There is a mass of legislation that deals with both England and Wales for which the Welsh assembly has responsibility. By July 2005 this had reached some 630 acts of parliament (Wales Legislation On Line) with fifty more, which impact on Wales either totally or in part, coming in the Queen's speech of 2005.

The Government of Wales Act 1998 and the assembly's own Standing Orders require that 'draft Statutory Instruments are considered by assembly Subject Committees and be usually put before the plenary assembly for approval, with or without amendments, before they can be made' (Navarro and Lambert, 2005, p. 2). In fact, one of the reasons that the assembly had been introduced was to have the ability and time both to scrutinise and amend secondary legislation. Statutory Instruments (SIs) made to enforce or implement legislation in Wales are derived from three sources. These sources are: directly from Whitehall departments, co-operation between Whitehall departments and the assembly itself or solely from the assembly. The majority of SIs come from Whitehall, with a smaller percentage coming from the assembly itself and just a fraction, below 5 per cent, coming from both the assembly and Whitehall acting together.

It was under the Welsh Office that many aspects of government policy in Wales had been enforced through secondary legislation, which had never gone under any real scrutiny at all. These 'unseen laws' were cause for considerable concern amongst pro-devolutionists who resented laws being passed upon a Welsh population without a chance to scrutinise them effectively. Thus a Welsh assembly would in theory remedy this anomaly and scrutinise secondary legislation. This noble objective did not, however, reach the reality its proposers had desired. Between 1999 and 2003 only nine attempts were made to amend secondary legislation (1 per cent of total secondary legislation). This was in respect of some 685 pieces of secondary legislation. All of these attempts failed. In fact, of all secondary legislation only some 29 per cent was debated in the assembly chamber itself. The remaining 71 per cent was passed either without debate in the assembly (accelerated procedure, 31 per cent) or passed through executive order whereby the Welsh executive had deemed that 'procedural stages' set out in Standing Order should not apply them on the grounds that this was 'not really practicable' (National Assembly for Wales, 2003). The desire of the assembly's founders to scrutinise secondary legalisation fully (SIs) had failed and there were a number of reasons for this:

1 The are no clear divisions between powers given to the English Whitehall departments and the assembly, concerning the powers to make secondary legislation for ministers. Therefore there was confusion as to who had done what (Richard Commission, 2004, p. 88).
2 There was too much secondary legislation coming into the assembly and there were too few assembly members to scrutinise it effectively. Assembly members were in effect, overwhelmed by it and therefore it came through largely as it had arrived.
3 Assembly plenary time was limited and therefore so was time for full debate. To review all of the secondary legislation would leave no time for any other business.
4 Assembly members were not sufficiently knowledgeable about the complex actions required to amend or adapt legislation and the supporting mechanisms only existed for the government ministers to do this scrutiny.
5 Secondary legislation was often part of a package of measures and therefore to change one aspect could affect the whole implementation of a policy which may have had general government and opposition support.
6 Much of the secondary legislation was of an uncontroversial or functional nature for which there was little point in scrutinising anyway.
7 The Welsh assembly executive (government) did not desire to have its legislative programme damaged and therefore was reluctant to allow any amendments to this through secondary legislation adjusted by anyone but itself.

The scrutiny of secondary legislation was not the only dilemma, enacting it was also a problem. There was no mechanism for the assembly to inform Whitehall or vice versa that secondary legislation is being made by either. The result has meant that joint English-Welsh legislation that comes within the assembly's remit is often enacted at differing times, with the assembly normally being the slower to implement it (Navarro and Lambert, 2005).

Powers in relation to legislation: primary legislation

We have already noted that the Welsh assembly cannot determine its own primary legislation. It therefore must request this directly off the parliament in Westminster. In the assembly session 2001–02 it changed its Standing Orders regarding its submission of its own proposals for primary legislation to be requested from the government. From then onwards Standing Orders 33.11 and 33.12 require the assembly by 31 March each year to approve its cabinet's request for primary legislation. If this is successful then the first minister (originally known as the first secretary) communicates this decision to the Welsh secretary. It is then upto the Welsh secretary to decide which bids he will put forward to the UK cabinet to include in their own legislative programme at Westminster. The concordat between the assembly cabinet and the Wales Office deals with primary legislation affecting Wales, under this:

> The assembly is free to request the UK Government to introduce primary legislation at any time. Such requests will be considered in the context of the parliamentary timetable for the prospective legislative programme. (Wales Office, 2001)

The response of the Welsh secretaries to requests for the primary legislative bids has been threefold:

- To reject them totally. The St David's Day bill which supported a national holiday for Wales on St David's Day was rejected the four times it was submitted between 2001–05, despite the full assembly endorsing it numerous times. Others, such as the education (miscellaneous provisions) (Wales) bill in 2003 have similarly been rejected, mainly on the pretext of a 'lack of parliamentary time'. This is the most common end for requests for 'Wales-only' legislation.
- To put the requests for legislation into forthcoming English bills. Thus the Sunday licensing (Wales) bill had its provisions contained in the Licensing Act 2003, similarly the housing ombudsman (Wales) bill was included in the Housing Act 2004.
- To have a separate Wales-only acts. Between 1999 and 2005 there were only four such acts:
  1 Children's Commissioner for Wales Act 2001 – providing for a Children's Commissioner for Wales;

2 Health (Wales) Act 2003 – which made provision for community health councils in Wales and also established the Wales Centre for Health and Health Professions Wales;

3 Public Audit (Wales) Act 2004 – this enabled there to be a single public audit body for Wales;

4 Public Services Ombudsman (Wales) Act 2005 – this created a single Ombudsman service for Wales, combining the three current offices of the commissioner for local administration in Wales, the health services commissioner for Wales and the Welsh administration ombudsman into one service.

In addition between 1999 and 2005 the Welsh assembly supported just one private member's bill. This was the prohibition of smoking in public places bill 2005, put forward by Julie Morgan (MP for Cardiff North and wife of the first minister, Rhodri Morgan). The bill fell in the Lords in February 2005.

Although the assembly has been considerably more effective that the Welsh Office in bringing forward Welsh legislation its output has been far less than most pro-devolutionists imagined (Deacon, 2002). Therefore of the twenty-two attempts by the Welsh assembly to get primary legislation between 2001–05, some eight (36 per cent) were successful either in being acts in their own rights or included in English-Welsh acts, two (10 per cent) were partially successful in having some of their provisions included in other acts and the majority fourteen (64 per cent) were unsuccessful in that period in having no legislation passed upon them (Watkins and Thomas, 2005). The frustration concerning this poor success rate for primary legislative powers was to emerge as a major issue in the Richard Commission Report 2004, which is examined later on in the chapter.

Civil service – Welsh quangos

Civil servants working for the Welsh assembly remain members of the UK civil service and as such are subject to the civil service code (Judge, 2005, p. 195). The Government of Wales Act 1998 had simply transferred the existing Welsh Office civil service to the new National assembly *en masse*, with a few going to serve the new Wales Office. The government of Westminster desired to keep the British civil service (excluding that devolved already to Northern Ireland) intact. This was in part to ensure that a unified civil service would act as a kind of 'constitutional glue' in holding the UK together and partly because creating a new Welsh civil service would have taken up considerable parliamentary time and delayed devolution (Laffin, 2002, p. 33). On St David's Day 2002 the civil servants based in Cathays Park and Cardiff Bay, with the exception of those in the presiding office were informed that they no longer served the assembly as a whole but instead their master was the Welsh assembly government. Although the civil service code still required civil servants to be accountable to the

'Assembly Secretaries and the National Assembly as a body', in reality apart from those civil servants working in the presiding office the loyalty of civil servants would now be with the assembly government rather than the assembly (Osmond, 2003a). There was now a clear division between the executive and the legislature. This new situation had the impact of putting the assembly on Westminster lines with a government and opposition rather than the all encompassing corporate body stated in the Government of Wales Act 1998. During this period the Welsh assembly government continued to sign a series of concordats stating clearly the relations between themselves and the various Whitehall departments and the responsibility for co-ordination over policy and secondary legislation. As noted earlier these didn't always work as planned and there was a tendency for Whitehall departments simply to forget about Wales when undertaking policy creation or the drawing up legislation. In October 2004, for instance, it became apparent that Department of Transport had forgotten about Wales when drawing up legislation to speed up the removal of abandoned cars. In England it could be as quick as twenty-four hours but in Wales it remained at around twenty-one days (*Western Mail*, 24 October 2004).

Thus the division of the civil service into differing camps meant that those working at the assembly could now be divided into a number of different groupings (Richard Commission, 2004, p. 216):

1 assembly members, of whom there were 60;
2 members' support staff, of which there was no clearly set number but was somewhere in the region of 120;
3 assembly ministers' special advisors, of whom there are around 12;
4 Wales Office staff of 48 civil servants (removed from the Welsh assembly and serving the Welsh secretary within the Department of Constitutional Affairs);
5 presiding office staff of some 251 civil servants, perhaps the most 'detached and independent' because they work directly to the presiding officer and assembly members;
6 National Assembly for Wales staff of 3,410 civil servants.

The arrival of the assembly had seen an unprecedented increase in the number of civil servants and employees serving devolved government in Wales. By 2004 the number had reached 4,290, some 1,456 more staff and £105 million more in running costs than the Welsh Office had been when Labour took office in 1997. The increases appeared even more dramatic because the last two Conservative Welsh secretaries, William Hague and John Redwood, had reduced the number of Welsh Office civil servants by around 20 per cent between 1990 and 1997 (Deacon, 2002, p. 109). In part the increase had been down to the assimilation of a number of Welsh quangos (referred to as assembly-sponsored public bodies – ASPBs). In part it was also because the Welsh Office under the Conservatives was far less dynamic in the policy creation area than the new Welsh assembly. Even taking these points into account plus rein-stating the civil servants lost under the Conservatives the gain in civil service numbers would still have been around a 1,000, far more than in any period under the old Welsh Office. The numbers are set to rise again with the demise of some of Wales's largest ASPBs, making the assembly one of the largest employ-ers in Wales.

After its had started operations in 1999 the assembly brought the ASPBs into a more disciplined line, reflecting the Whitehall departments rather than the more traditional arms-length quangos (Osmond, 2003, p. 19). This, however, was still not deemed to provide sufficient accountability for the ASPBs and there was general desire by assembly members to make sure most public bodies within the assembly's remit were taken inside its main civil service body. The assembly therefore undertook a general review of ASPBs under Sir Jon Shortridge, the permanent secretary, with the view to see how many could be abolished or merged. Only those bodies that maintained an audit-related role and therefore took 'decisions that were better taken at arms length' from the assembly or were totally 'non-governmental in character' were exempt. In addi-tion those bodies that had been established by royal charter such as the National Library of Wales were also able to escape merger or abolition (Shortridge, 2004). Around a month before Sir Jon undertook his review on 14 July 2004 the Welsh assembly government announced it was already going to merge the three largest ASPBs with the assembly. These are the Welsh Development Agency, created by Labour in 1975, the Wales Tourist Board (WTB) and Education and Learning Wales (ELWa). All three had endured a bad press for some time despite having in some areas an excellent performance record. They were seen, however, as being unaccountable and a visible reminder that the Welsh assembly was elected, in part, to put 'unaccountable government' under its own control. The Labour assembly executive wanted all functions in some areas such as economic development brought 'in house' in powerful 'one-stop shop' departments (Morgan and Upton, 2005, p. 89). The merger was greeted mainly with support from government and opposition alike. Although there was concern that the announcement appeared somewhat rushed and unplanned, the general principles were seen as being right. The ASPBs themselves seemed unaware of their demise until they heard it from the press. They did, however, find one surprising ally. Professor Kevin Morgan who had chaired the assembly referendum 'yes' campaign launched a fierce defence for keeping the quangos until their full record was analysed and their status fully determined. In the 1990s Professor Morgan had himself constantly attacked the Welsh quangos and in particular the WDA. Ironically for Morgan and other defenders of the ASPBs, his previous works on what was described as the 'democratic deficit' associated with quangos lack of accountability was now used in part to justify their removal (Morgan and Upton, 2005).

The civil servants' relationship with their new political masters was mixed. There were consequently a number of battles over who controlled the civil service organisational structure, the permanent secretary, assembly ministers or presiding officer. The civil service's policy creation and adaptation role was curtailed with the influx of special advisors who bypassed the civil service and shaped policies directly with assembly ministers (Laffin, 2002, p. 40). A separate strategic policy unit was established in order to maintain this distance and plan for long-term policy initiatives without direct reliance on the civil service, although it remained part of the Welsh assembly government. In July 2005, the Welsh secretary reaffirmed that all civil servants, with the exception of those in the presiding office would only serve the Welsh assembly government, remaining in the UK civil service. Presiding office staff would no longer be within the UK civil service but would instead work directly for the Welsh assembly. The divisions concerning the staffing of devolution in Wales would now mirror those in Scotland with a clear divide appearing between Welsh assembly government (executive) and Welsh assembly (legislature) (Wales Office, 2005, p. 18).

Officers and executive of the assembly

Presiding officer

When an assembly is elected its first responsibility is to elect a presiding officer and a deputy presiding officer – the equivalent of the speaker and deputy speaker in the Commons. In the first and second assembly terms the presiding officer elected was Lord Dafydd Elis Thomas, the Plaid Cymru assembly member for Meirionnydd Nat Conwy. Lord Thomas, a former leader of Plaid Cymru, was elected initially in part as an indication of the strength of the assembly opposition and in part as recognition of his strong personal commitment to both Welsh devolution and the Welsh language. His second election was seen as a *fait accompli* despite the fact that in taking office he ensured that the Labour party, who lacked an overall majority, would automatically be able to form the Welsh government.

Lord Thomas more than perhaps any other individual was responsible for moulding the Welsh assembly into a more parliamentary body. Under him the presiding office became removed from the civil service structure that served the Welsh assembly government. There is now a separate budget for the office, the officers within it are appointed mainly under the guidance of the clerk to the assembly (Paul Silk, a former House of Commons select committee clerk rather than a civil servant) and the assembly's House Committee. From December 2002 the assembly's Business Committee agreed to change the assembly's Standing Orders so that in future the House Committee (made up of AMs and responsible for the presiding office, assembly members' pay and conditions and the general operation of the assembly) would be 'entirely autonomous and separated from the Administration' (Osmond, 2003a, p. 68). This was an important step in determining the separation of powers between legislative and executive in the Welsh assembly.

The first minister and the cabinet

The Government of Wales Act 1998 requires that members must elect a first secretary (now known as first minister, a name which was thought to sound more prime ministerial in nature). It is they who are the assembly's political leader and they act as a quasi prime minister, albeit in a stronger cabinet-led government than Westminster. As well as being elected by their party the first minister must being elected by a majority vote of the whole assembly. The first minister in turn appoints the necessary assembly ministers. The first minister and up to eight ministers (the maximum allowed by Standing Orders) then form the cabinet of the Welsh assembly government. On 27 November 2001 Rhodri Morgan declared that in future the administration would be known as the 'Welsh assembly government': Wales now had its own government. The Government of Wales Act 1998 requires that the ministers' portfolios are shaped around the assembly's subject committees with the exception of the first minister and business manager (equivalent of the Westminster's government leader of the House of Commons).

The first minister has several important roles to play:

* to lead the assembly;
* to lead the Welsh assembly government through selecting assembly ministers to form the cabinet;
* to liaise with the Welsh secretary to help draft Welsh legislation at Westminster;
* to act as party leader and ensure the implementation of the party manifesto;
* to represent the assembly at Westminster, in the European Union and overseas;
* to hold the equivalent of prime minister's question time in the assembly;
* to write and deliver an annual 'state of the nation' address.

The first, first (secretary) minister was Alun Michael, who had reluctantly been drafted into the position the position by Tony Blair after Ron Davies had resigned from his position as both Wales Labour leader and Welsh secretary after having an 'infamous moment of madness' on Clapham Common on 27 October 1998. He was later to have a number of further 'moments of madness' in other public places which would lead to the demise of his career as Labour politician. Eventually Mr Davies left the Labour party altogether, joining a fringe party called Forward Wales and entering political obscurity. When Davies had resigned it looked as though his defeated leadership rival Rhodri Morgan would now be in a position to take the leadership, but Morgan was not trusted by Tony Blair and therefore Michael, MP for Cardiff South and Penarth, and who had worked previously under Blair when he shadowed the Home Office, was persuaded to stand against him. In the final result Michael won the leadership by 52.68 per cent of the vote against 47.32 per cent. Within that total, however, the only part of the electoral college to support him was represented by the union block vote. The Labour party membership backed Morgan, as did twenty-one out of the twenty-eight Labour assembly members.

When the May 1999 assembly election was held Labour failed to secure an overall majority, being three seats short. Unlike everybody expected, including Tony Blair, Labour did not seek a coalition with the Welsh Liberal Democrats but instead decided to government as a minority administration. Bit by bit Alun Michael's leadership was undermined. First he antagonised the farming community by choosing a vegetarian, Christine Gwyther, to be his agriculture secretary. Most Welsh farming concerns livestock rather than cereal production. At the same time he made Tom Middlehurst the assembly secretary responsible for the Welsh language, despite the fact that Middlehurst does not speak Welsh (although neither did his two successors, Jenny Randerson and Alun Pugh).

In October 1999 the three opposition parties combined to pass a motion of censure against Christine Gwyther by thirty votes to twenty-seven, for her failure to get European agreement to a support scheme for Welsh farmers that had been passed by the assembly. Michael simply ignored the censure motion aimed at his cabinet member and attempted to carry on as though nothing had happened, even managing to survive a vote of no confidence proposed by the Conservative leader, Nick Bourne, who famously said, 'The minority administration, acts and fails, to react as if it were a majority administration' (cited in Hazell, 2000, p. 62).

In February 2000 Plaid Cymru proposed a vote of no confidence in Alun Michael over what they claimed was the first minister's failure to get money from the Treasury so as to match European funding for the poorest regions of Wales. When the day of the vote came, Michael resigned before it was held, something few, including the prime minister, were aware of at the time. Within a few days Rhodri Morgan was his successor and it was he who would shape the future direction of the Welsh assembly government. In Wales the arrival of Rhodri Morgan was seen by many as the right man finally being given the job, with a change to a more clearly Welsh agenda for the assembly. Yet over the coming years the relationship between Morgan and Blair remained as harmonious as that which Blair had shared Alun Michael. After the 2003 assembly elections resulted with no one party in overall control Morgan has appointed the cabinet from his limited number of assembly members infrequently, mainly because the post-holders tend to stay fixed for a number of years with demotions or sideway moves on portfolios rather than outright sackings. As both Labour-led assembly administrations have not had a majority Morgan cannot afford to alienate any of his ministers if he is to keep his party in power without the support of another party. The Welsh cabinet, like its counterpart in Westminster, operates on collective accountability, but this has never resulted in any resignations within Mr Morgan's period as first minister, although there have been a number of sackings.

Assembly committees

As the assembly was being conceived it was thought that it would herald the era of a more a more inclusive form of politics than the adversarial politics that had so dominated the last years of the Welsh Office. Therefore it was anticipated that the assembly as a whole should take some part in policy creation and at the same time also be able to keep the executive accountable by analysing its policy in some detail. At the core of this policy creation and scrutiny were to be the subject committees. There are usually seven of these and their range varies according to portfolios of the various Cabinet members. As set out in Standing Order 9.2, the chairs of these committees are selected from a panel of members elected by the assembly to ensure that committee chairs are apportioned in accordance to the electoral balance of the parties in the assembly. This committee is called the Panel of Chairs and has as many members as there are subject committees, but ministers are not eligible to be members of the panel. These subject committees under Standing Orders are expected to review the assembly government and its public bodies, contribute to policy development and provide advice to the Welsh assembly government. The Committees have spent most of their time (around 40 per cent) on policy development with rest being on policy scrutiny and procedural issues (Richard Commission, 2004, p. 55).

Within time it became apparent that although the subject committees were 'accessible, responsive and relevant' and undertook a significant amount of useful work, they had some severe drawbacks (Richard Commission, 2004, p. 56). As the Welsh assembly government found its feet the committees found it increasingly difficult to hold them to account; at the same time ministers' presence on these committees weakened the ability to hold these same ministers to account (Lang and Storer, 2003, p. 89). The restricted extent of the committees' work, limited times they meet, lack of sufficient members to development expertise (most members serve on two or more committees) and the ministers' ability to ignore those decisions that didn't coincide with government policy were other drawbacks of the subject committee system. In essence they did not play the role in either policy creation or development of scrutiny that had originally been envisaged.

Apart from the subject committees there are also three other types of committee. These are as follows:

- The *standing committees*, six of which were established either in accordance with the Government of Wales Act 1998 or with the advice of NAAG. They are Audit, Legislation, Equality of Opportunity and European and External Affairs, Business (of the assembly), House Committee and Standards of Conduct.
- *Special task committees*, set up to examine specific issues, such as the Planning Decision Committee which looks at planning appeals and *ad hoc* committees such as the Public Audit (Wales) Bill Committee which examined the drafting of this bill.

- *Regional committees*, which cover the assembly's five electoral regions. Through their public hearings within the regions these advise the assembly on matters affecting the regions, the effect of assembly policies in those regions, and the work of public bodies in the regions (National Assembly for Wales, 2005).

Wales has always been dubbed a nation run by committees, and in this respect therefore the Welsh assembly could be set to be its crowning national achievement.

The role of the secretary of state for Wales

Under Section 22 of the Government of Wales Act, a transfer of functions order was issued by means of which virtually all the secretary of state's functions were transferred to the assembly. Initially with the functions of the Welsh Office all transferred, there were just two ministers in the Westminster government who were responsible for Wales, the Welsh secretary and a junior minister. Paul Murphy succeeded Alun Michael as Welsh secretary in 1999. As secretary, Murphy revealed that he and his junior minister sat on more than twenty cabinet committees to defend the Welsh interest (Hazell, 2000, p. 59). In 2002 he was appointed Northern Ireland secretary and was replaced by the famous anti- apartheid South African-born Neath MP, Peter Hain. He was a key member of the Yes for Wales referendum campaign team and had then been a junior minister at the Welsh Office between 1997–99 before going to the Foreign Office.

On 12 June 2003, amongst some controversy, Hain was also appointed leader of the House of Commons, lord privy seal as well as being secretary of state for Wales. This was seen as both diluting the prestige of the post of Welsh secretary and providing an indication that, in the cabinet at least, Wales had become a part-time issue. At the same time the Wales Office was put under the control of the Department for Constitutional Affairs, which had its own secretary of state, and further blurred lines of accountability. This was justified in part by the government's view that devolution had sufficiently lessoned the workload of a Welsh secretary to the extent that a full-time post was no longer required. It was thought at the time of these changes that even the shared post of Welsh secretary would disappear altogether within a few years. After the general election of May 2005 Peter Hain became Northern Ireland secretary as well as Welsh secretary. This had the affect of uniting the two nations for the first time politically under one cabinet minister but again causing some concern as to the status and position of the Welsh secretary in the government. The post had survived, however, into a new parliament.

But what did the Welsh secretary now do in the devolutionary era? The answer came in 2004 when the Richard Commission was able to define the role of the Welsh secretary within the post-assembly set-up. It defined it as (Richard Commission, 2004, p. 143):

1 The voice of Wales within the UK government and Westminster; a friend and advocate of the assembly's position in cabinet.
2 Acting as a guardian of the Wales devolution settlement – ensuring that Whitehall departments are properly consulting their assembly counterparts and taking the lead in dispute resolution.
3 Ensuring that the interests of Wales are fully taken into account in UK government decisions.
4 Bidding for slots in the primary legislation programme for measures affecting Wales and taking these decisions through parliament.
5 In addition to Richard's four points the Welsh secretary also has a representative role in projecting Welsh interests on subjects which have not been devolved such as pensions, benefits and defence.

The Welsh secretary's role, however, will not stand still. From 2007 it is envisaged that it will alter still further with some of its functions transferring to the Welsh assembly. The appointment of the auditor general for Wales and other monitoring posts in respect of the assembly by the crown on the advice of Welsh secretary will now be on the advice of the Welsh assembly. At the same time, however, the Welsh secretary will continue to act as the gatekeeper for the Welsh assembly's requests for primary legislation at Westminster and their power to determine some of the assembly's revised Standing Orders (Wales Office, 2005).

Finance

The secretary of state for Wales currently passes on the money voted to the Welsh assembly from parliament after taking a small proportion of the funds available to cover the costs of his or her own office. From 2007 the assembly will also have to pass a vote to enable the assembly government to gain access to this money for the finance of its various programmes. The assembly will continue to hold them accountable for its use of the money (Welsh Office, 2005, p. 17). As is the case in Scotland, payments to the Welsh assembly are determined by a block grant with additional funding being determined by the Barnett formula, under which funds are allocated to Wales according to its population size and GDP calculation relative to England. The value of this funding in 2005–06 was approximately £12 billion per year.

There is a general perception amongst assembly members that Wales is the nation that does least well under the Barnett formula, but they have been unable to get it renegotiated due to the Westminster government's fear of the impact this would have on reducing Scotland's more generous formula. In September 2005 both Plaid Cymru and the Welsh Liberal Democrats sought to get the assembly to re-open the debate on Barnett. Neither Labour nor the Conservatives, however, fearing upsetting the London leadership, were willing to support this. Other ministers and government departments may also make payments to the assembly. For example, the Intervention Board makes payments to Wales on behalf of Europe in respect of the Common Agricultural Policy. The assembly was also successful in gaining additional funding from the Treasury in order to enable it to make full use of the Objective 1 European Structural Funding programme between 2000–06. This was a complex and difficult issue which in part caused a power struggle within the assembly resulting in the resignation of the First Minister, Alun Michael (Bristow, 2003, p.77).

The budget-planning process in Wales goes from mid July to late September. This process involves widespread consultation and the impact of the various assembly committees. It is the job of the finance minister to steer this process through and get the final budget ratified by the assembly in the plenary session in December. Normally the opposition is unable to make much of an impact on the budgetary process. In June 2005, however, the opposition in the assembly were able to combine in order to make a fundamental change to the Labour administration budget proposals over higher education in Wales. It was able first to defeat the Labour administration in the assembly chamber on the issue of university student top-up fees and general Welsh university funding. This was despite the Welsh assembly government holding a commission under Professor Teresa Rees into how tuition fees could be implemented. After the opposition had rejected the Rees Commission's findings, two days before they were even published, the Welsh assembly government was then forced into negotiations with the opposition. The result was that 'a series of principles have been established which will mean Welsh domiciled students will not have to pay top-up fees at Welsh universities. In addition the agreement ensured that in future the assembly would have to redress the funding gap between Welsh higher education institutions and comparable colleges elsewhere in the UK' (joint Welsh assembly Opposition Press Release, 2005). The result was that for the first time the opposition had forced the assembly government to reshape its budget to a significant degree.

The Welsh assembly is almost totally reliant on the funding given to it from Whitehall and the European Commission and does not have any significant fundraising powers itself. The chances of the assembly gaining the same tax-raising powers as the Scottish parliament were put off the agenda by the Wales Labour party when the Richard Commission was given its remit. The issue of tax-raising was not to form part of this remit and the party remains totally opposed to opening up the question for debate (Osmond, 2005a, p. 47). Although Plaid Cymru and the Welsh Liberal Democrats remain committed to giving the assembly tax-raising powers, the Conservatives and Labour parties do not and this in affect will keep the issue off the political agenda for as long as both parties dominate the legislative process at Westminster.

How the assembly works

Plenary sessions of the assembly are more informal than in Westminster, with members seated at desks in a semi-circle facing the presiding officer and referring to each other by name. The presiding officer places a firm hand on time, limiting any discussion to within Standing Orders, and has the power to cut members' microphones off if they go over their allotted time. At the same time there are rules concerning what members can and cannot say or do. Anything deemed to be derogatory in respect of the royal family is taboo. Consequently a Plaid Cymru AM, Leanne Wood, was expelled from the chamber when she refused to withdraw a remark she had made concerning the Queen being called 'Mrs Windsor'. In addition the Welsh Liberal Democrat AM, Mick Bates, was banned from the chamber for wearing a Santa Suit. The presiding officer ruled that he would not call members to address the chamber if they were 'abnormally dressed'.

When Ron Davies once referred to another member as an 'honourable gentleman', Dafydd Elis Thomas famously replied 'there are no honourable gentlemen in this assembly' (Deacon, 2001, p. 189). Debates are often bilingual and an instantaneous Welsh-to-English interpretation service is available. Both first ministers have been fluent Welsh speakers and politicians consequently will often deliver part of their speeches in Welsh to be picked up on the Welsh channel 4, S4C. Assembly members do not have to give way to one another on points of order or information as they must at Westminster, the result of which is the possibility of members being able to speak at length without interruption or contradiction, as happened in a debate about Europe in 1999: 'A speech by a Labour member which attacked the Conservatives and Plaid Cymru but gave them no time to reply resulted in both of these parties walking out of the chamber in protest' (Deacon *et al.*, 2000, p. 103). Voting is done by way of computer terminals, without members having to leave their desks. This means that the percentage of those voting in day-to-day debates and attending assembly plenary sessions is much higher than those attending corresponding sessions at Westminster.

Plenary and committee sessions are restricted to Tuesdays, Wednesdays and Thursdays so that members can carry out constituency work on Mondays and Fridays rather than at weekends. As the assembly expands its powers, particularly of primary legislation, it is likely that it will go into sessions of plenary across three days and committees across all five days of the working week (National Assembly for Wales, 2005, p. 61). The proceedings of the assembly are printed verbatim in *The Assembly Record*, with the exception of translated material which it is not always possible to translate verbatim. The *Record* is modelled on *Hansard*. When Rhodri Morgan became first minister he also established the practice, in the name of 'open government', of publishing cabinet minutes on the internet, at www.wales.gov.uk. As well as debates, plenary sessions of the assembly are called to hear and question the first minister and the various cabinet secretaries. The assembly, however, was designed to be a committee-led body and committees are the means by which members can take an active and important role in its running.

The assembly elections

The first elections to the Welsh assembly took place on 6 May 1999, the same day as first elections to the Scottish parliament and elections to Welsh county councils. The second were held on 1 May 2003. As in Scotland the electoral system chosen for Wales was the additional member system (AMS), in which forty assembly members are elected for constituencies by first-past-the-post. Four top-up members are then chosen for each of the five regions represented by the 1997 Euro-constituencies, selection being by way of the d'Hondt method, under which the number of votes cast for each party list is divided by the number of constituency members already elected plus one; the process being repeated until all the seats are filled. This being applied to a smaller total of seats and votes the system is not so proportional in Wales as it is in Scotland, although here too the Conservatives benefited from the proportional nature of the vote. The system of election to the Welsh assembly has been partially successful. It has produced an assembly of around a fifty:fifty male–female ratio, perhaps the best in the world. It is also more proportional as a representation of people's voting patterns than the Westminster elections. It is, however, the least proportional of the three devolved national bodies in the UK. In 1999 the measure of this disproportionality, known as the Gallagher Index, recorded a percentage of 5.8 for the Northern Ireland assembly, 11.5 for the Scottish parliament and 12.9 for the Welsh assembly.[1] In 2003 the figure for Wales had risen to 17 per cent whilst staying the same for Scotland. The figure should be 0 in a system in which those elected exactly represent the voting intentions of the electorate. The fact that the system was not proportional in 1999 or 2003 by a significant measure, unsurprisingly, remained of little importance to the political party it benefited, the Wales Labour party (Coakely and Laffan, 2005, p. 206).

The 1999 results were a great shock to Labour, whose 35 per cent share of the vote was their worst performance in Wales since 1918. On the basis of their opinion-poll rating and from long experience of the Welsh electorate, they had expected to sweep the board in elections that were the creation of a Labour government. Instead of which Labour, despite being the largest party in the assembly, they fell three seats short of an overall majority, thanks to a totally unexpected swing to Plaid Cymru in the Labour heartlands of the valleys. In a major electoral upset the party lost the apparently rock-solid safe seats of Rhondda, Llanelli and Islwyn (Neil Kinnock's old constituency). The election was held on the same day as the council elections and many within the Labour party see this as being responsible for the poor showing. These elections also

Table 7.1   *Welsh assembly election results*

	May 1999		
Party	Constituency seats	Regional seats	Total seats
Labour	27	1	28
Plaid Cymru	9	8	17
Conservative	1	8	9
Liberal Democrat	3	3	6
Turnout			40%

	May 2003		
Party	Constituency seats	Regional seats	Total seats
Labour	30	0	30
Plaid Cymru	5	7	12
Conservative	1	10	11
Liberal Democrat	3	3	6
Independent	1	0	1
Turnout			38%

brought in some seven MPs, which meant that for a while there were seven AM-MPs. There was a great deal of criticism about these 'two-job' politicians but the Labour government at Westminster did not want any of their MPs to step down and force a by-election that could result in an embarrassing defeat. Only Plaid Cymru's Cynog Dafis in Ceredigion gave up his Westminster seat before the 2001 general election, a decision that in part enabled the Welsh Liberal Democrats to come a clear second, re-establishing themselves as the challenger in the seat, and then to build upon this to win the Westminster seat off Plaid Cymru five years later.

The fact that the Labour party did not have an overall majority in the 1999 elections was assumed at first to mean that it would try to form a coalition executive as it had done in Scotland. The idea was, however, rejected by the party. Wales Labour, due to its virtual monopoly of political power in much of Wales, was far more hostile to working with others such as the Liberal Democrats than was the Labour party in either England or Scotland. This position of feeling they were the 'natural' party of government in Wales also ruled out Plaid Cymru and the Conservatives as coalition partners. Going it alone, however, meant the eventual loss of a first minister, Alun Michael, in an unstable administration that was later forced to seek a coalition with the Welsh Liberal Democrats in order to survive. The 2003 assembly elections therefore came after a period of coalition government. This, however, seemed not to be detrimental to the Wales

Labour party's electoral fortunes, as had occurred with Labour in Scotland. Turnout was down in every Welsh constituency, only reaching 50 per cent in 10 per cent of Welsh constituencies and going as low as a quarter in Alyn and Deeside (The Electoral Commission, 2003). Despite the fact that 62 per cent of total Welsh voters failed to vote, Labour was able to win four constituencies off Plaid Cymru, although it lost one seat to an independent in Wrexham. Here the sitting Labour AM, John Marek, had been deselected and had stood as an independent. Marek, a long-standing supporter of devolution, would later become the deputy presiding officer and form his own political party, Forward Wales, with former Welsh secretary Ron Davies.

Thus the 2003 assembly elections were a tie between Labour and the opposition parties. Plaid Cymru had faired badly in the elections, losing five AMs. This caused a leadership crisis that never quite settled down. Their leader, Ieuen Wyn Jones, resigned but then stood again and was re-elected. Lacking the charisma and presence of his predecessor Dafydd Wigley, Jones saw his party go into a period of decline losing, over following elections, control of Rhondda Cynon Taff and Caerphilly county councils in 2004 and its MP for Ceredigion in 2005.

In 2003 Labour had won four seats and lost two and the Conservatives had won two more. The Liberal Democrats had consolidated their previous gain in Cardiff Central but failed to progress with their vote increase under 1 per cent (Broughton and Storer, 2004, p. 273). The assembly could have gone into deadlock, but Plaid Cymru's Lord Elis Thomas immediately selected the neutral presiding officer's position, which gave the Labour party an effective majority of one. John Marek, the independent, took the deputy presiding officer's post, further strengthening the Wales Labour party's position. It was also true that the opposition parties were not willing to work together in a coalition partnership. Plaid Cymru and the Conservatives' mutual fear of each other was just a strong as their distrust of Labour. In the Westminster general election of 2005 Labour AM Peter Law, in a row over all-women shortlists, stood as an Independent in Bleanau Gwent, meaning immediate expulsion from the party. In the tradition of Welsh Labour politicians falling out with the party Law won the seat. It meant that Labour was now in a minority administration of twenty-nine AMs against thirty-one opposition. There was, however, this time no rush towards a coalition with the Welsh Liberal Democrats. Neither side seemed keen to reinstate the pre-May 2003 status quo. These 2003 assembly elections also stood out for another reason. In 1999 Westminster MPs had stood in the assembly elections and with the exception of Alun Michael had either stayed there or retired. In 2003, however, a number of assembly members now sought to make the Welsh assembly a stepping stone to Westminster. This was particularly true amongst Conservatives where at the 2005 general election three of their AMs stood for Westminster and one, David Davies in Monmouthshire, succeeded in getting elections. Once again there were AM-MPs but this time their journey would end in Westminster and not Cardiff.

Policy differences and policy problems

For much of the assembly's life policy was determined solely by the Labour Wales assembly government with the occasional tweaking by assembly committees or by the flexing, post-2004, of the assembly opposition muscle, such as over university funding. Between October 2000 and May 2003 there was a coalition arrangement between the Labour party and Welsh Liberal Democrats. For both the assembly and Lib Dems this was a period of policy liberation. The Wales Labour party was able to use the excuse to pursue more left-of-centre policies than it had been allowed to before by stating that this was necessary to keep its coalition partners on board. In reality there had been little bargaining when the two parties held coalition talks, with the Wales Labour party taking the Welsh Liberal Democrats' assembly policies wholesale. When it came to their October 2000 Builth Wells conference to endorse the coalition Welsh Liberal Democrat leader Michael German was able to announce that the Lib Dems had got a good deal in the coalition arrangements, in the end getting some 114 of their policies implemented. Labour did not have a conference to endorse the coalition, something which caused much anger in Labour ranks. There then started a Labour campaign to destabilise the coalition by attacking the Lib Dem element within it. German had taken the position of deputy first minister and minister for economic development on 16 October 2000. Cardiff Central AM Jenny Randerson also became minister for culture, sport and the Welsh language, at the same time becoming the first female Liberal minister in history. The following day accusations were raised by Labour's council leader in Bridgend, Jeff Jones, that there had been financial irregularities concerning Michael German's time as the European Manager of the WJEC (a Welsh local government education quango). The following July German was forced to step down until his name was cleared in June 2002. Although he had enjoyed the widespread support of his own party and of Rhodri Morgan he had been out of the cabinet for almost a year. Despite this absence, just before the first minister's second annual report in October 2002, German, much to Labour's annoyance, was able to claim that six of the eight leading achievements of the assembly government that year had come directly from the Liberal Democrat manifesto (Thomas, 2003, p. 187). Whoever originated the policies some of the key differences had emerged between Wales and England were (ESRC, 2003a):

- the UK's first children's commissioner;
- the creation of twenty-two local health boards, to work alongside Wales's twenty-two local authorities;
- free public access to Wales's national museums and galleries
- the Homelessness Commission, and extending support for the homeless;
- the abolition of school league tables;
- free medical prescriptions for those under twenty-five and over sixty;
- free bus travel for pensioners;

- free school milk for children under seven;
- the piloting of a new Welsh baccalaureate in nineteen schools and colleges;
- six weeks' free home care for the elderly after discharge from hospital.

When he campaigned in the 2003 Welsh general election Rhodri Morgan described these key policy differences as 'clear red water' between the Cardiff and Westminster governments. There was, however, more than a hint of Liberal yellow in this same 'water'. After 2003, however, all policy was to be determined solely by Labour, for which they could take the 'credit or the flak'.

Not everything in Wales was seen as a policy success. Although in 2003 Wales Labour had introduced a policy of free prescription fees for all in Wales by 2007, other areas of the Welsh NHS were far from healthy. NHS dentistry in rural areas virtually ceased and as if to prove this publicly there was queue of some people in Carmarthen when an NHS dentist opened in July 2003. When other rural dentists opened their books to the NHS similar queues were seen in the Welsh and British media. The rise in NHS waiting lists, to far higher levels than in England, also caused a public row between Kim Howells MP (Pontypridd), a Westminster minister, and Jane Hutt, assembly health minister, over the length of time she took to respond to one of his letters. The figures were damning: as of the end of March 2004 only eighteen English patients had been waiting over six months for an outpatient appointment, in Wales 6,000 patients had been waiting over eighteen months. On another list only seventeen English patients had been waiting over twelve months for an inpatient appointment, while 8,500 Welsh patients had been waiting over the same time (Osmond, 2005b).

Relationships between Labour MPs and the Labour-controlled Welsh assembly government became so poor at one stage that a joint group of Labour AM and MPs was formed in 2004 to try to smooth out differences (*Western Mail*, 27 September 2005). Nevertheless the state of the NHS remained such an embarrassment to the Westminster government during the run-up to the May 2005 general election that they allegedly pressurised Rhodri Morgan to sack Jane Hutt and replace her with Dr Brian Gibbons, himself a GP as well as an AM for Aberavon. As well producing the humorous BBC Ceefax headline, 'Welsh NHS better off under Gibbons', it also made Gibbons put £32 million into the NHS some six weeks before the election was held.

On the economic front the assembly's rolling programmes to increase wealth regeneration in Wales through documents such as *Better Wales* and *A Winning Wales* was aimed through Objective 1 monies to increase the Welsh percentage of GDP to 90 per cent of the UK's by 2010. In April 2005, however, the Welsh GDP in the Objective 1 area of West Wales and the South Wales Valleys had actually dipped below the 75 per figure it had been in 2000. The Welsh assembly's subsequent economic policy *Wales: A Vibrant Economy* (WAVE), which came out in September 2005, had dropped the 90 per cent target altogether (*Western Mail*, 23 September 2005). Across the whole policy field there was now more extensive analysis and development than ever before. Lobbyists, of whom there were now many, lobbied for this policy or that. In other areas such as local government there was now more of a partnership approach, which worked well. Labour firmly controlled the Welsh Local Government Association (WLGA) until the council elections of 2004 (Laffin *et al.*, 2002). They had worked together in the assembly's Local Government Partnership Council which was in theory meant to produce local government policy together. When Labour WLGA control was diluted in 2004 with the rise of a number of Liberal Democrat-led authorities the relationship became more hostile, particularly over the rebanding of council tax in Wales. This saw a third of Welsh households rise by one band or more and the Wales assembly government consequently capped council tax in a number of non-Labour-held authorities, to ensure that price rises did not impact on them too heavily at the Westminster May 2005 elections. The Welsh rebanding did, however, influence the Westminster government to shelve its plans to do the same in England, at least in the short term.

Under the Lib-Lab coalition there was also the launch of three commissions. The first was the Rees Commission, which examined the issue of student finance. It recommended among other things the re-introduction of student grants, which the assembly duly endorsed. The second was the Sunderland Commission, which examined the issue of Welsh local government reform and recommended an STV system of election similar to that being introduced for Scottish local government. After the 2003 Welsh assembly elections, in respect of implementing a new electoral system, the assembly government put the report into a very dark cupboard never to see daylight again. The final commission of the coalition government was the Richard Commission on the power and electoral arrangement of the Welsh assembly. Although much of this was also sidelined it was still able radically to alter the assembly and push it on to the road of being a proper parliament.

Operational reviews and the Richard Commission

In 1997 some 26.8 per cent of the Welsh population wanted an assembly, 14.1 per cent wanted independence, 19.6 per cent wanted a parliament and around 40 per cent wanted nothing at all. By 2003 27.1 per cent wanted an assembly, 13.9 per cent wanted independence, 37.8 per cent wanted a parliament and now only around 21.2 per cent wanted nothing at all (Richard Commission, 2004). At the same time whilst most of the Welsh population knew that the UK government had the most influence in Wales the majority believed this should be the assembly and placed their trust in the assembly rather than 10 Downing Street (Wyn Jones and Scully, 2004, p. 41). It wasn't just the Welsh public that would have liked to see a Welsh assembly. It was also the desire of politicians from all political parties, even many of the Conservatives. At the same time as wanting to become more like a parliament they became more aware of the weaknesses of their own assembly. In February 2002 the assembly fully revised its procedures and introduced new Standing Orders covering issues ranging from the role of deputy ministers to the way it dealt with primary and secondary legislation (National assembly for Wales, 2002). For dealing with future legislation a clear set of guidelines was drawn up by the constitutional lawyer Professor Richard Rawlings from the London School of Economics (Appendix 3). From now on these so-called Rawlings Principles would be at the heart of the assembly legislative process. As part of this review the assembly also unanimously agreed a resolution calling for as clear as possible a separation between the work of its executive and legislative arms as the legal constraints of the Government of Wales Act permits.

Yet the review of the assembly's procedure did not stop in February 2002. The Welsh Liberal Democrats, the coalition partners in the assembly government, wanted to turn the assembly into a legislative parliament. For this they had insisted on a commission examining the assembly's future role as part of the agreement on them coming into the coalition. The Commission therefore took place in October 2000. Within the document *Putting Wales First: A Partnership for the People of Wales* came the commitment to (Welsh assembly Government, 2000):

> Establish an independent Commission into the arrangements of the National assembly in order to ensure that it is able to operate in the best interests of the people of Wales. This review should investigate *inter alia* the extension of proportionality in the composition of the assembly, and of the relevant competencies devolved.

The coalition government was able secure Lord Richard of Ammanford as the head of this important commission. Lord Richard was one of the most distinguished Welsh politicians still active. He was a former MP, EEC commissioner leader of the House of Lords and former UK ambassador to the UN. It was also felt that his weight within the Labour party would help bring enough gravitas to persuade everyone that this was a major commission. The other nine commission members were made up of five independent members and four political party nominees, all of considerable stature. The commission's terms of references were twofold (Richard Commission, 2004, p. 265):

1 to consider the sufficiency of the assembly's current powers;
2 to consider the adequacy of the assembly's electoral arrangements.

The Richard Commission was the largest ever examination of a democratic system in Wales. It took oral evidence from over 150 witnesses in some 155 evidence sessions. It had some 418 written submissions in addition (McAllister, 2005, p. 42). When it reported back in April 2004, at the cost of some

£1 million, it recommended that by the year 2011 or sooner if possible the assembly:

1 should have its delegated powers enhanced;
2 should be given primary law-making powers;
3 that the membership of the assembly should increase from sixty to eighty members and that all should be elected by STV;
4 should be reconstituted with a separate legislature and executive

There was, however, one major problem with the commission's recommendations, as those supporting a Welsh parliament soon found out. Lord Richard had reported back eleven months after the Welsh Liberal Democrats had left the coalition government and in the process they had lost any influence over the government of Wales. The post-May 2003 period saw Labour in the political driving seat both in Cardiff and Westminster. The Wales Labour party, traditionally of a 'conservative' nature in respect to devolution, rejected Richard's recommendation of primary law-making powers and an STV system by two to one in their internal consultation exercise (*Western Mail*, 4 August 2004 and BBC, 4 August 2004). This was then endorsed by the Welsh Labour party's special Cardiff conference on 12 September 2004. Many Welsh Labour MPs had now also become open critics of the Welsh assembly. In part this was out of frustration concerning the assembly's perceived failure on policy issues such as health that they could do nothing about but were getting the blame for, and in part it was also from a fear of being marginalised and even losing their own seats if the number of Westminster MPs were cut. *Better Governance for Wales*, the Welsh Labour consultation document produced in 2004, made it clear there would be no primary law-making powers for the assembly in the foreseeable future. Labour had also dismissed STV and was hostile to proportional representation as a whole. In both assembly elections Labour had only gained one list seat, in 1999, and none in 2003. Labour backbench criticism of regional list members' status increased after the 2003 elections (Bradbury and Russell, 2005). Many in the party deeply resented the present AMS system and the list members' status. In Section 9 of *Better Governance for Wales* the Welsh Labour party declared (Wales Labour party, 2004):

> The electoral system established in the Government of Wales Act was not designed or intended to be used as a means for failed constituency candidates to be elected via the back-door often opening constituency offices and setting up as rival members to those they were defeated by.

Importantly for the opposition assembly members not only would there now be no STV electoral system but in addition the AMS system was going to be amended to prevent candidates standing on both the constituency and the regional list (Wales Labour party, 2004). Twenty of the thirty opposition AMs were elected by the list vote. Now not only would there be no STV system of election to the assembly, also the AMS system is to be changed to stop opposition assembly members having 'two bites of the electoral cherry'. For the opposition parties who struggled to find enough candidates to stand in the current sixty vacancies, the thought of having to find an additional twenty-five candidates (the five lists have five candidates from each party on each) to avoid standing in both constituency and list was a nightmare. Unsurprisingly they bitterly resisted these changes.

In mid-June 2005 the Welsh secretary, Peter Hain, produced the government's White Paper, also entitled *Better Governance for Wales*. Amongst all the detail it produced three key proposals for the development of the National assembly. These were (Constitution Unit, 2005, p. 1):

1 Splitting the assembly into two with its parliamentary functions separate from its executive ones, thus ending the corporate body and introducing a parliamentary separation of powers. This was uncontroversial and in October 2004 the assembly adopted a resolution calling for legislation to effect a formal separation between its executive and legislative branches (Wales Office, 2005, p. 13).
2 On elections, as mentioned earlier, the ending of assembly members' rights to stand in both a constituency and on the regional list.
3 The move towards primary law-making powers via a three-stage proposal. The first phrase would use the so-called 'framework powers' in Westminster legislation which would pass laws for the assembly, designed by them but with no scrutiny at Westminster, although the major caveat here was that they would have to be approved by the Welsh secretary in advance. This raised concern that an opposition Welsh secretary, or even one from the same party, would block any legislation they felt to be controversial. The second stage would be to transfer substantial functions to the assembly in those fields where it already had powers by orders in council. These would be made with the consent of the both the assembly and Westminster.

   The third stage would be the granting of full primary powers to the assembly in those areas of which it already has the functional remit. There would have to be a national Welsh referendum first, however. Although this may well be nearly a decade in the future it soon brought out members of a potential Labour 'no' camp. Key amongst these figures was Lord (Neil) Kinnock who publicly stated that he would campaign against the assembly getting primary powers (*Western Mail*, 23 September 2005).

Generally the response to the formal split between the parliament and the executive was welcomed by most politicians. The alteration to the electoral system was unsurprisingly welcomed by Labour but no one else. The three-stage approach to extending the assembly's proposals was seen as potentially 'problematic at each stage' (Trench, 2005, p. 1). Most academic opinion thought that it would be unworkable in practice. Nevertheless it was an advance towards the Welsh parliament that many assembly members desired. In the words of John Osmond, the director of the Institute for Welsh Affairs (2005c):

> ... the White Paper probably represents the best we could hope for in present circumstances. Certainly it testifies to Peter Hain's brilliance in negotiating some pretty difficult rapids between the high ground of the Richard Commission and the lower reaches of his own backbenches. It may be a clever political fix, but it remains a fix.

Conclusion

Devolution in Wales had a very shaky start and from time to time has involved itself in various controversies of a Welsh or national nature. It enjoyed or was perhaps lucky not to receive much media attention. Both the *Western Mail* and *Daily Mirror* dropped full time reporting of the assembly during the first term. No British national paper has a reporter in the assembly and few ever bother to cover its meetings. The radio and television media do a more even coverage of the assembly but rarely does its business get into the daily news. It is the Institute of Welsh Affairs (the Welsh think tank) that undertakes the most comprehensive analysis of the work of the assembly, together with the University College London's constitution unit. If you chart their work since the assembly started in 1999 you will see that an institution which originally was modelled very closely on the workings of local government has aspired to become modelled on the workings of a parliament. Much of the period since the 1999 election has been a series of steps on the road to becoming a Welsh parliament. It is period in which the new elite at the Welsh assembly had sought to take on the role of the government of Wales and, in the process, supplant the existing Labour political elite of Welsh MPs. In this they were only partially successful. The recommendations of the Richard Commission, which have been taken into the new Government of Wales Act, will see this process of transformation reach a halfway house between the executive oversight body the Welsh assembly is and the move towards the powers and status of the current Scottish parliament. Therefore the Welsh assembly will no longer be a super county council but it will also not be fully-fledged parliament. Instead it will represent a hybrid between the two. It is then that the battle between those who wish to minimise the role of the Welsh assembly and those who want to maximise it will start in earnest.

Notes

1   The standard Gallagher Index, named after its originator, Michael Gallagher, is defined as the square root of the sum of the squared deviations of percentage seats from percentage votes,

8

Northern Ireland:
the more off than on agreement

For a few years around the end of the last millennium and the start of this one it looked as though the Northern Ireland problem had finally been solved. Every British prime minister since the 1960s and even a number of American presidents had a desire to solve the conundrum that was lasting peace in Northern Ireland. On Good Friday, 10 April 1998, a settlement of sorts on the Northern Ireland problem had been reached. As soon as this was agreed upon, things moved very swiftly. On 22 May that year referendums on the agreement were held simultaneously in Northern Ireland and the Republic. A month later, on 25 June, elections to the assembly took place and on 1 July the Northern Ireland assembly held its first meeting in order to choose its first minister and deputy first minister. From now on the Northern Ireland political process would be a series of stop-go-stop measures. Although the 'peace' part of the Good Friday Agreement continued more or less, the political part seems as distant as ever. This chapter charts the stormy waters of Northern Ireland devolution, which have continued to frustrate politicians and public alike both in Northern Ireland and elsewhere.

Referendums on the Good Friday Agreement

The current political structure of Northern Ireland owes its direct origins to the Good Friday Agreement (see Chapter 5), which was consolidated in referendums held throughout the whole of Ireland, both north and south, on 22 May 1998. Given the normal apathy of the electorate, the turnout in Northern Ireland was remarkably high, with 81.1 per cent choosing to express their views, rather more than was normal in a general election. Of these, 71.12 per cent voted to support the agreement and 28.88 per cent voted against it. South of the border turnout was rather lower, at 56.3 per cent, but the vote was overwhelmingly in favour of the agreement. Some 94.4 per cent of those who took part voted in favour, only 5.6 per cent voting against (Hunt, 1999, pp. 113,

117). In most states a victory by the 'yes' over the 'no' by 71 to 29 would at least put the issue in abeyance for a decade or so. But not in Northern Ireland. Ian Paisley's Democratic Unionist party (DUP) and the one party in favour of full integration with the United Kingdom, the UK Unionist party (UKUP), together formed a vocal and influential minority that was totally opposed to the agreement. Alongside them there was a sizeable group within the Ulster Unionist party (UUP) opposed to the party leader, David Trimble, and the official pro-agreement stance of the party. For this vociferous minority the Good Friday Agreement was represented as being a compromise too far. Their hostility to the agreement was only consolidated by time rather than weakened.

The structure of government in Northern Ireland

The government department in charge of administering most of Northern Ireland's affairs was the Northern Ireland Office. Constituted in 1998, the it consisted of the secretary of state (Mo Mowlam) with four junior ministers, the most senior of which was future Northern Ireland secretary Paul Murphy, These junior ministers dealt with constitutional matters, security, police and the courts, as well as six social and economic departments:

- agriculture;
- economic development;
- education;
- environment;
- finance and personnel;
- health and social services.

Assisting the Northern Ireland Office were five education and library boards, four health and social services boards and twenty-six district councils, responsible for street cleaning, refuse disposal, consumer protection, environmental health and recreational facilities. In April 1998, as the negotiators came close to finalising the Good Friday Agreement, the Northern Ireland Office issued a paper on the structure of government in Northern Ireland which basically restated the governing structures under direct rule, into which a devolved administration could be inserted in the event of a settlement. In particular it named the government departments that would be in charge of devolved matters. In the same period Mo Mowlam, as secretary of state, drew up a draft set of Standing Orders for the new assembly, based on the standing orders drawn up for the ill-fated assembly of 1973–74.

The settlement reached under the agreement consisted of five basic points:

- **There was to be an elected Northern Ireland assembly of 108 members of the legislative assembly (MLAs)**, elected by PR in sixteen six-member constituencies. The assembly would have legislative powers determined by weighted majority so as to prevent unionist domination.

- **There was to be a 'cabinet' or controlling executive of twelve members**, including a first minister, a deputy first minister and ministers for finance, health, education, agriculture and so on, according to the previous Northern Ireland office ministerial structure. The cabinet would include representatives from all sizable parties. This consociational basis of government or 'big tent' power sharing as it was also called was perhaps one of the most important measures of the Good Friday Agreement (Tonge, 2004, p. 185). It was matched with parallel consent being required for the approval of certain legislative measures in the assembly. All of the measures were designed to protect the Catholic minority.
- **The assembly would set up and supervise a north-south ministerial council to deal with cross-border issues**, a council which would take the form of joint meetings of ministers from Dublin and Belfast who could formulate all-Ireland policies on issues like transport, inland waterways, ports and harbours, as well as police matters such as drug trafficking and food safety.
- **The twice-yearly Council of the Isles (also known as the British-Irish Council)**, being a discussion group drawn from the Dublin, Belfast, Westminster, Edinburgh and Cardiff parliaments or assemblies, together with representatives from the legislative bodies of the Isle of Man and Channel Islands.
- **Efforts would be made to settle outstanding issues over paramilitary groups**, including the decommissioning of arms, the accelerated release of paramilitary prisoners and the flying of flags on public buildings.

It would be this last point that would come back to haunt Northern Irish politics time and time again.

The assembly elections: 1999–2003

At the time of writing, the Northern Ireland assembly has had two elections. The first election of June 1998, just like the second of December 2003, was fought across the entire province, with over 300 candidates seeking to become MLAs across 108 seats in 18 Westminster constituencies. In 1999 this resulted in a 70 per cent turnout; in 2003 this figure dropped to 56 per cent. The elections were held under the single transferable vote (STV) system of proportional representation, with the aim of electing six members for each of the eighteen constituencies.[1] The chief merit of STV, which has made it the preferred system for non-Westminster elections in Northern Ireland since 1979, is that it is easier in multi-member constituencies to ensure that electors from either side of the sectarian divide will have a representative with whom they can identify. In 1998 this meant that of the eighteen constituencies in the Northern Ireland

Table 8.1 *Northern Ireland assembly election results*

Party	1998	
	% of first preference votes	*Seats won*
UUP	21.3	28
SDLP	22.0	24
DUP	18.1	20
SF	17.6	18
Alliance	6.5	6
UKUP	4.5	5
PUP	2.5	5
NIWC	1.6	2
UUAP	1.3	3

Party	2003	
	% of first preference votes	*Seats won*
UUP	22.7	27
SDLP	17.0	18
DUP	25.6	30
SF	23.5	24
Alliance	3.7	6
UKUP	0.7	1
PUP	1.2	1
NIWC	0.8	0
UUAP	did not stand	0
Others	0.9	1

assembly there was only one that did not have both unionist and nationalist assembly members with whom the constituents could identify with (the exception is the entirely nationalist West Belfast with four Sinn Fein and two Social Democratic and Labour party (SDLP) MLAs). In 2003, however, with the polarisation of Northern Ireland politics, whilst every constituency now had a DUP member, their were no SDLP or Sinn Fein nationalist representatives in four constituencies (East Belfast, East Antrim, North Down and Strangford). There are drawbacks for STV as well. Despite being in use for three decades, there are still thousands of papers spoilt by people not understanding the system. In 2003 alone some ten thousand ballot papers were spoilt by being incorrectly filled in (Electoral Commission, 2004).

In 1998, although they did not win the largest number of seats the SDLP still polled the highest number of votes, with 177,000 or 22 per cent of first preference votes. The party's position as natural champion of the nationalist community was, however, strongly challenged by the 17.6 per cent polled by Sinn Fein, the highest ever vote for the IRA-linked party, a fact which contributed to their overtaking the SDLP to become the most popular nationalist party in West Tyrone. On 25 November 2003, for the first time since 1975, a Northern Irish election was held on the same boundaries and with the same seat distribution as its predecessor election. In this election, however, Sinn Fein overtook the SDLP across Northern Ireland by some 45,211 votes. The frustration over the province's politics and a fall in the voter turnout led to Catholic nationalists voting to back Sinn Fein in greater numbers than ever before.

Whilst the SDLP was struggling the UUP appeared to be going into terminal decline. In 1998, led by David Trimble, the UUP won its lowest ever share of the vote, 21.3 per cent, as against the 32.7 per cent recorded as recently as the 1997 general election. What made it worse for Trimble was that UUP supporters were rapidly moving from the pro-agreement camp to being anti-agreement. For the first time since its foundation a century earlier, the party lost the support of the Orange Order, which opposed the agreement. The anti-agreement DUP, led by both Ian Paisleys, father and son, became the third most popular party with an 18.1 per cent share of the vote. But an even more significant statistic was the fact that the DUP topped the poll in seven constituencies, while the UUP only managed to do so in three.

In 1998 the only unionist party to give 100 per cent support to the agreement was David Ervine's Progressive Unionist party (PUP) which was linked with the paramilitary Ulster Volunteer Force (UUF). All the other splinter unionist groups were opposed to the agreement. The largest of these was Robert McCartney's UKUP which wanted an even closer integration with the UK than is provided by direct rule. UKUP gained 4.5 per cent of the vote and won five seats. Shortly afterwards, however, four of the UKUP MLAs quarrelled with McCartney and went off to form the Northern Ireland Unionist party (NIUP), leaving UKUP as a rather idiosyncratic party of one. In December 1999, Roger Hutchinson of the NIUP agreed to join a statutory committee of the assembly and was thereupon expelled from the party and forced to sit in the assembly as an independent. Three members who were elected as independents formed themselves into the United Unionist assembly party (UUAP). The 2003 elections saw all of these minor unionist parties either reduced to a token single seat or removed altogether from the proposed assembly, as was the case with the UUAP. Their supporters, as had many from the UUP, went *en masse* to the DUP.

The American senator George Mitchell was heard to say that what surprised him most about Northern Irish politics was the fact that, unlike the rest of the world where it seems to be a law of nature that political parties should always move towards a consensus in the centre of the political spectrum, here the political groupings moved steadily away from the centre and towards the extremes (Hazell, 2000, p. 111). Bearing this fact in mind it wasn't just the UUP, SDLP and minor unionist parties who had their votes squeezed in 2003. In 1998 there were only two non-sectarian parties who gained representation. The more senior of the two, the liberally inclined Alliance party, won 6.5 per cent of the vote and six seats. Their leader, Lord Alderdice, was nominated as the assembly's first presiding officer, or speaker. John Ford then became the Alliance's new leader. The Alliance is closely associated with the UK mainland Liberal Democrat party, with members of one also being members of the other. In 2003, however, with the polarisation of votes between nationalists and unionists the Alliance vote slumped to a mere 3.7 per cent of the vote. Alliance support, however, is concentrated in the east of Northern Ireland which enabled them to retain their six seats. In 1998 another pro-agreement centralist party emerged, partly from the Northern Ireland forum group which had preceded the arrival of the assembly. The Northern Ireland Women's Coalition (NIWC) was formed in 1996. In 1998 it was only able to achieve just 1.6 per cent of the vote but that got it two seats. One of these two members, Jane Morrice, was chosen to be one of the three deputy speakers in the assembly. In 2003, however, the NIWC vote fell to less than 1 per cent and with it went both their seats. Neither the Alliance party nor the NIWC hold any Westminster or European parliamentary seats. As the assembly did not reconvene after its 2003 election the Alliance's representation was limited to its thirty district councillors elected in 2005, in the same elections the NIWC lost its sole council representative and with it any elected representation in Northern Ireland. The centre ground of Northern Irish politics had not looked less promising than since the dark days of political unrest in the 1970s.

The assembly that wasn't

On 1 July 1998, within a week of the elections of 25 June, the assembly was called together for the first time. The meeting took place in the castle buildings on the Stormont estate, although all subsequent meetings would be held in the parliament buildings. With Lord Alderdice as initial presiding officer the assembly proceeded to elect David Trimble of the UUP as first minister designate and Seamus Mallon of the SDLP as deputy first minister. The assembly also appointed the statutory committees required by the Northern Ireland Act, most importantly a committee on standing orders and a committee to advise the presiding officer.

Appointment of the first minister and his deputy, together with the statutory committees, was by cross-community voting procedures developed especially for the Northern Ireland situation, and would be used for any other contentious issues such as settling the budgetary process and deciding upon a programme for government. In order for these cross-community procedures to take place all members of the assembly had to declare at the time of their election whether they were unionist, nationalist or other, so that their votes could be correctly weighted in any future cross-community procedures. There were two forms of cross-community agreements:

- parallel consent – involving a majority of those voting who had to include both unionists and nationalists;
- weighted majority – requiring 60 per cent of those present to vote, which must include at least 40 per cent of unionists and 40 per cent of nationalists.

With the basic decisions and appointments made, the assembly meeting of 1 July came to an end. The whole process then simply marked time since the first minister had announced that he and his deputy would not move on to appoint members to the executive committee or cabinet until the IRA began the decommissioning of arms.

Over the summer a succession of events encouraged those opposed to the Good Friday Agreement and threatened to destroy the peace process. As usual the month of July was dominated by the Orange Order's marching season and confrontation over the peace settlement was once again threatened by a stand-off on the Drumcree march in Portadown. At the height of the confrontation a petrol bomb thrown at a house in Ballymoney killed three Catholic boys. The volatile situation at Drumcree was defused by a statement from the deputy chaplain of the Orange Order, the Revd William Bingham, who famously stated that 'a fifteen-minute walk along the Garvaghy Road is not worth the lives of three wee boys'. The rest of the marching season passed off peaceably.

On 15 August the province was rocked by a car bomb in Omagh, County Tyrone, which proved to be the worst terrorist incident of the whole troubled period; killing 29 and wounding 200, some of them sufficiently badly as to leave them permanently maimed. The bomb was shown to be the work of the so-called 'Real IRA', a splinter group that had rejected the Good Friday Agreement and sought to continue the armed struggle. The Real IRA was disowned by Sinn Fein but there were those from the unionist community in the province who felt that Sinn Fein's condemnation of the atrocity was less than wholehearted and who therefore believed that any co-operation with the party before decommissioning took place was out of the question and would betray the innocent victims who had died.

On 18 December 1998 Trimble and Mallon agreed on details of the structure of the proposed executive when it could be formed. There would be a total of ten departments, the ministers of which would form the cabinet along with the first minister and his deputy. Agreement was also reached at this meeting on the six north-south implementation bodies and the six areas of north-south co-operation which would be chosen from a list including such issues as inland waterways, food safety, trade and business development, special EU programmes, language, agriculture and marine matters. The two men were agreed that the executive would have 'parity of ministerial esteem' by which membership would be divided between six unionist and six nationalist members.

These talks also fleshed out what had been unformed proposals of the agreement and which divided into three strands:

1 assembly and executive;
2 north-south implementation bodies – ministerial meetings;
3 British-Irish council and a British-Irish intergovernmental committee.

It was understood under the terms of the agreement that the three strands stood or fell together and, during the shadowy period when only the first strand had a partial existence, the second and third strands lapsed and fell by the wayside. The period was not entirely without activity, however, and the assembly met in plenary session on nineteen occasions over the next seventeen months, mostly involved in establishing a set of Standing Orders based on those drawn up for the ill-fated power-sharing executive of 1973–74.

On 1 April 1999 the British prime minister, Tony Blair, and the Irish taoiseach, Bertie Ahern, engaged in talks intended to bring the two sides together, resulting in an agreed position by the British and Irish governments, *The Way Forward*. During June both leaders were involved in talks at Stormont over arms decommissioning. Tony Blair was confident enough to claim that he detected 'a seismic movement' in the Northern Irish position, but unfortunately his optimism was not reflected in the unionist rejection of *The Way Forward*. The proposed simultaneous devolution scheduled for 1 July had to be deferred in Northern Ireland, leaving just Wales and Scotland to go ahead together.

On 15 July 1999 the secretary of state for Northern Ireland, Mo Mowlam, called on the assembly to meet in order to nominate ministers to membership of the executive committee, a nomination carried out by the d'Hondt method. Prior to the meeting she made it clear that the executive would be nominated subject to Standing Order number 22, which stated that the executive could only exist if it contained three designated unionists and three designated nationalists. This proved to be an impossible condition to meet since the UUP had refused to recognise the meeting and remained in their party headquarters in Belfast throughout. The presiding officer attempted to proceed under the d'Hondt rules but both the DUP and UKUP refused to nominate, as did the Alliance since it claimed that the sectarian nature of Standing Order 22 was an insult to any non-sectarian parties such as themselves. Since the SDLP and Sinn Fein were the only two parties prepared to nominate, the rule in question could not be honoured and the secretary of state had to revoke her notice calling the assembly, forcing the presiding officer to adjourn until further notice. Seamus Mallon resigned from the position of deputy first minister in protest at the UUP's stance.

In August the British and Irish premiers once again asked George Mitchell to arbitrate between the two sides. Mitchell's review lasted eleven weeks, during which time Mo Mowlam was replaced by Peter Mandelson. Opinion in Northern Ireland was that Mo Mowlam favoured the nationalists at the expense of the unionists but that Mandelson was more sympathetic to the unionist position. That seemed to influence events when Senator Mitchell reported on 18 November.

Everything hinged on David Trimble and the UUP position and Trimble chose to interpret a decision by the IRA to send a representative to see the Commission on Decommissioning under independent international arms inspector General John de Chastelain, as meaning that decommissioning would get under way before the end of January 2000. Trimble thereupon agreed to devolution going ahead and got the Ulster Unionist Council (UUC) to agree to this on the basis that he himself would be willing to tender his resignation as first minister and bring down the executive if sufficient progress with decommissioning had not been made by the end of January 2000.

The new millennium's seventy-two-day devolution

The UUC agreed to what they understood had been recommended by George Mitchell on 27 November 1999 and this enabled Westminster to process the devolution settlement that had been in abeyance for a year and a half: the vote on 30 November being in favour by 318 votes to 10. The day on which devolution was officially granted was 2 December.

Once the step had been taken and devolution declared, all the rest fell into place and the process of establishing government structures was completed remarkably swiftly. On 29 November Peter Mandelson granted a Standing Order which permitted the assembly to reject Seamus Mallon's resignation. Rather than go through the long drawn-out procedure of re-electing the deputy first minister, an act which might well have failed, Mandelson's order simply set the resignation aside as something that had never happened. Both the first minister and his deputy were therefore present when the assembly met that same day in order to nominate members to the executive (Wilford and Wilson, 2000, p. 88). There were four nominating parties who voted in the stipulated order – UUP, SDLP, DUP, SF – based on the share of the vote in assembly elections, and they had to select ten cabinet members in the agreed proportions of three each to the UUP and SDLP and two each for the DUP and SF.

Having chosen its executive committee, the assembly went on to appoint the ten statutory departmental committees, each of which had eleven members, with party allegiances proportional to the representation of the parties in the assembly. The chairs and deputy chairs of these committees were similarly proportionately divided between the parties. The ten departmental statutory committees were:

- agriculture and rural development;
- culture, art and leisure;
- education;
- enterprise, trade and investment;
- environment;
- finance and personnel;

- health, social services and public safety;
- higher and further education, training and employment;
- regional development;
- social development.

Also set up at this time were the six standing committees:

- Audit Committee;
- Business Committee;
- Committee of the Centre;
- Procedure Committee;
- Public Accounts;
- Standards and Privileges.

The final stage in setting up the institutions of the devolved assembly came on 24 January 2000 when the chairs and deputy chairs of the standing committees were chosen (see Appendix 9). At the same session three deputy speakers were elected by cross-community voting. These were Donovan McClelland of the SDLP, Sir John Gorman of the UUP and Jane Morrice of the NIWC. A DUP member, William Hay, was nominated but failed to get cross-community support.

From the start, the DUP members of the assembly refused to participate to the full in power-sharing and neither of the two DUP ministers would attend meetings of the executive at which Sinn Fein would be present, although DUP members sat quite happily on both statutory and standing committees, despite those committees having Sinn Fein members.

The Sinn Fein minister of health, Bairbre de Brun, stirred up a number of controversies over issues ranging from the placing of hospital maternity units to the use of the Gaelic langauge in the assembly. Ms de Brun was also well to the fore in the 'battle of the flags' that arose from Sinn Fein's demands and counter-demands. This involved what the Liberal Democrat peer, Lord Carlile, once famously called 'politics by semaphore' (Brack and Ingham, 1999, p. 37). Both Sinn Fein ministers, Martin McGuinness and Bairbre de Brun, refused to allow the flying of the union flag over their ministries on public holidays. And, since unionists rejected the republic's tricolour equally vehemently, Sinn Fein adopted the position of 'neither flag or both together'. The flying of the two flags side by side was rejected by all unionists as a symbol of joint rule with Dublin so therefore no flags at all were flown although the argument continued to rage, on and off. Yet in another twist of sectarian 'semaphore politics' republican Belfast often flew Palestinian flags and unionist Belfast flew Israeli flags to identify themselves with differing sides in another unsolved conflict, a sight that made strange viewing for those from outside of Ulster visiting Belfast for the first time.

Despite all the work done by the assembly in December 1999 and January

2000, the issue of decommissioning would not go away and, as it became clear that the UUP's understanding that decommissioning would begin in January was just not going to happen, progress in the assembly began to slow down. A meeting of the UUC was scheduled for 12 February 2000, at which it was expected that David Trimble would make good his promise to resign if decommissioning had not started. If he did resign the executive would collapse, with no guarantee that it could later be put back into place. To avoid that collapse Peter Mandelson made a pre-emptive strike on 11 February by suspending the assembly and reimposing direct rule. Suspension of the institutions of the Northern Ireland assembly took effect as of midnight, 12 February 1999.

Devolution resumed

With the assembly suspended, the prime minister and taoiseach redoubled their efforts to get the process back on the rails. Extensive talks were held with all parties but most pressure was put on to Sinn Fein, and through them on to the IRA, in order to get movement on the decommissioning of arms. As a result of these talks the two leaders issued a statement on 5 May 2000 which virtually said that devolution could be reinstated in return for a commitment that could be rather less than the 'permanently unusable' position asked for previously. In reply an IRA statement of 6 May spoke merely about putting arms 'beyond use', although, as a 'confidence-building' measure the IRA pronounced itself willing to open certain arms dumps to the arms inspection team of former African National Congress leader, Cyril Ramaphosa, and former Finnish president, Martii Ahtisaari.

As early as March David Trimble had announced that he was ready to re-enter government with republicans, surviving a leadership challenge from the Revd Martin Smyth at the UUP AGM. On 27 May, in the light of the IRA statement, Trimble once more asked the UUC to support him in re-entering government. He got that support, although it was reduced yet again to 53 per cent and he had to agree to end the Sinn Fein flag protest and to halt reform of the police service by retaining the name Royal Ulster Constabulary, which Chris Patten's report had said must go.

Two days later, on 29 May 2000, devolved powers were returned to the assembly. The DUP, however, continued to object to sharing power with Sinn Fein and said that not only would they continue to boycott the executive committee but they would make government difficult by rotating their members filling their two assigned ministerial positions. This DUP action put an end to hopes that the long-awaited programme for government was about to appear. In its place the executive issued an 'agenda for government' as a short-term interim measure on 29 June, outlining the programme proposed for the assembly between July 2000 and April 2001.

On 26 June the arms inspection team made their report, saying that they had been allowed to see a substantial proportion of the arms held by the IRA and that they were satisfied that those arms could not be used without their prior knowledge. Nevertheless the DUP, representing the anti-agreement parties in the assembly, chose to bring a motion on 4 July condemning Sinn Fein for its support of the IRA and seeking to exclude Sinn Fein ministers from executive office. The motion was bound to be rejected since it would never receive the cross-community support required but it did reveal yet further rifts in the unionist ranks.

The unionist bloc in the 1999–2003 assembly was fifty-eight members strong, made up of twenty-eight UUP, twenty DUP, two PUP, one UKUP, three NIUP, three UUAP and one independent. Originally the twenty-eight Ulster Unionists were all pro-agreement and were joined by two members of David Ervine's Progressive Unionists. In the vote of 4 July, however, four UUP members voted for the motion, leaving David Trimble leading a minority of just twenty-six members in the Protestant bloc, as against thirty-two anti-agreement MLAs. There was widespread pessimism in the Irish press as to the unionist position: 'Broad unionist opinion has swung over two dispiriting years, from a positive to a negative view of the Good Friday deal'(*Belfast Telegraph*, 22 September 2000).

The assembly rose for the summer recess on 7 July and Northern Ireland was immediately plunged into troubles arising from the marching season and the release of paramilitary prisoners. According to the time-scale laid down in the Good Friday Agreement the government had been steadily releasing paramilitary prisoners belonging to both communities. On 28 July 2000 the last major group of prisoners from both sides of the divide was released. Yet, while the Protestant prisoners tended to disperse and disappear quietly, the IRA prisoners were greeted with nationalist flags, songs and celebratory speeches. It was a counter-productive move because the celebrations of the IRA's supporters were perceived as triumphalism by unionist onlookers. The merest hint that the republicans were claiming a victory was enough to drive many unionists into an anti-agreement stance.

On the so-called loyalist side there was factional infighting when the Ulster Defence Association (UDA) and its political wing, the Ulster Democratic party (UDP), embarked on a feud with the UVF. Random attacks and beatings gave way to organised violence when the two sides clashed openly at a UDA parade in Belfast on 19 August 2000. Even before that, the *Belfast Telegraph* had reported a series of attacks in Belfast, Ballymena, Carrickfergus and Newtownabbey under the headline 'Sectarian attacks reach new levels of hatred'. In the course of the disturbances 200 families were driven from their homes and two men died in attacks by the UVF. Peter Mandelson, as secretary of state, was forced to make it clear that these disturbances were largely attacks by one loyalist group upon another, that they were disorganised and that they therefore were no threat to the continuation of paramilitary ceasefires. Things were made worse by an assembly member, Billy Hutchinson of the UVF-connected PUP, who condoned attacks on the UDA. Part of the problem was that, of the two loyalist paramilitary groups' political wings, the UDA's UDP never won a seat in the assembly, whereas the UVF's PUP won two seats. Now, however, a rift developed between the moderate David Ervine, who supported the Good Friday Agreement, and the more extreme Billy Hutchinson, who moved to adopt an anti-agreement stance and a return to paramilitary confrontation. As the press in the Republic reported, 'There is a dangerous sense of drift, with the real possibility of the initiative passing back to the gunmen' (*Irish Times*, 20 November 2000). On 22 August 2000 Mandelson acted decisively to defuse the situation by re-imprisoning Johnny 'Mad Dog' Adair, leader of the UDA in West Belfast and a major orchestrator of the violence.

October 2000 saw rather more progress on a practical level as the final devolved institutions were put into place. On 9 October the Civic Forum, agreed as long ago as 16 February 1999, met for the first time in Belfast's Waterfront Hall. This was an advisory discussion group that was representative of the entire Northern Ireland community, which was scheduled to meet in six plenary sessions each year, with *ad hoc* groups meeting between times. The Civic Forum has a membership of sixty nominated representatives and a chair and is administered by the Office of the First Minister and Deputy First Minister (OFMDFM):

- agriculture and fisheries 3
- arts and sport   4
- business   7
- churches   5
- community relations   2
- culture   4
- education   2
- trade unions   7
- victims   2
- voluntary/community   18
- plus three places nominated by the first minister and three by the deputy first minister.

At the inaugural session a businessman, Chris Gibson, was nominated to be chair of the forum. The meeting appeared to go well but the institution was heavily criticised by those opposed to the agreement on four grounds: excessive bureaucracy; excessive cost; the under-representation of victims; a failure to accept representatives of the Orange Order.

Later that same month the assembly finally succeeded in producing the programme for government that had been promised from the start of devolution. The programme, launched on 24 October 2000, laid out a total of 230 actions to be taken by the Northern Ireland government in an agenda that stretched through until the proposed elections of 2003, but alas the assembly did not last that long. These actions were divided between five goals that the assembly had set itself:

- growing as a community;
- working for healthier people;
- investing in education and skills;
- securing a competitive economy;
- developing north–south, east–west and international relations.

The first of those goals was judged to be the most important since it tackled the issue of sectarianism head on with actions such as:

- the promotion of equality and human rights;
- tackling poverty;
- renewal of disadvantaged neighbourhoods;
- enhancing local communities;
- tackling divisions in society.

This programme counted as a major triumph for the devolved assembly and executive in that the whole thing was published with the apparent agreement of all, despite internal divisions and the difficulties created in reaching four-party agreement while the DUP continued to absent itself from meetings of the executive.

Tying Northern Ireland into the British Isles

On the morning of 2 December 1999 the Irish Republic's government changed Articles 2 and 3 of its 1937 constitution, which had expressed the aspiration to 'unite the peoples of the island' without their full consent. From now on both the Irish and British government were committed to the 'consent principle'. The principle of any future unification of Ireland only being effected with the consent of the majority of the population of Northern Ireland was accepted, removing fears in the unionist community that any cross-border co-operation would lead inevitably to control by Dublin. Removal of that fear meant that progress could be made in setting up the three cross-border institutions: the North-South Ministerial Council (NSMC), the British-Irish Council (BIC) and British-Irish Intergovernmental Conference (BIIGC).

The NSMC met for the first time in Armagh on 13 December 1999 and agreed on the six all-Ireland implementation bodies:

- inland waterways;
- food safety;
- trade and business development;

- special EU programmes;
- language;
- aquaculture and marine matters.

Also agreed were the six areas for north-south cooperation:

- agriculture;
- education;
- environment;
- health;
- tourism;
- transport.

The NSMC is based in Armagh which, as St Patrick's city, is the ecclesiastical capital of Ireland and seat of both Catholic and Anglican archbishops of all Ireland, making it 'neutral territory'. The NSMC was scheduled to have plenary sessions at six-month intervals, these sessions being led by the first minister and his deputy for Northern Ireland, together with the taoiseach for the Republic. Due to the assembly's frequent suspensions there was only one plenary held each year in either Dublin Castle or Armagh before NSMC's suspension in 2002. As well as the plenary sessions there were also regular sectoral meetings for the areas of cross-border cooperation. Most of the sectoral committees managed to have around eight meetings in various places across Ireland before they were suspended in 2002.

Four days after the first meeting of the NSMC came the first meeting of the British-Irish Council, also sometimes known as the Council of the Isles, in that it includes eight delegations, not only from the London and Dublin governments but also from the Scottish parliament, the Welsh and Northern Ireland assemblies, the Isle of Man, Jersey and Guernsey. The BIC meets at the same three levels as the NSMC, there being plenary sessions twice a year, a regular programme of sectoral meetings and *ad hoc* meetings as required. The British Cabinet Office and the Republic of Ireland's Department of Foreign Affairs jointly provide a secretariat for the council. The first meeting of the BIC took place in London on 17 December 1999. The council also examines sectoral areas and various nations were given responsibility for leading this. The Northern Ireland executive led on transport. The last area of input for the Northern Ireland executive was in the Summer of 2002. It concerned minister Bairbre de Brún presenting a paper on the importance of involving the community in developing and implementing drugs strategies. That November the Northern Ireland assembly's executive was due to hold a conference on good practice in drugs strategies. It never happened and although the Council of the Isles continued to have meetings across the British Isles and work closely together there was no longer any representation from Northern Ireland (British-Irish Council, 2003).

On the same day that the Council of the Isles met in December 1999, the first meeting took place of the BIIGC, which was also held in London. This body was inherited from the 1985 Anglo-Irish agreement and exists in order to hold bilateral meetings on areas of mutual concern. Led by prime ministers Blair and Ahern the meeting consisted of representatives of the London and Dublin governments, together with David Trimble and Seamus Mallon. After the suspension of the Northern Ireland assembly and the NSMC the BIIGC became the main focus point of planning and agreeing north-south issues in Ireland. Meetings continued be held in Dublin, Belfast and Downing Street or Lancaster House, London to try to get the peace process back on track and plan for joint strategies between Northern Ireland and the Republic. The joint communiqués between London and Dublin continued at regular intervals stating they wished to push all sides together to pursue a settlement.

On a knife edge – the paradox of success and failure

The final success of the Northern Ireland assembly in producing an agreed programme for government served to emphasise the paradoxical situation in Northern Ireland, whereby the assembly, both in plenary session and in its committees, appeared to be coping extremely well with the business of government administration and legislation, while the party political structure lurched from crisis to crisis, continually threatening to collapse. The same period that saw the programme for government published, the Civic Forum launched and the north-south cross-border bodies functioning well, also saw the parties divide among themselves over the same three problems:

- the decommissioning of IRA weapons and demilitarisation by the British;
- the reform of policing in Northern Ireland;
- the flying of flags over public buildings.

David Trimble tried to force the pace on decommissioning by refusing permission for Sinn Fein members of the executive to participate in any north-south cross-border meetings. The two ministers involved, however, Bairbre de Brun and Martin McGuinness, continued to meet their counterparts from the Republic on an informal, unofficial basis. Much of Northern Irish politics was often conducted in this covert and informal way in difference to the public stance of the sectarian parties.

During a visit to Belfast in December 2000, in the last month of his US presidency, Bill Clinton attempted to find his way into the history books by securing a final Northern Ireland agreement. Like countless others before him, however, he failed to make progress and was heard to claim that settling the conflict in Northern Ireland was every bit as difficult as finding a solution to the Arab–Israeli problem in the Middle East.

If the decommissioning of IRA weapons was the *sine qua non* for unionists then the reform of the police service fulfilled the same function for nationalists. Chris Patten had led the enquiry into reform and had come up with a number of proposals, including the removal of the name 'Royal Ulster Constabulary'. The nationalist position was that the RUC was too deeply implicated in the repression of the minority community in Northern Ireland for it to be deemed acceptable to the nationalist community. Nor could it be trusted as a police force for the entire community unless there was a change in its ethos, currently typified by a name that emphasised its link with the British Protestant supremacy. As a result the SDLP as well as Sinn Fein felt unable to accept a police force that continued to call itself the RUC and, above all, both nationalist parties were ready to speak out and campaign against recruitment to the police from the Catholic community. The result in respect of the police reforms was that a renamed RUC – the Police Service of Northern Ireland (PSNI) – was made accountable to a policing board which was meant to be composed of members of both unionist and nationalist parties. In addition the emblems of service would be neutral, with no Union Jacks flying above police stations. In an attempt to support David Trimble – who fought off a challenge to his leadership of the UUP from Jeffrey Donaldson by promising to halt the police reforms, retain the name of the RUC and ban Sinn Fein from north-south meetings until decommissioning had taken place – the then secretary of state, Peter Mandelson, ruled that the union flag should be flown from public buildings on all of the seventeen public holidays each year. And by saying 'all public buildings' he meant even those which housed departments headed by Sinn Fein or SDLP ministers.

It was as a result of that decision on flags that Peter Mandelson's resignation from office on 24 January 2001 was cheered by the nationalist community. Mandelson resigned after he admitted that he had made misleading statements supporting the passport application of controversial Indian billionaire Srichand Hinduja. Compared with Mo Mowlam's term as secretary of state, which was felt to have favoured the nationalist parties and particularly the SDLP, the sympathies of Peter Mandelson were felt to be with the UUP. At the time of his resignation there were very few voices raised in his defence but the loyalist community did treat his departure with genuine regret. Mandelson was replaced by Scottish secretary, John Reid, a Catholic – the first one to hold the post of Northern Ireland secretary.

Even though the unionists deeply despised the changes occurring with the RUC Sinn Fein rejected these same changes for not bridging the gap between Patten's recommendations and the heavily amended Police Act 2000. They subsequently refused to sit on the policing board, which in the light of later developments in respect of the IRA's involvement in criminal activities ironically proved beneficial to the PSNI's own integrity.

This rise in the fortunes of the hard-line parties of Sinn Fein and the DUP in the 2001 general election made the position of David Trimble and any other moderates much more difficult to sustain. It was pointed out that 74 per cent of the Northern Ireland electorate voted for parties supporting the Good Friday Agreement (including the UUP as a whole and Sinn Fein), leaving a mere 26 per cent openly opposed. And yet it seemed as though the minority opinion dictated public positions. On 1 July, before travelling to France for the eighty-fifth anniversary of the Somme, David Trimble resigned as first minister over the issue of the IRA's failure to put its arms out of use. Sir Reg Empey was appointed to be caretaker first minister while attempts were made to resolve the matter. If not resolved in six weeks, the assembly would have to elect a new first and deputy first minister on a cross-community basis. Since that cross-community support looked unlikely it seemed inevitable that John Reid would suspend Stormont and re-impose direct rule.

In mid-July the British and Irish prime ministers called a special conference of all parties involved in the peace process at the neutral location of Western Park on the Shropshire-Staffordshire border. Some progress was made but the entrenched positions of the unionists and Sinn Fein on the decommissioning of arms and police reform made both sides unwilling to give way. As a member of the SDLP said, 'The Ulster Unionists and Sinn Fein are engaging in a blame game ...' (*Guardian*, 12 July 2001). The London and Dublin governments continued to negotiate after the Northern Ireland parties had quit the meeting and in the next week produced an agreed document on matters such as reform of the police service that it was hoped would overcome the doubts of both sides.

The agreed statement, however, satisfied the demands of the nationalist community far more than it met the requirements of the unionists since there was still no timetable for the decommissioning of IRA weapons. The overall position worsened with the spread of sectarian violence against Catholics in Ulster and a bombing campaign by the Real IRA on the streets of London. In the first week of August, at the same time as a massive car bomb exploded in Ealing, General de Chastelain's commission announced that they had agreed with the IRA the means by which weapons were to be put beyond use. For the unionists it was still not enough since no timetable for the process to begin was announced. The six weeks from David Trimble's resignation ended and, at midnight on 10 August 2001 John Reid suspended the devolved institutions, reimposing direct rule. Twenty-four hours later, at midnight on 11 August, the devolved institutions were restored. The short break was a constitutional device that won a further six weeks of negotiation before the suspension of devolution had to become permanent, but the artificiality of the device annoyed both sides of the sectarian divide, the IRA for their part withdrawing the announcement they had made on weapons only a few days previously.

The timing of the suspension meant that half the six weeks gained was lost because the leaders of all sides went off for a much-needed summer holiday. Therefore, when the deadline of 22 September 2001 was reached, nothing whatsoever had changed and John Reid was forced to suspend Stormont for a second twenty-four hour period, thereby gaining a further six weeks' grace.

Around the same time the chief nationalist politician and Nobel laureate John Hume resigned as leader of the SDLP due to health reasons; the party's deputy leader Seamus Mallon, also at the centre of the peace process and deputy first minister, announced that he did not want the leadership and would be stepping down as well. This left the leadership and deputy first minister's post open to be taken by the SDLP finance minister, Mark Durkan. It also had the affect of weakening the SDLP in the public's perception as its two leading politicians left the political stage.

The start of September saw unionist violence come not only to attention in Northern Ireland but across the world. Primary-school pupils' access to the Catholic Holy Cross school in Ardoyne was blocked by unionists who declared that republicans were using the journey as a screen to attack their community. The scenes of frightened children and their parents running the 'gauntlet of a baying mob' and of a pipe bomb attack traumatising the children shocked and disgusted the wider world. The violence would carry on for months with some 500 people rioting the following January and 80 policemen being injured. It also indicated that not just the nationalists were capable of attracting world attention because of their sectarian attitudes.

Back in the assembly, on 18 October 2001, David Trimble required his three unionist ministers to withdraw from the executive over decommissioning and the Good Friday Agreement seemed to be about to collapse. On 22 October John Reid told Sinn Fein that the IRA had to do something to break the deadlock and that if they did they would not find the British government ungrateful. On 23 October the IRA announced that they had begun to decommission arms, a fact that was confirmed by General de Chastelain's commission. This was enough for David Trimble to offer himself once more as first minister and Mark Durkan of the SDLP as deputy first minister. After the complex vote was over, part of which involved five Alliance members having to reclassify themselves as Unionist in order the get the required majority, the assembly could get back into business. This act, however, strengthened the DUP's hand in arguing that power-sharing will do little to protect Protestants if they slip into the minority (*The Economist*, 8 November 2001). To add to the problems there was a concern that the dissident Ulster Unionist MLAs would align themselves with the DUP, making David Trimble's position precarious.

There was one less unionist party to worry about, however, as on 28 November 2001 the Ulster Democratic party, linked to the loyalist paramilitary Ulster Defence Association was dissolved. The reason given by the Northern Ireland secretary was that most UDA members no longer supported the Good Friday Agreement and therefore the UDA and UDP were incompatible with the assembly's existence. The reality was that there had been an internal UDA feud between leader Johnny Adair and other UDA 'commanders' which was mentioned earlier. This issue later resulted in a series of murders between September 2002 and February 2003. When rivals party offices were attacked, taxi firms targeted and homes shot at, the then Northern Ireland secretary

Peter Mandelson ordered Adair's re-arrest and he was returned to prison (10 January 2003); his supporters, and family, were forced to flee the lower Shankill area of Belfast for the UK mainland. In January 2005 Northern Ireland secretary Paul Murphy released Adair, who went to join his family in Manchester. Rivals in Belfast were now committed to killing him on sight. The decision to dissolve the UDA was supported back in January 2002 when the US government named five paramilitary groups as illegal organisations: the Continuity IRA, the Loyalist Volunteer Force, the Orange Volunteers, the Red Hand Defenders and the Ulster Defence Association. Some of the parties sprang back to life almost instantly: John White, of the now disbanded UDP, formed a new group named the Ulster Political Research Group (UPRG) a few weeks after the ban had come into force, the name coming from a group set up by the UDA in the 1970s called the New Ulster Political Research Group, which had advocated an independent Ulster. A year later when the paramilitary UDA/Ulster Freedom Fighters (a cover name for the UDA) declared a cease-fire its announcement was through the URPG, which had now in effect become the new UDP.

Banning paramilitary groups seemed to make little difference to their activity. In January 2002 there was an upsurge in paramilitary activity. Colombia seized three members of the IRA who had been involved in training Marxist FARC rebels there. The rioting around the Holy Cross school intensified and then on the 12 January 2002 twenty-year-old Catholic postman Danny McColgan was murdered as he arrived at work in north Belfast. The murder was claimed by the illegal unionist paramilitary group the Red Hand Defenders. Loyalists paramilitaries also started making threats to teachers and postal workers, which was roundly condemned by David Trimble. On 18 January Trimble, Mark Durkan, Sinn Fein education minister Martin McGuinness and thousands of trade unionists attended rallies against sectarianism and paramilitary killings. Northern Ireland secretary, John Reid, held secret talks with the unionist paramilitaries to try to get them desist in their actions, but to no avail.

Whilst Northern Ireland was sliding back into sectarianism on 1 February 2002 John Hume was awarded the Gandhi peace prize in India for being 'instrumental in heralding a new era of justice, peace and reconciliation in Ireland' (BBC News, 1 February 2002). Hume's presence was beginning to be greatly missed in the SDLP and it began to lose out to the more radical campaigning style of Sinn Fein. Sinn Fein was also campaigning in Southern Ireland's election and although Irish premier Bertie Ahern ruled out a coalition with the party if it did well in the general elections it was now seen by parties in the south as being an electoral threat. In the May election Sinn Fein did do reasonably well and returned five members to the Dáil (the Irish parliament). Although Ahern was returned without a parliamentary majority for his party he did not seek Sinn Fein as a coalition partner.

In March, Trimble called for a referendum on whether Northern Ireland should remain part of the UK to take place on the same day as 2003 assembly elections. This was seen as a way of undermining Sinn Fein's constant public assertions that it was possible to woo a unionist population into a United Ireland. At the same time Trimble described Southern Ireland as a 'pathetic, sectarian mono-ethnic, mono-cultural state' partly in an attempt to reassure his own UUP supporters he was not going soft on maintaining the British Union (BBC News, 9 February 2002).

On 18 March 2002 there was a break-in at the Special Branch offices of Castlereagh police station, Belfast. The police station had prided itself as being one of the most secure in the world and therefore there was considerable speculation that it was an inside job. In the ensuing separate investigations by the police and the Northern Ireland Office six people were arrested, including one prominent senior republican, prompting a furious response from Sinn Fein. Later on at the end of June the police in Northern Ireland started warning leading loyalists, members of the judiciary and politicians that their names had been found on a computer seized during searches of homes in republican areas in the wake of the break-in.

Despite the fact that the IRA had decommissioned a 'substantial' amount of weapons beyond use at the start of April, something which was verified by General de Chastelain, the UUP were now convinced that the IRA were breaking the ceasefire. They put a motion as such to the assembly at the end of April, and although it was defeated the SDLP leader Mark Durkan stated that he also believed IRA were 'still active'. A few days later John Reid stated that this was no longer enough from the IRA, there also needed to be a 'sense that the war is over' (BBC News, 1 May 2002). Dr Reid, like many other observers of the peace process believed the IRA leadership was now committed to peace and the end of any continuing paramilitary activity. At the same time the British government was doing all it could to boost the assembly and on 2 May 2002 Tony Blair and Gordon Brown, came to Belfast to launch the Reinvestment and Reform Initiative which gave fiscal borrowing powers to the assembly (Wilford and Wilson, 2003, p. 82).

Throughout June and July loyalist and republican violence increased across Ulster and in particular in East Belfast. Then on 4 July in response to this violence Trimble demanded action from the secretary of state, including a ruling on the state of the IRA ceasefire. Tony Blair and Dr Reid issued a 'yellow card' last warning to the paramilitaries some three weeks later. Blair told MPs that a ceasefire should mean an end to targeting, training and the development or acquisition of weapons.

On 16 July 2002 the IRA issued a statement apologising for the non-combatant deaths they had caused during their thirty-year campaign. The total killed was some 1,800 people. The British and Irish government gave somewhat muted responses but the unionists gave a sharp rejection of the apology. Trimble warned Tony Blair not to use the statement as an excuse for not taking tough action against the IRA for breaching the ceasefire, and their political wing Sinn Fein.

At a special conference of the Ulster Unionist Council, Trimble announced that he and his fellow UUP minister would withdraw from the executive if the IRA failed to demonstrate that it had left violence behind for good. Although the nationalists, in particular Mark Durkan condemned Trimble for bringing the peace process into crisis it was not to be Trimble who was responsible for the end of the assembly. This was to occur on the 4 October when their was a police raid on Sinn Fein's parliamentary offices and officials' homes. Four officials were charged with holding documents likely to be of beneficial use to terrorists. On 6 October Sinn Fein's head of administration at Stormont, Denis Donaldson, was taken into custody. This caused an immediate crisis and Trimble sought to speak to the prime minister demanding the expulsion of Sinn Fein. On 11 October the DUP's two executive ministers resigned in protest, thereby in effect ending the operation of the assembly. On 14 October 2002 John Reid suspended devolution and the return of direct rule by London ministers from midnight that day, with the government drafting in two extra ministers. Three days later Tony Blair flew to Belfast and told Northern Ireland's political leaders they were at a fork in the road. He went onto state that:

> We cannot carry on with the IRA half in, half out of this process. Another inch by inch negotiation won't work. Symbolic gestures, important in their time, no longer build trust. It's time for acts of completion. (Prime minister's speech on Northern Ireland, 18 October 2002)

Sinn Fein's Martin McGuinness immediately stated that it was 'highly unlikely' that paramilitaries would disarm under the terms set by unionists. The following week John Reid became chairman of the Labour party and the task of solving the Northern Ireland conundrum passed onto the fourth Northern Ireland secretary of the Blair government, former Northern Ireland minister and Welsh secretary, Paul Murphy. On 20 October 2002 the IRA responded to Blair and not only rejected his disbandment call but suspended its engagements with decommissioning. Murphy responded by stating that the IRA's withdrawal of co-operation was 'regrettable and disappointing' but 'not surprising', comments which were regarded at the very least as being temperate by unionists (Wilford and Wilson, 2003, p. 94).

After the assembly stopped talking

The remainder of 2002 consisted of failed attempts to get the assembly back into operation. Murphy's initial arrival had not made a great impression on any side and therefore bilateral talks with political leaders produced nothing of a tangible nature. These talks weren't helped either by the police arrest of a civil servant who had access to David Trimble's office at Stormont on IRA spying allegations on the 7 November 2002. The unionists were already totally disillusioned with Sinn Fein and the IRA and this just added more grist to that mill. When multi-party talks were held on 19 December 2002 a leaked Irish government paper revealed that the IRA were still active, resulting in David Trimble walking out of multi-party talks and in effect ending them.

At the start of January 2003 Ulster Unionist MP Jeffrey Donaldson declared that the unionist community 'has lost all confidence in this process ... The only way this will work is if the republican movement disbands' (BBC News, 5 January 2003). In return SDLP leader Mark Durkan blamed both the UUP and Sinn Fein for the impasse with the Unionists being fixated on the IRA and Sinn Fein having the same paranoia in respect of the British government. Talks in the same month failed when the UUP and PUP boycotted round-table talks at Stormont, stating that at this time they were just a facade. In the February poll conducted by Queen's University and the Joseph Rowntree Trust it was found that only a third of Protestants would now support the Good Friday Agreement if another referendum were held, however the majority were still in favour of devolution for the future of Ulster (Irwin, 2003). Over the coming months peace talks floundered on the issue of the IRA's decommissioning and although US president George Bush put his name to a joint statement by the British and Irish governments saying Northern Ireland must abandon paramilitarism there seemed to be little movement. As a result, Tony Blair put the assembly election that was due at the start of May back to the end of that month.

Prior the 29 May 2003 assembly elections there were frantic attempts to get the peace process back on course. All of this failed and on 1 May Blair declared that until the IRA committed itself clearly to giving up all paramilitary activity elections could not take place. The British and Irish governments had been trying to get a statement out of the IRA saying that they would give up 'military attacks, training, targeting, intelligence-gathering, acquisition or development of arms or weapons, other preparations for terrorist campaigns, punishment beatings and attacks and involvement in riots'. The most the governments could get, however, was a statement by Gerry Adams, Sinn Fein's head, that declared that there would be 'no activities which will undermine in any way the peace process or the Good Friday Agreement' (*The Economist*, 1 May 2003). This was not enough for the prime minister and he postponed the elections until the IRA provided the required assurances.

Whilst the British government continued to try to get all sides talking again the legislative programme proposed by the suspended executive had been continued by John Reid and then Paul Murphy at Westminster. Part of this included creating a children's commissioner and the creation of the Strategic Investment Board to fulfill the reinvestment and reform initiative. The Northern Ireland grand committee debated this legislation and just as it had set the assembly's first budget it was also responsible for setting the last. Ironically the committee contained many Northern Ireland MPs who were also MLAs but not those from Sinn Fein who continued their boycott of the Westminster parliament (Wilford and Wilson, 2003). By June 2003 the Northern Ireland Office started to recall those civil servants who had been seconded to the assembly, at the same time as seeking the return of the Civic Forum which had been a feature of politics during the long years of direct rule (Wilson, 2003a, p. 14).

The next move occurred on 4 September 2003 when a four-strong independent monitoring commission (IMC) charged with scrutinising paramilitary ceasefires and other elements of the Good Friday Agreement was established. It was chaired by Richard Kerr, a former deputy director of the US's Central Intelligence Agency. The three other commissioners were: John Grieve, formerly a senior officer in the Metropolitan Police, former assembly presiding officer Lord Alderdice and the former secretary general of the Department of Justice in Ireland, Joseph Brosnan. This move was enough to encourage the main parties tentatively to begin talks at restoring devolution once more. Northern Ireland secretary Paul Murphy declared that this new body would restore the parties faith in the peace process. Sadly it was in a short time overtaken by events.

On 21 October 2003, after behind-the-scenes talks between Sinn Fein, the Ulster Unionists and British and Irish officials, Tony Blair announced that elections to the assembly would now take place on the 26 November. On the same day John de Chastelain announced that a third act of IRA decommissioning has been witnessed. David Trimble said, however, that the arms report was not enough and that more transparency and openness was needed. As a result the UUP put any moves towards a pre-election deal 'on hold'.

When the elections occurred as we noted earlier it was seen as a widespread success for the more extreme sectarian parties over the more moderate. This started Northern Ireland's development into a new phase of polarised politics.

Trimble and the decline of the Ulster Unionist party

Virtually every side in the conflict saw David Trimble as being the key player in the resolution of the Northern Ireland problem. Born in October 1944, David Trimble was a barrister and Queen's University lecturer who launched himself into the centre of Northern Irish politics. Originally seen as a hardliner, in 1995 he was seen to parade hand-in-hand with DUP leader Ian Paisley at the Orange Order's annual Drumcree parade, straight after they had won the stand-off with the nationalist community of the Garvaghy Road in Portadown. In the June 1998 assembly election, anti-agreement unionists in his own constituency almost polled as many votes as his own party. Yet in the October 1998 Trimble and SDLP leader John Hume were rewarded for their efforts on peace by being awarded the Nobel peace prize. Being a Noble laureate seemed to give Trimble little breathing space both inside and outside of his own party. At first 72 per cent of the 860 members of the UUP council supported him when he called on them to back his joining the assembly's executive as first minister. That support fell to 58 per cent when he put the George Mitchell Review to them in November 1999, and to just 53 per cent in May 2000. This drop in support led to the Reverend Martin Smyth MP, former head of the Orange Order, challenging him for the leadership. Although Smyth lost he won 43 per cent of the vote.

In September 2000 the UUP lost the South Antrim by-election to the DUP's Revd William McCrea. He took what had been until then one of the UUP's safest seats. In the 1997 general election the UUP had gained 57 per cent of the vote, now they got 35.26 per cent compared with the DUP's 37.95 per cent. This caused UUP anti-agreement MP Jeffrey Donaldson to call for a 'phased withdrawal from the executive in order to pressure the IRA' (BBC News, 2 November 2001). Mr. Trimble in return dismissed Donaldson's strategy as a mere 'wishlist', but on 8 May 2001 Trimble stated that he would resign as first minister on 1 July if the IRA had not started decommissioning. In between this time was a general election in which the UUP remained the largest party in terms of votes and seats (six MPs) and regained South Antrim but at the same time the DUP's number of seats increased from two to five, just one behind the UUP. The DUP had treated this general election as a second referendum on the Good Friday Agreement and used their electoral success to further undermine the Northern Ireland assembly. Whilst all of this was happening, Trimble became aware that the IRA would not be decommissioning to save the post of a unionist first minister. He therefore duly resigned on 1 July and this time enjoyed the backing of many UUP hardliners, including Jeffery Donaldson.

On 16 June 2003 Trimble once again faced a vote of no confidence by the UUP council, which he duly survived. Yet the press continued to comment that he had failed to win the hearts of the UUP membership. On 23 June 2003, a number of prominent members whose hearts he had failed to win resigned their party whips. The foremost of these were Jeffery Donaldson, David Burnside, party president the Revd Martin Smyth and former UUP leader Lord Molyneaux. Whilst these resignations were supported in elements of the nationalist press, the Catholic and Irish press were concerned about the possible threats to Trimble's position as a moderate unionist voice in negotiations (McLaughlin, 2003a, p. 16).

On 18 December 2003 Donaldson and two other disillusioned MLAs, Arlene Foster and Norah Beare, left the UUP. Donaldson stated:

> I have been a member of this party for over 20 years, but it is not the party I joined. It's a party that has abandoned its principles. It is a party which can no longer command the support of a clear majority of unionists. I do not see the Ulster Unionist party ever again being the largest party in Northern Ireland. (BBC News, 18 December 2003).

On 5 January 2004 Donaldson and the two other disillusioned MLAs officially defected to the DUP. Their departure had the effect of making the DUP the biggest unionist party in both the assembly and at Westminster. Trimble was now the junior unionist leader to the DUP's Ian Paisley. The DUP they had joined was defined by the party's Ian Paisley Jnr as one dominated by:

> traditional unionist principles ... They very much see themselves in the light of
> Carson Unionists ... It is not prepared to have double standards in dealing with
> Dublin [it's] a very straight up and down 'like us or loathe us' party. And it thinks
> that it is very different from the kind of broad church image ... which the UUP try
> to market. (Cited in Cocharane, 2001, p. 97).

In the European elections in June later that year, although the UUP got its candidate, longstanding MEP and former MP Jim Nicholson it was with half as many votes as the DUP's winning MEP Jim Allister, who received almost a third of the total preference votes cast. The internal splits and feuding within the UUP, however, contrasted heavily with the successful teamwork of their political opponents the DUP and Sinn Fein. As the peace process began to stall irrevocably the DUP appealed to unionists even more. Trimble seemed to be sidelined now by both the electorate and the governments in Dublin and London as they concentrated their persuasive powers on the DUP and Sinn Fein. The British pre-general election polls for the May 2005 election indicated that the UUP lagged behind the DUP by 16 per cent to 28 per cent (*The Economist*, 12 May 2005). In the actual election the DUP took 66 per cent of the combined DUP-UUP vote. This was the best-ever vote for the DUP and the worst ever for the UUP, whose vote had more than halved since 1997 (Wilford and Wilson, 2005, p. 86). Under David Trimble's leadership the UUP had gone right to the heart of Northern Ireland's government only to be bounced into the sidelines of unionist politics. After he lost his own Westminster seat to the DUP his leadership became untenable.

On 7 May 2005 a simple statement came from the UUP press office stating that its leader David Trimble had stated: 'At a private meeting with the President and Chairman of the Ulster Unionist party this morning I indicated to them that I do not wish to continue as Leader.' The UUP celebrated its centennial in 2005 but it now had just one MP and eight Lords. Sir Reg Empey, MLA for East Belfast, a prominent unionist and former Lord Mayor of Belfast, became the new leader. The UUP were now playing second unionist fiddle to the much larger DUP. David Trimble, however, continues in his role as a backbench MLA.

The continued polarisation of Northern Irish politics

At the same time in 2000 as the Labour party had been forced into coalition governments with the Liberal Democrats in Cardiff and Westminster the four sectarian political parties in Ireland were thrust into a 'grand coalition' (Wilford and Wilson, 2003, p. 80). Northern Ireland had developed the strongest religious sectarian political parties in Europe and whilst elsewhere religion was fading from the political scene, in Northern Ireland it was becoming even more prominent (Tonge, 2004, p. 191). The Northern Ireland executive was for a time the only known example in the world of an enforced coalition of four political parties, each of them bitterly opposed to the others. It ended with the anomaly of all parties acting as though they were in government and opposition at the same time. The 2003 assembly election saw the end of even this strange experiment with the political parties unable to form another administration. The DUP now became the dominant voice of unionism. Although for a time it was thought that the DUP might find some co-operation with Sinn Fein tolerable, just as the UUP had before, this co-operation did not come about. In February 2004 the DUP published their conditions for establishing a stable government, *In Vision for Devolution*, which once again insisted on complete IRA decommissioning amongst other things. All of the options put forward by the DUP contemplated some form of power-sharing with the nationalists (Wilford and Wilson, 2005, p. 73). All of the other political parties came up with their versions of how the Good Friday Agreement should be reviewed. When, however, on 20 February members of the Provisional IRA kidnapped Bobby Tohill, a prominent dissident republican in Belfast, David Trimble called for the exclusion of Sinn Fein from the review process. This did not occur and instead Trimble took the UUP out of the review process. This in affect led the DUP to take up the unionists' main role in the peace process.

After the May 2004 Euro election both Dublin and London governments engaged in separate and joint meetings with the various party leaders. Tony Blair and Bertie Ahern tryied to hurry matters along, but to no avail. Talks at Leeds Castle in Kent sought to 'shoe horn' any agreement around the DUP and Sinn Fein. It led the SDLP and the UUP to threaten to boycott any government that did not include their own seal of approval.

In December 2004, after a year of slow negotiations, it began to be reported that that the DUP leader, the Revd Ian Paisley, would take the first minister's position with Martin McGuinness of Sinn Fein, believed to be a former head of the IRA, as deputy minister (*The Economist*, 2 December 2004). The sticking point of decommission had been overcome by allowing two clergymen to photograph decommissioning and release the photos once power-sharing had began. This was then overturned by Revd Paisley when he decided he could not co-operate with Sinn Fein after all. Thus Blair and Ahern's presence at the Belfast Waterfront on the 8 December was merely to present proposals to which no one had or would sign up to.

On 20 December 2004 an event occurred which would affectively end any short-term prospects for power-sharing and the re-opening of the Stormont talks. Some £25.5 million was stolen from the Northern Bank in Belfast. In the ensuing investigation the police said the IRA had carried out the theft, and this was backed up by the IMC. Whilst Sinn Fein's Gerry Adams denied this, few believed him. On 20 February 2005 the Irish justice minister, Michael McDowell, named Gerry Adams, Martin McGuiness and Martin Ferris, leading members of Sinn Fein, as members of the IRA's ruling council. Both governments in Britain and Ireland accused Sinn Fein of planning the robbery. In Britain, Northern Ireland secretary Paul Murphy withheld future allowances from Sinn Fein in Stormont and Westminster to the tune of some £600,000 a year. The robbery and subsequent fall-out was enough to kill off the prospect of devolved government returning to Northern Ireland, at least for the moment.

One of the major problems of the peace process was that the sectarian gangs and armies of either side, once taken out of military action, turned their attention to the greater pursuit of organised crime. The Northern Bank robbery was just the most spectacular example of this. Most believed that paramilitary gangs could now carry on this area of activity with impunity from the law, something that was clearly illustrated on the night of 31 January 2005. On this night a Catholic man, Robert McCartney, had his throat slit outside a pub crowded with Provisional IRA men who had just returned from the annual Bloody Sunday commemorations in Derry. No witnesses would come forward, all being too frightened to speak. McCartney's five sisters then took up an active campaign to bring his killer to justice. The ensuing publicity caused widespread hostility to Sinn Fein and got worldwide attention, particularly in the United States where the sisters were welcomed, in contrast with Gerry Adams who was now *persona non grata* at official events.

It wasn't just the IRA that were causing problems of a paramilitary nature. The UDA and UDF had also failed to decommission any weapons. Paramilitary activity overall had increased significantly post-Good Friday Agreement. In its first report in April 2004, the IMC, which watches paramilitary organisations, reported that paramilitary shootings and assaults between 1999–2002 was even greater than the pre-1995 'ceasefire'. This led a host of prominent churchmen to declare their despair at the rise in paramilitary activity. Dr Ken Newell, the Presbyterian moderator, declared in Belfast that the 'wave of hope that had followed the agreement has given way to a trough of despair ... Paramilitarism still burdens our communities with its interface tensions, internal feuding and rising criminality' (cited in Wilford and Wilson, 2005, p. 67). It was perhaps therefore unsurprising that in June 2004 a poll indicated that some 66 per cent of Protestants and 50 per cent of Catholics were indifferent to devolved government in Northern Ireland. Although they were pleased with the peace and prosperity that the Good Friday Agreement had brought, they were less pleased with the sectarian 'carve-up' leading from it. There was therefore no real groundswell of opinion pushing for the Northern Ireland assembly to be reinstated.

The Northern Ireland public sector gets a shake-up

With the Asssemby not sitting the Westminster government was able to tackle revisions to Northern Ireland's local government and public administration structure that both unionists and nationalists may have found too politically sensistive. Public expenditure per head in Northern Ireland is nearly one-third higher than in the UK overall. Much of this goes on the large public sector. At the same time local government has for a long time been much weaker than the mainland authorities, making many of them little more than 'talking shops'.

On 22 November 2005 Northern Ireland secretary Peter Hain MP announced the government's response to Dr Tom Frawley's review of public administration in Northern Ireland. The government had commissioned Dr Fawley, the Northern Ireland assembly ombudsman and commissioner for complaints, to chair a commission to review Northern Ireland's public sector back in 2002. In line with commission evidence Mr Hain's response was drastically to slim down Northern Ireland's large public sector. He stated that he would reduce the total number of public bodies in health and social services, education and local government from sixty-seven to twenty. The present twenty-six councils would be reduced to seven large councils with an enlarged and enhanced range of functions, to include planning, regeneration and the maintenance of local roads. Other functions from the many quangos would also go to local government. At the same time each of these new councils would have no more than fifty councillors and their members would not be allowed to also sit in the Northern Ireland assembly, if and when it resumed (Northern Ireland Office, 22 November 2005). It was these council changes that proved most contentious with both unionists and nationalists stating it would be an agenda to 'split' Northern Ireland into sectarian-grouped councils pursuing their own political agendas.

In other areas of the public sector it was announced that a new strategic health and social services authority would replace the existing four health and social services boards, which will be abolished. In education one single board would now cover the whole country. Although these changes were meant to save some £200 million per annum the government denied that the whole exercise was a cost saving exercise, Critics disagreed.

Conclusion

The 2005 Westminster general election saw Northern Ireland as the only significant part of the United Kingdom in which it was expected that the elections would make a difference. It was predicted that the SDLP and UUP would be reduced to one or two seats at most with both leaders losing their seats (*The Economist*, 29 April 2005). As we noted earlier the DUP did do well and gained 33.7 per cent of the total vote with the UUP gaining just over half of that on 17.7 per cent. The DUP gained four seats whilst the UUP lost five including David Trimble's, who lost his Upper Bann seat by almost 5,500 votes. The UUP defector Jeffery Donaldson won his Lagan Valley seat with 55 per cent of the vote over the UUP 22 per cent. It appeared to most political observers as though the UUP were now finished as a political party. Their one remaining MP, Lady

Sylvia Hermon, wife of the former chief constable of the RUC Sir Jack Hermon, became their Westminster leader by default. In the macho world of unionism – the UUP MLAs are all male – the UUP's prospects looked uncertain in the hands of a 'sweet-natured liberal' (*The Economist*, 12 May 2005).

The SDLP's future does not look so bleak, however. In the 2005 general election the SDLP managed to hold two of their three seats. They lost Newry and Armagh to Sinn Fein but at the same time picked up South Belfast when DUP intervention in the seat split the unionists vote ensuring that the UUP lost the seat. The SDLP leader Mark Durkan won his Foyle seat, gaining almost 6,000 votes ahead of second place Sinn Fein. This meant that on the nationalist side at least there were still two choices, between the SDLP and Sinn Fein. Although Sinn Fein, at the time of writing, has its highest number of Westminster seats ever (five) and at the same time secured nearly a quarter of the total Northern Ireland vote (24.3 per cent) it did not deliver the same political blow to the SDLP as the DUP had to the UUP.

The post-2005 general election saw a new Northern Ireland secretary, Peter Hain, who now combined the post with that of Welsh secretary. He was the fourth Northern Ireland secretary in the New Labour period and the first not to have this position as his sole responsibility. Perhaps it was a symbol of the government's pessimism in the restoration of the Northern Ireland assembly that they only allocated Ulster a part-time secretary. Or perhaps it was their optimism that Hain could make a marriage of the DUP and Sinn Fein and restore devolution once more. Whatever the reason, the British and Irish governments continue to try to bring a lasting settlement to Northern Ireland with that anticipation that the next step climbed will finally get to the top of mountain of lasting peace in one of the world's most intractable religious conflicts. This was thought to have arrived in September 2005 when General John de Chastelain, with the aid of independent monitors, confirmed that the IRA had decommissioned its entire armoury. This was widely welcomed by governments in Ireland, Britain and the United States and many within Northern Ireland. The unionist paramilitaries and IRA splinter groups did not follow the IRA's example in decommissioning, however. In addition the Revd Ian Paisley, now the key to restarting the assembly in Northern Ireland, dismissed the decommissioning as the 'falsehood of the century'. The 'Northern Ireland problem' therefore once more remained unresolved.

Note

1 See Appendix 6 for a discussion of the STV system of voting.

9

The English question

By the start of the third millennium, Northern Ireland, Scotland and Wales could now determine their own policy and legislation over a wide variety of domestic areas through their devolved institutions. There was one nation within the United Kingdom who had not so far benefited directly from devolved government, this was the biggest one of the four – England. What would happen to England in these new devolved isles? The English question had been there for decades but as yet it did not have an answer. In 1977 the MP for the Scottish constituency of West Lothian, Tam Dalyell, during the second reading of Labour's Scottish devolution legislation in 1977, raised the 'English question' which then became famous as the 'West Lothian question'. He stated:

> For how long will English constituencies and English Honourable Members tolerate not just 71 Scots, 36 Welsh and a number of Ulstermen but at least 119 Honourable Members from Scotland, Wales and Northern Ireland exercising an important, and probably often decisive, effect on English politics while they themselves have no say in the same matters in Scotland, Wales and Ireland? (cited in Pilkington, 1997, p. 275)

Dalyell's question recognises the point that any devolution of power from Westminster would lead to a disproportionate presence of MPs from the devolved regions in the Westminster parliament, voting on English matters. At the same time the Barnett formula had provided non-English nations with a better level of government funding per capita. With the advent of devolution it was widely believed in many academic and political circles that after the other nations gained devolution then the English regions would wish to have this as well. Many English politicians, including the deputy prime minster John Prescott, believed that there would be a grass-roots swell of opinion which would demand their own assemblies in order to 'gain fair treatment for all of the regions in England' (McLean, 2005, p. 3). As apparent evidence of this desire for devolved government between April 1998 and March 1999 the North-East

Constitutional Convention was established, as was the Campaign for Yorkshire, Campaign for an English Parliament and Campaign for the English Regions. It therefore seemed as though there was a genuine groundswell of political and public opinion supporting devolution (Tomaney, 2000, p. 118). This feeling that something would soon happen to move England towards devolved government gathered pace. In 2003 the minister for local government, regional governance and fire, Nick Raynsford MP, stated to the House of Commons Standing Committee on Regional Affairs (House of Commons, 2003) that:

> Elected assemblies are part of our framework for continued improvement in regional economies. Their functions will be focused around the twin pillars of economic development and improving the quality of life ... As the Prime Minister made clear, it will be a matter of choice. No region will be forced to have an elected assembly. As strategic regional bodies, elected assemblies will be able to set the direction for their regions. Their block grant, and the spending flexibility that will go with that, will allow them, rather than central Government, to address regional priorities. For the first time, English regions will be able to make decisions on regional issues, and to hold regional politicians to account for those decisions.

A year later on 4 November 2004, however, the North East, the first English region to be given the chance to vote on establishing its own assembly voted 'no' by 77.9 per cent to 22.1 per cent. It was crushing blow for those politicians and campaigners who wished to see England develop regional government.

Dealing with the devolution fall-out in England

After the successful devolution referendums in Scotland and Wales it became evident that the government would have to examine whether or not England was to remain a centralised nation with power remaining concentrated in London. In 1998 the House of Commons procedure committee began an enquiry into the procedural consequences of devolution, which reported in July 1999. Two of the areas they investigated concerned the so-called English question:

- What legislation would continue to be debated at Westminster and what new procedures should there be for its scrutiny?
- What would be the role of the territorial select and grand committees?

The second of these issues was the most important because even before devolution Scotland and Wales, whose affairs were dealt with by the Scottish and Welsh Offices respectively, had had their own select, standing and grand committees to consider all legislation for those territories. The procedure committee decided that it would be unfair to retain the Scottish, Welsh and

Northern Irish grand committees if there were not some similar arrangement for English MPs; although it was conceded that an English Grand Committee with over 500 members was totally impracticable. Instead, for a period a new forum for discussing territorial matters was created which, because it is housed in the Grand Committee Room off Westminster Hall, has acquired the title of 'Westminster Hall'. In the end an English grand committee didn't arrive and those of the other nations began to look increasingly archaic as devolution took away much of their purpose. What happened instead was the resurrection of a defunct Standing Committee on Regional Affairs that looked at the English regions and had operated between 1975–78. English regionalism remained an alien concept to the thinking of Margaret Thatcher and her successors and therefore the committee had not resumed work. Margaret Beckett tried to resurrect the committee on a number of occasions after 1999, but met with such resistance from the Conservatives that it was not until 10 May 2001 – the last day that parliament sat before dissolution and the general election – that the fifteen-member committee could be convened for the first time. The committee since its re-inception has been dominated by eight Labour MPs as opposed to two Liberal Democrats and three Conservatives. It proved something of a 'damp squib' as a committee and really only concentrated on the north of England. Its first report in 2003 examined the forthcoming referendums on devolved assemblies in the north. Its second report, in June 2004, dealt with regional economic performance in the north of England, again ignoring the south and west. Even this geographically biased examination was an improvement on what had happened before. Prior to the establishment of the Standing Committee on Regional Affairs the only select committee to look at devolution in England in any detail was the Environment, Transport and Regional Affairs Committee that examined devolution issues, including regional development agencies, whilst in existence from 1997–2001.

Outside of the reports of the Standing Committee on Regional Affairs the wider question of the role of the Westminster parliament after devolution arose as an issue of concern to Westminster. Would the joint Houses even become an English parliament? A move such as this, however, was felt to once again centralise power in London rather than devolve it out to the English regions. In a number of the devolved areas, however, Westminster did become a de facto English parliament. At the start of 2001 a survey conducted by University College London's constitution unit showed that four select committees had already established an exclusively English membership: those dealing with the devolved matters of education, employment, health and home affairs. It was also noted at the time that there were no ministers in these departments who were Irish, Welsh or Scottish rather than English (Hazell, 2001). Westminster, however, remained firmly the United Kingdom parliament in respect of the majority of legislation and reserved matters of policy determination.

'English votes for English laws'

The concept of 'English votes for English laws' in Westminster was seen as a possible solution favoured by the Conservative party and a few others to resolves the West Lothian question. As leader of the party William Hague had set up a working party chaired by the academic Lord Philip Norton, which became known as the Commission to Strengthen Parliament. Reporting in July 2000 the commission proposed a change in legislative procedures for bills that are certified by the speaker as relating to just one constituent part of the UK. Such bills would be referred to a bill grand committee formed by all the MPs from that constituent part of the nation concerned with the legislation. These MPs would see the bill through the legislative process. In their passage through parliament the committee stage of such bills would be taken in a special standing committee whose membership would also be restricted to MPs from that constituent nation or region, the numbers of committee members reflecting party strengths in the Commons. Something similar was proposed in June 2000 when the Labour backbencher Frank Field proposed a bill to bar Scottish and Northern Irish MPs from speaking or voting on any devolved matter. The same bill also would have prevented Scottish or Irish MPs from being given ministerial rank in departments dealing with reserved matters. The bill was rejected by 190 votes to 131, showing that there was both no real support for this solution and that the Labour party was fearful of losing its substantial Scottish and Welsh MPs vote.

Regional agencies and regional assemblies

During the early 1990s, as part of the Tory government's reorganisation of the civil service, offices known as government offices for the regions (GOs) were instituted to perform the same service for the English regions as the Northern Ireland, Scottish and Welsh Offices did for the national regions. The regional director in each office became responsible for the regional policies of three departments of state – Environment, Transport and the Regions; Trade and Industry; Education and Employment – reporting to and remaining accountable to the relevant secretary of state. The ten regional offices and the populations served by each were: London (6.9 million); the South-east (7.7 million); the East (5.2 million); the South-west (4.8 million); the West Midlands (5.3 million); the East Midlands (4.1 million); Yorkshire and Humberside (5.0 million); the North-east (2.6 million); the North-west (2.6 million); and Merseyside (1.5 million) (Bradbury, 1996, pp. 16–19). The role of GOs became uncertain, relationships with local authorities were often difficult and knowing which cabinet members were accountable for which area of the GO's operations was often vague (Mawson and Spencer, 1997)

Following the 1997 election these arrangements began to change and widen so as to allow the GOs to form the nuclei of possible English devolved regions alongside developments in Scotland and Wales. In late 1998, John Prescott, (who was not only deputy prime minister but also the secretary of state for the short-lived super 'Department of Environment, Transport and the Regions' (DETR)) announced the setting up in April 1999 of eight regional development agencies (RDAs) under the Regional Development Agencies Act 1998 which would replace the existing government offices for the regions. RDAs were 'Prescott's babies' and departmental Whitehall battles meant that it would be from his own DETR that most of their functions would come (Tomaney, 2000, p. 124). The new agencies were much the same as their predecessors but the creation of an elected mayor and strategic authority for London removed the capital from the list of regions, while Merseyside was absorbed into the north-west region based in Manchester. These RDAs have a role in developing regional strategies and selected members represent the English regions in the deliberations of the European Union's Committee of the Regions. They also have a say in regional policies on transport, land use and the environment, further and higher education, crime prevention and public health (Hetherington, 1998).

The eight RDAs concerned are quangos which may or may not have 'councils' of business people, trade unionists and local government councillors to look after them. They represent a form of administrative or executive devolution for the:

- South-east;
- South-west;
- East;
- East Midlands;
- West Midlands;
- Yorkshire and Humberside;
- North-west;
- North-east.

A ninth region is represented by the Greater London Authority (GLA), with its mayor and strategic authority. Within each of those regions the agencies are responsible for the supervision of industrial development, urban and rural regeneration and transport and strategic planning.

The establishment of the RDAs was seen as putting into place the raw building materials out of which some kind of English devolution might have been created, even though at inception these regional developments were seen as being 'top-heavy and unaccountable' (Bogdanor, 2001). Their budgets, although increased over their tenure were still only a fraction, representing just one or two per cent of the Scottish parliament or Welsh assembly's budgets.

Following Scottish and Welsh devolution the government hinted at a willingness to consider a move towards English devolution and thus complete the 120-year-old Gladstonian vision of devolution.[2] The first stage, as we have said, was the creation of the eight English RDAs set up by John Prescott with the aim of improving provincial economies. Alongside the RDAs came a political level, the regional chambers, popularly known as 'assemblies', which were set up by Prescott to shadow the RDAs and had a membership comprising 70 per cent councillors and 30 per cent of 'others' including business people, trade unionists and religious leaders. Full-time secretariats were established to service the assemblies and regional plans were prepared. Gordon Brown later spoke of John Prescott as 'deserving congratulations for delivering the RDAs and their assemblies' (Hetherington, January 2001). The assemblies have responsibilities covering three areas: advocacy, accountability and regional planning. The advocacy role means providing a voice for their region as a lobby group to Whitehall, Westminster and Brussels. With regard to accountability, the RDAs are required to be accountable to the assembly for their actions in respect of their regional economic strategy. The assembly's final role is in respect of being a regional planning body, and to this effect they are responsible for proposing strategic planning and transport policies to the London government.

Assemblies all round

The RDAs suffer a number of deficiencies. The powers they have are too modest to achieve any ambitious economic development strategies. Their capacity to join up initiatives within interlinked policy fields such as transport and rural policy are insufficient. The varying needs of each region were also not sufficiently understood by Whitehall, for instance, the prosperous South-east has different economic planning needs from the North-east (ESRC, 2003a). The other major issue concerning RDAs was their overall lack of democratic accountability to the electorate they served. Although the regional chambers had a large political element upon them they were not directly elected. They therefore lacked political accountability and in essence were no more democratic that the RDAs they were set up to monitor. The next step in the devolutionary process therefore would be to make them directly elected, but this could only happen with the people's consent. A poll in the *Economist* (27 March 1999) found that the North-east (51 per cent for, 21 per cent against, rest undecided) was the only region outside London that agreed with the hypothesis that an elected regional assembly would look after the region's interests better than central government. In 2000 the British Social Attitudes survey showed a mere 18 per cent of the population favouring regional devolution for England while 62 per cent wanted the status quo to continue (Hazell, 2001). There was nevertheless a certain degree of interest in a number of areas that felt neglected in the past, including Merseyside and the North-west and Cornwall and the South-west, areas that felt they were losing out to Wales or Scotland when it came to inward investment and funds from Europe. There was also widespread resentment of the Barnett formulas favouring of non-English regions in a number of English regions (McLean, 2005). Of the regions, the North-east was seen to be the most enthusiastic for regional devolution since it was the area of England closest to Scotland and the voters and MPs of the region looked across their border to a land where 'there were no student tuition fees, the prospect of free nursing care for the elderly, higher wages for teachers and a hands-on industrial policy pumping tens of millions annually into hi-tech industry' (Hetherington, January 2001).

Delegates to Labour's 2001 election national policy forum agreed that the party had to recognise the 'legitimate aspirations of the English regions' and belief was expressed in the idea that elected regional assemblies might well be the next step in Labour's reform programme of revising the constitution and empowering the ordinary citizen. Jack Straw, as home secretary, then developed the criteria by which English devolution might be developed during Labour's second term in office. What he proposed was a three-point plan that had to be followed for the establishment of regional bodies:

1 Plans for devolution should be drawn up and regional chamber members petitioned for their support.
2 The plan would be forwarded to parliament by the regional chamber, indicating that the plan has the support of a majority of local government councils in the region. The relevant secretary of state must submit the plans to opposition parties to secure their support.
3 Evidence, most probably by way of a referendum, has to be provided to show that the public want devolution and would approve of the proposals.

The main point of these safeguards was to ensure that the people of England were not swamped by 'unnecessary layers of government'. For the same reason a fourth criterion was added to make the point that regional chambers would only be permitted in areas of unitary authorities, since any elected regional bodies would replace the old county councils.

John Prescott and his supporters believed that these developments meant that they were on their way to committing a future Labour government to the introduction of English devolution during Labour's second term. Any such move would be different from the arrangements for Scotland and Wales. The various regions would be allowed to choose for themselves whether they wished to move towards devolved government, and what form that devolution would take. Although many doubted that the government was serious on continuing with English devolution, in May 2002 the White Paper *Your Region, Your Choice* was published. This White Paper set out in considerable detail government plans for English devolution. These plans included enhancing the role of regional chambers, devolving more power to the government offices and giving the regions a greater say in the decision-making process. The RDAs' budgets were increased and at the same time they were freed up to target their resources more as they saw fit. The regional chambers were given additional resources to enhance their scrutiny over the RDAs and provided for them to become regional planning bodies. The White Paper included a crucial element for devolved government in England to prosper, summed up in the prime minister's introduction to the White Paper: 'This White Paper is about choice. No region will be forced to have an elected assembly. But where there is public support for one, we believe people should be given the chance to demonstrate this in a referendum.'

The pro-devolutionists were only half pleased by *Your Region, Your Choice*, however. This was because the proposed assemblies would only have strategic powers and limited budgets, much less than their own role model, the Welsh assembly. The Regional Assemblies (Preparation) Act 2003 reinforced this notion by making it clear that the new elected assemblies would only have power over the RDAs, regional and economic strategy, spatial planning, EU funding policy and housing investment (Bradbury and Mitchell, 2005, p. 299). In addition to the limited powers there were also two other ominous signs in respect of any forthcoming assemblies. The first was that local government had to be reorganised before an assembly came into place (Hazell, 2003, p. 5). The two-tier system of borough, city and district councils had to be merged with the county councils into a system of urban authorities. This had caused great upheaval and protest when it was done in Wales and Scotland in 1995. Mercifully for pro-devolutionists it had been undertaken by the last Conservative government, relieving the incoming Labour government of having to do this before it launched its devolution plans. In England, just as had previously occurred in Scotland and Wales, it was unlikely that all of the councils would accept disbandment and many with well-formed local identity, fearing abolition, would not therefore support the introduction of assemblies. The second bad omen for any future referendums was the fact that between 2001–02 there had been twenty-eight mayoral referendums in England and not one big city had voted for a directly elected mayor. It seemed as though the public was not in the mood for any changes to the existing way they were governed.

Despite the signs against establishing assemblies the English regional champion, John Prescott, was in the new Office of the Deputy Prime Minister (ODPM) and once again in charge of regional and local government. Prescott was able to gain the support of the chancellor, Gordon Brown, for regionalism, in a cabinet that was otherwise hostile or just plain sceptical. Brown was interested in the prospect of using the regions as mechanisms to speed up economic activity through its strategic planning role.

The North-east says 'no'

In June 2004, John Prescott, announced that the consultation exercise resulting from *Your Region, Your Choice* would mean referendums would be held in the North-east, North-west, and Yorkshire and Humberside regions. It was clear in the government's follow-up White Paper, *Your Region, Your Say*, that only the three chosen regions had the majority of respondents favouring a referendum. In the June 2004 European and local government elections the North-west and Yorkshire and Humberside had all postal voting. There were a significant number of problems during this exercise and concern over reports of irregularities developed. A month later the local government minister Nick Raynsford announced that due to these concerns there would now only be a referendum on a regional assembly in the North-east. The other reason was that Labour was dominant in this region, holding twenty-eight of the thirty seats, and controlling sixteen of the twenty-five local authorities. In the other two regions Labour MPs were reporting back to the deputy prime minister that they thought any referendum there would probably be lost. Therefore it was felt that it would be up to the North-east to show the way (Rallings and Thrasher, 2005, p. 1).

Once the referendum date of 4 November 2004 had been announced the campaign got into full swing. Not only had the 1.9 million electors in the North-east to agree that they wanted an assembly, they also had to vote at the same time on the form of single-tier local authority they wished to see for their area. This meant that within a short time county and district councils started fighting themselves 'like ferrets in a sack'. This then started to dominate local coverage of the referendum (Hetherington and Pinkney, 2004). Professor John Tomaney led the 'Yes 4 the North East' campaign from the University of Newcastle upon Tyne. Its followers were mainly from the Labour and Liberal Democrat parties. The 'yes' campaign was also able to gather some prominent supporters in the form of the president of Newcastle United football club, Sir John Hall, and the sports commentator and former Olympic athlete Brendan Foster. They promoted the message that voting 'yes' was all about identity with slogans such as 'be proud, vote yes' and 'this is your chance, don't waste it'. There were also attempts to link the official 'no' campaign directly to the Conservatives, the BNP and other right-wing parties, which were alien to most traditional Labour voters. John Prescott, although an MP in the neighbouring region, was seen as the spokesman for much of the campaign for the 'yes' camp. As the campaign developed the main problem with the 'yes' camp was that most of the population seemed indifferent to the opportunity to get an assembly, reflected by a luke-warm support by many Labour councillors and MPs in the region.

The 'North East Says No' (NESNO) campaign was under the chairmanship of Bishop Auckland businessman John Elliott, a former Conservative candidate who enjoyed a lot of business and Conservative party support. The campaign then became synonymous with the Conservatives, although this didn't appear to dent their message to any real degree. There was also another 'no' campaign, the 'North East No' campaign run by Sunderland businessman Neil Herron and backed mainly by UKIP. Herron was well known in the North-east as the 'metric martyr', a businessman who refused to use metric measures and continued selling goods in the imperial system. Both 'no' campaigns tended to bicker and swap supporters but once again it seemed to make little impact on the result.

On 14 September 2004, the electoral commission's chair, Sam Younger, designated the official 'yes' and 'no' groups – NESNO and 'Yes 4 the North East'. Both groups were given £100,000 of public funds. Neil Herron's group, much to many commentator's surprise as it was seen as the best campaign, got nothing.

In the referendum campaign proper the 'no' campaigns had the most enduring images. They burned fake money to symbolise the 'waste of a new assembly'. Their main slogan was 'Politicians talk, we pay', a message that resonated well in a period when the public complained frequently about there already being too many politicians. Despite the fact that the 'yes' campaign pointed out that there would be fewer politicians because a layer of local government was being scrapped this message did not get through. The 'no' campaigns were able to connect the public's mind with the notion that the assembly would be an expensive 'taking shop'. To support this view they went into Teesside and at the Transporter Bridge unveiled a fifteen-feet inflatable white elephant. Their spokesman, Graham Robb summed up the message: 'The white elephant is a symbol for the regional assembly. It's unwieldy, cumbersome and serves no useful purpose at all and is full of hot air' (*Northern Echo*, 5 November 2004)

Although a number of polls had indicated initially that the 'yes' campaign would win, as it advanced the number who said they were certain to vote, and would vote 'no', increased considerably over the 'yes' vote. The postal vote also meant that few voters left their vote to near the actual polling day. Some 68.4 per cent had voted a week before close of poll. When the result came it was a resounding defeat for the 'yes' campaign.

When the day of the poll came some 77.9 per cent voted 'no' and just 22.1 per cent voted 'yes', on a turnout of almost 50 per cent. Every council area in the North-east voted 'no' by more than two to one and in nine councils, including Sunderland, the result was greater than four to one (Rallings and Thrasher, 2005). Despite the North East being a Labour stronghold the high-profile Labour politicians who came and campaigned in the region, including Tony Blair, Gordon Brown, John Prescott and Ken Livingstone, failed to persuade their normal voters to back them on this issue. Similarly Charles Kennedy had been unable to persuade Liberal Democrat supporters to do likewise. Regional devolution as an elected institution, in one stroke, had left the political agenda.

In the post-referendum period the Labour party continued with its commitment both to RDAs and regional chambers. This commitment was in part because the existing structure seemed too difficult to dismantle. The Conservatives, however, became dedicated to disbanding all regional chambers. In March 2005 the ODPM select committee published the results of its investigations into the (by now withdrawn) regional assemblies' referendums bill (Sandford and Hetherington, 2005, p. 111). The committee reflected on the lessons to be learnt from the lost North-east referendum. It concluded that (Tomaney *et al.*, 2005: ODPM, 2005):

- any future assemblies should be given 'real' powers if and when on the political agenda;
- any future legislation to set up elected regional assemblies in England needs to be more ambitious than the draft bill;
- the scope of the powers and responsibilities which the government was prepared to give assemblies was disappointing and would limit their effectiveness;
- any further initiative to promote assemblies must be backed, and commitments made, by all government departments, not just the ODPM;
- the role of local government, once an assembly was up and running in a region, had to be clarified;
- a clearer case is needed for elected regional assemblies in terms of value for money for the electorate.

When the 2005 general election saw Labour once more returned to power regional devolution seemed to enter a phase of slow evolution from which no one is really sure what will happen.

The governance of London

Whilst the English regions didn't want regional government the capital, London did. The road leading to the establishment of the Greater London Authority (GLA) began when the Greater London Council (GLC) was abolished by the Thatcher government in 1986. When that happened it meant that London became the only major city in the developed world not to have some form of city-wide government. The departure of the GLC left a confused system in which a multitude of public and private bodies took over the council's duties. Some services reverted to the various London boroughs, others to government agencies and specially created quangos, while still others were contracted out to private companies.

It was clear that something had to be done to clear up this confusion. When John Major's government introduced their government offices in 1994, one of the nine instituted was the Government Office for London (GOL). Members of the Major administration, most notably the deputy prime minister, Michael Heseltine, also became enthused with the idea of a directly elected mayor for London on the grounds that most major cities such as Paris and New York were run by powerful elected mayors and their administrations. This aspiration was evident despite the fact that the Thatcher government had clashed so repeatedly with Ken Livingstone when he was leader of the GLC that it had inspired them to abolish it altogether. Livingstone had been acting as a *de facto* mayor of London through his leadership of the GLC but the Conservative supporters of a mayor didn't have his possible return on their agenda.

The idea of an elected mayor was taken up by the Labour party which was also supporting the notion of elected mayors across local government (Pimlott and Rao, 2002, p. 142). This concept of elected mayors was combined with internal party pressures for the return of the GLC. Therefore it was unsurprising when a proposal that there should be an elected mayor for London was included in Labour's 1997 general election manifesto. Acting quickly on that manifesto promise the Blair government issued a Green Paper, *New Leadership for London*, in July 1997, which led in turn to the decision to consult the London electorate and, in the aftermath of the Scottish and Welsh referendums, the Greater London Authority (referendum) bill was introduced to parliament in October 1997. The GLA proposed by the Labour government consisted of a directly elected mayor and assembly but there were amendments proposed by the Conservatives that would have led to a directly elected mayor and an indirectly elected assembly of borough council leaders. At the same time the Liberal Democrats put down an amendment that would have had a directly elected assembly but no mayor (Hazell, 2000, p. 246). Both amendments were defeated and the referendum framed by the government was set for 7 May 1998, on the same day as the London borough elections.

The result of the referendum appeared to be a resounding endorsement of the government's proposals, 72 per cent voting in favour and only 28 per cent against. However, it has to be said that turnout was a mere 34.6 per cent of the electorate and this meant that, in effect, only 23 per cent of Londoners had voted for the GLA. At the same time the London boroughs had become increasingly self-sufficient since the 1980s and did not welcome the prospect of another GLC encroaching on this independence (Peele, 2004, p. 209). Nevertheless, the government went ahead, publishing the White Paper *A Mayor and Assembly for London* in March 1998. This became the Greater London Authority Act of 1999, receiving the royal assent on 11 November 1999, and came into force in a series of measures introduced between December 1999 and July 2000. The act as passed was a massive 476 pages long – longer than either the Scottish or Welsh devolution bills.

The Greater London Authority

The GLA constituted in the Greater London Authority Act of 1999 consists of:

- **The mayor**, directly elected by supplementary ballot.[3] His duties are to:
  - propose policy;
  - prepare a budget;
  - make appointments to the GLA agencies;
  - speak for London;
  - appoint his own cabinet;
  - establish mayor commissions which examine a particular area such as housing or health and independent from the assembly's scrutiny committees;

- make mayoral strategies both statutory (in areas such as air quality, culture, transport and waste management) and non-statutory (in areas such as children and childcare, energy, drugs and alcohol).

- **The assembly** – twenty-five members elected by the additional member system:
  - fourteen members are constituency members, elected by simple majority;
  - eleven members as top-up members, chosen from London-wide party lists.

- **GLA agencies**, known as the 'functional bodies', the executive powers of the GLA are held within these four bodies:
  - Transport for London (TfL);
  - London (economic) Development Agency (LDA);
  - Metropolitan Police Authority (MPA);
  - London Fire and Emergency Planning Authority (LFEPA).

Each of these bodies has its funding directly from central government and the mayor is unable to alter this, although he can add to it with his own limited revenue raising powers. The mayor appoints most of the members of these boards but the MPA and LFEPA has a majority of assembly members on it and the mayor must also appoint assembly members to the LDA board. The GLA is a much weaker form of devolution than elsewhere in the UK. The problem lies in the fact that it has only a limited amount of executive power, which has been referred to as 'the devolution of responsibility without power, in the form of obligations to write "strategies" but no proper functions' (Sandford, 2005, p. 142). The mayor has consequently drawn up numerous strategies over his tenure, although even these are limited by the fact that he cannot draw up policies that duplicate those of other bodies and the strategies are also meant to be 'consistent with national policy' under Section 41 (5) of the Greater London Authority Act 1999.

The mayor is held accountable by a number of devices, including the monthly report he must make to the assembly and a monthly question time session in the assembly. Once a year the mayor must present a progress report to the assembly which is then published as a 'State of London' address and debated by the assembly. Twice a year, in association with the assembly, the mayor speaks directly to Londoners in a 'people's question time'. The mayor also has the task of drawing up a budget that is presented to the assembly before the end of February each year. The assembly can approve a budget by a simple majority but an amendment requires a two-thirds majority. The assembly also elects a chair and deputy chair who have the ability to take over many mayoral functions in the mayor's absence.

Electing the mayor and assembly

The mayor is elected through a universal ballot of those residents eligible to vote within the GLA area. This method of election has proved to be much less controversial than the actual process of selecting the candidates to stand in it. For those seeking to be come the first elected mayor of London campaigning started well before the eventual elections. In March 1999 Lord Jeffrey Archer announced that he was a possible Conservative candidate, challenged shortly afterwards by Steven Norris. In October Archer was chosen as a candidate by a very large majority of Conservative party members, after which party leader William Hague and much of the remaining the party leadership endorsed his candidature enthusiastically. In the following month, however, Archer was charged with having perjured himself in the libel case of 1987 and was forced to retire from the mayoral contest. He was subsequently found guilty and served two years of a four-year jail sentence for his crime. Against the wishes of many in the party Steven Norris was chosen as Conservative candidate but made such an effective job of it that the party readily endorsed him again for the following 2004 mayoral elections.

In the meantime the struggle had begun for the man who believed that the post of mayor was his by right, and had been ever since Margaret Thatcher rejected him as leader of the GLC. Ken Livingstone had announced his bid for the Labour party candidature in March 1999, as had Trevor Phillips. But Livingstone was disliked and distrusted by the Labour party hierarchy and New Labour's 'Stop Livingstone' campaign began almost immediately. In July Glenda Jackson resigned from the government to seek the Labour party nomination, and other Labour party hopefuls seeking the nomination included Nick Raynsford, then minister for London. In October, however, Tony Blair's own choice, Frank Dobson, made his move and resigned as health secretary to seek the mayoral nomination. In the light of Downing Street's endorsement of Dobson both Trevor Phillips and Nick Raynsford withdrew from the contest.

The Labour party introduced a new electoral process to select its candidate, a political manoeuvre that mirrored exactly the process introduced in Wales to ensure the election of Alun Michael rather than Rhodri Morgan. There was to be an electoral college with three sections: rank-and-file members of London constituency Labour parties; membership of affiliated trade unions in London; and London-based Labour MPs, MEPs and GLA candidates.

On 20 February 2000 Frank Dobson received 51.5 per cent of the vote against Ken Livingstone's 48.5 per cent, Glenda Jackson having been eliminated in the first round of voting. Frank Dobson was immediately adopted as Labour's official candidate but, despite an undertaking to abide by the decision, Ken Livingstone registered a protest. The union section of the electoral college had divided into those unions who had consulted their membership before voting and those who had not.[4] Those who consulted their membership ended by supporting Livingstone, those who had not consulted voted for Dobson: it was the same sort of manipulation of the union vote that had been used in

Wales to secure the selection of first Ron Davies and then Alun Michael rather than Morgan. Ken Livingstone claimed that if the unions had followed the wishes of their members he would have won and, after two weeks' hesitation, he announced on 6 March that he regarded the vote as 'tainted', saying that this allowed him to disregard his earlier undertaking and to stand as an independent candidate.

In the election of 5 May 2000 there was a total of eleven candidates, although only four of these could be considered to have a reasonable chance of winning: those being Livingstone, Norris, Dobson and the Liberal Democrat candidate, Susan Kramer. On the first ballot Ken Livingstone came first with 39 per cent of the vote, Steven Norris came second with 27 per cent and Frank Dobson was third with 13 per cent, only a short distance ahead of Susan Kramer who gained just under 12 per cent. Counting second preferences added another 12.6 per cent to Livingstone's total, making him the clear winner ahead of Steven Norris who gained another 13 per cent. Frank Dobson got 16 per cent of second-preference votes, but this was overshadowed by the 28.5 per cent of second preferences given to Susan Kramer. Second-preference votes also allowed a fifth candidate to make a showing, with Darren Johnson for the Green party claiming 13.6 per cent of second preferences.

Ken Livingstone was therefore elected mayor, but with a turnout of only 34.7 per cent. What was clear is that the London electorate was determined to punish Tony Blair and the official Labour party position for the way in which Livingstone was excluded and Dobson was forced onto the ballot paper. The same revolt among Labour supporters was seen in the assembly election results, where Labour did comparatively badly in the constituency section, winning only seven of the fourteen constituency seats, as did the Conservatives. In the 2000 assembly elections Labour had a total of nine seats, the Conservatives nine, the Liberal Democrats four and the Green party three, the latter two parties having only list members. As in the other devolved assemblies third and fourth parties did very well from the additional member voting system. In the second assembly elections in 2004 the Labour's party's popularity decreased still further with it losing two assembly members. The Conservatives stayed static on nine; the Liberal Democrats edged forward with one additional list seat, putting them on five seats; the Greens lost one seat to gain two; and UKIP came into London's political arena for the first time with two new seats. Within a year, however, both UKIP members would defect to Robert Kilroy-Silk's Veritas party.

The result for both elections showed different things to different parties. It indicated to the Conservatives that they were better at gaining first-past-the-post seats than list seats. For the Liberal Democrats and the Greens the situation was reversed and their future lay heavily with the list system. It soon became evident to the wider Labour party in 2000 and 2004 that Ken Livingstone was more popular than the party in London. It would need to be pulled along by his coat tails rather than the other way around.

In September 2002 Ken Livingston had applied to be readmitted to the Labour party but his application was rejected. The party continued to look for its new mayoral candidate and Nicky Gavron was duly selected. The party's attitude to Livingstone was to go through a rapid transformation. It became clear that his traffic-controlling congestion charges would turn out to be a success rather than the widely predicted disaster. When this was combined with Labour's candidate Nicky Gavron being on around 10 per cent and the same polls indicating that Livingston would almost certainly be re-elected again, those at the highest level of the Labour party (including the prime minister) decided to bite the bullet and get try to Livingston back into the party.

Ken Livingstone had continued to be opposed to the government's policy in some areas and in particular was a fierce opponent of the war in Iraq, which only seemed to boost his popularity still further. By the end of 2003 the Labour Party's mind was focusing on the forthcoming London elections and the necessity to win them. Whilst ex-leader Neil Kinnock was 'fundamentally and irretrievably' opposed, as was the deputy prime minister, John Prescott, to Livingstone's re-entry, many of the Labour grass-roots members and even the Prime Minister were now in favour of his re-admission. In January 2004 the Labour party national executive committee met and interviewed Livingstone and allowed him back into the party. The problem of there already being an existing Labour mayoral candidate, Nicky Gavron, was dealt with by offering her back her previous position as deputy mayor in the post-election assembly.

In the 2004 mayoral elections turnout was up slightly, to 36.95 per cent, with almost 2 million people voting. Once again Ken Livingstone was the winner, albeit now back in the Labour party. He had 35.7 per cent of the first preference and some 13.04 per cent of the second preferences. This was enough to become mayor. Once again Steven Norris was second and the runner up with some 28.24 per cent of the first preference and 11.59 per cent of the second-preference votes. The Liberal Democrat Simon Hughes came third with 14.82 per cent of the first preference vote and 24.25 per cent of the second preferences (more than any other candidate). Fourth was UKIP candidate Frank Maloney with around 6 per cent of the first preferences and 10 per cent of the second-preference vote. This was an indication of the strength of UKIP in British politics at the time. All of the other seven candidates got less than 5 per cent of the vote. The 'Livingstone effect' was indeed apparent in the 2004 mayoral election, but it did not spill over onto the Labour party's general assembly result where the party lost two seats. The main question therefore at the end of the contest was how long would Livingstone stay in office? The job was beginning to look like his for as long as he wanted it.

The Livingstone administration

The governance of London after May 2000 was dominated by the personality politics that surrounded the new mayor. The battle between central government over who controlled the London Underground, the congestion charge, the London bombings and the worldwide contest to gain the 2012 Olympics dominated newspaper headlines both in the UK and wider afield. The official London face of the reaction to major issues in London, including the 7 July 2005 London bombings, was channelled mainly through Ken Livingstone's public appearances. The mayor has come to symbolise the people of London in many ways .

When elected, Mayor Livingston's main effort was to fulfil the promise that his administration would be inclusive. Despite his quarrel with the Labour hierarchy he appointed a Labour member of the assembly (AM), Nicky Gavron, to be his deputy. He then went on to appoint his cabinet, although stressing that the GLA cabinet would not be like the Westminster cabinet in that it would be purely advisory and not decision-making. Mrs Gavron became a member of the cabinet, as did two other Labour AMs, Toby Harris and Val Shawcross, but the cabinet also included a Lib Dem AM, Graham Tope, and Darren Johnson who had been the Green party candidate for mayor. Cabinet nominees who were not assembly members included such familiar Labour names as Glenda Jackson and Diane Abbott; the latter personifying another aspect of Livingstone's inclusivity in that the cabinet and functional bodies appointed by the mayor included a high proportion of women and representatives of ethnic minorities. Although the faces have changed in the cabinet its functions have not and at the time of writing the mayor has his own advisory cabinet which consist of some Labour and Liberal Democrat AMs, a few Labour MPs, the chair of the London Development Agency and a larger number of his own nominees, normally experts in specific fields. The cabinet considers reports from members or more often from officers. The experts have a dominant role here and the committees become in essence a way of joining up policy on the differing areas of the mayor's functional areas. The assembly itself was inaugurated on 3 July 2000, choosing the journalist Trevor Phillips to take the chair with the Liberal Democrat Lady Hamwee as deputy chair.

One of the unsung successes of the GLA was to move into the new, purpose-built London City Hall without any of the fuss concerning cost-overruns that dogged both the Scottish parliament and the Welsh assembly. In July 2002 the hall, a new striking rounded glass building on the south bank of the Thames near Tower Bridge became home to the GLA, mayor and 600 officials. The old County Hall, home to the GLC and sited opposite the Houses of Parliament had been sold off by the Thatcher government a decade before.

When it came to its actual duties the new assembly took a while to find its feet. Its only real power is to reject the mayor's budget, but in a system of governance that is built on partnership this issue hasn't really arisen. With no substantial or legislative powers the assembly has had to build up its scrutiny remit of the mayor's activities. To aid the scrutinising process the assembly created nine committees, which by 2005 had evolved into those concerning:

- budget;
- commission on London governance;
- economic development, culture, sport and tourism;
- elections review;
- environment;
- health and public services;
- planning and spatial development;
- transport;
- standards.

The committees work somewhat similarly to select committees in parliament, having chairs allocated according to the distribution of parties in the assembly. The committees since their inauguration have produced many detailed reports upon all aspects of London's life under the assembly's remit. The assembly also maintained the right to form *ad hoc* committees to examine unexpected issues of short-term significance. These have included themes ranging from the issue of young professionals like teachers and nurses whose salaries are too low to be able to afford to buy housing in the capital to the closure of post offices in London. The mayor, however, need not take on board any committees' recommendations and is also able to set up his own mayoral commissions if he wishes to enquire into any particular issue. This fact weakens the scrutiny role of the assembly's committee structure.

The mayor's progress

In the first year of the GLA Ken Livingstone followed the example of Tony Blair, doing very little that might upset the middle ground in politics, content to exhibit administrative competence rather than any innovative measures that might alienate the voters. In one area at least he soothed the fears of the doubters and that was by proving himself capable of working with the police, supporting them in their methods of controlling the riots of May Day 2001 with a policy of 'zero tolerance'. By using his ability to raise council tax for specific purposes he was able to increase the size of the Metropolitan police by 1,050 officers, as well as increasing starting pay to cover the problem of housing costs in London. It was to be policing and transport by which Livingstone sought to define his first period in office (Sandford, 2005, p. 149).

Most of the concerns of the GLA, as well as most of the controversy, have centred on the question of transport. From before he was elected mayor Livingstone was hostile to the government's favoured public-private partnership (PPP) plans for funding the modernisation, development and daily running of London Underground. He claimed that the involvement of private operators would lead to problems similar to the difficulties of rail privatisation, particularly in its safety implications. In order to reform and modernise the underground, Livingstone appointed as his transport commissioner the American

Bob Kiley, who had made his name by turning round the failing New York subway and had performed a similar service for the urban transport systems of Boston, Massachusetts. By the time of the 2001 election Kiley had achieved so much support in London that Tony Blair was forced to appoint him as head of London Transport.

The issue of PPP funding for the rapidly deteriorating underground remains typical of the way in which devolved administrations can come into conflict with central government. The Blair government remained committed to PPP, despite having the unions, most of the other parties and the voters of London opposed to the semi-privatisation of the underground. In July 2001 Bob Kiley was sacked from his position at London Transport for opposing the government and two weeks later Livingstone and Kiley lost out in a judicial review which stated that the government had the right to insist on PPP funding for the tube. However, Kiley remained as traffic commissioner and Livingstone was talking of an appeal. It was to be February 2003 before the mayor and central government were able to come to an agreement on the future of underground by unifying TfL and London Underground Ltd (LUL) management structures and so avoid the court of appeal. Livingstone's first period in office was reflected in many prominent issues and as the British media is based in the capital they often received detailed attention. There are too many different occasions when his political agenda or views have made an impact in the media or become a talking point to detail in this chapter. Therefore we'll examine just two of the more interesting occasions when Livingstone made both national and international headlines.

The Congestion charge

> The implementation of the Mayor's proposals for congestion charging will bring the biggest civil change to London since the Second World War.

So said the Transport Policy and Spatial Development Policy Committee in the GLA's first-ever scrutiny committee report in November 2000. The committee itself neither endorsed nor rejected the plan, but only made comments and suggestions on the technical detail of the proposal. Mayor Livingstone, however, fully endorsed congestion charging as the centre of his green transport policy agenda. The charge, in theory, would both decrease traffic through a price deterrent affect and at the same time provide increased revenue to boost public transport in the city. The scheme initially had many supporters and even more opponents. Transport secretary Alistair Darling predicted in February 2003 that the congestion charge would mean: 'There'll be people crashing into the barriers because they don't know they are there, huge jams because drivers are turning round rather than paying and it'll all end up with complete gridlock' (BBC News, 11 February 2003). At the same time the Conservatives built much of the electoral strategy on campaigning against the charge. Traders and unions representing the low paid also resisted it and tried legal action to halt it but to no avail. Despite these protests the scheme started on 18 February 2003 and withstanding predictions of chaos it ran smoothly. It works in the following way:

- the charge applies in eight square miles of central London (twenty-one square kilometres);
- charges apply 0700–1830 GMT Monday to Friday, except public holidays;
- there is a flat daily fee payable in advance or on the day;
- there are non-payment fines of up to £120;
- the scheme is monitored by CCTV;
- residents have a 90 per cent price reduction,

In February 2004 the London assembly's transport committee, under the chair of the Liberal Democrat AM Sally Hamway, produced the assembly's first scrutiny into the congestion charge. They congratulated the success of the scheme in reducing congestion but did have reservations about the poor amount of revenue generated and the way in which customers were being treated (London Assembly, 2004). That fact was that penalty charges for late payment contributed one-third of the revenue for the scheme, which meant that insufficient revenue was becoming available to invest in public transport as Livingstone had originally envisaged (*The Economist*, 9 July 2005, p. 27). By July 2005, although it was evident that the scheme had cut city-centre traffic by 15 per cent and congestion by 30 per cent, further measures were needed to increase the revenue. Buoyed by the general public's acceptance of the scheme Livingstone announced an increase in the charge from £5to £8, despite having stated when it was introduced two years earlier that the charge would probably stay fixed for a decade. At the same time as the charge rose he extended the scheme to the wealthier parts of central London surrounding Hyde Park. Once again the Mayor spoke of reducing congestion whilst increasing revenue for improved public transport. Such a move three years away from the next mayoral election showed the political shrewdness that Livingstone was able to bring to bear when the occasion demanded.

The mayor who couldn't say 'sorry'

Whilst Livingstone could be shrewd on some occasions, on others his stubbornness showed anything but the required diplomacy of a senior politician. On the weekend of 4 February 2005 he attended a party marking twenty years since former culture secretary Chris Smith had become Britain's first openly gay MP. On the way out he had a fierce exchange with an *Evening Standard* reporter, Oliver Finegold:

Livingstone: 'Are you a German war criminal.'

Finegold: 'No, I'm Jewish, I wasn't a German war criminal. I'm quite offended by
    that.'
Livingstone: 'Ah right, well you might be, but actually you are just like a concen-
    tration camp guard – you are just doing it because you are paid to, aren't you?'

Such an exchange may well have gone unnoticed on another occasion but this
was a sensitive time for any politician to make comments such as these, even in
the heat of the moment. The exchange soon became national news, helped in
part by it being only a week after the sixtieth anniversary of the liberation of
Auschwitz. A spokesman for the *Evening Standard* stated that 'We supported him
in the mayoral election last year but in this case we feel he fell far short of what
is expected of a figure in his position and he has caused great offence.' Within a
short time the prime minister, Tony Blair, culture secretary Tessa Jowell, transport minister Tony McNulty, the Board of Deputies of British Jews, the London-
wide Anti-Semitism Policy Unit, deputy London mayor Nicky Gavron, the GLA,
Holocaust survivors and Jewish community leaders and numerous other
organisations and politicians had asked Livingstone to apologise. He refused,
stating:

> If I could, in anything I say, relieve any pain anyone feels I would not hesitate to
> do it but it would require me to be a liar ... I could apologise but why should I say
> words I do not believe in my heart? Therefore I cannot. If that is something people
> find they cannot accept I am sorry but this is how I feel after nearly a quarter of a
> century of their behaviour and tactics. (BBC News, 24 February 2005)

Livingstone went on to claim he had been the victim of a twenty-four-year hate
campaign by newspapers, particularly Associated Newspapers, publishers of
the *Evening Standard* and the *Daily Mail*. On 14 February 2005 he was censured
by the GLA at its budget meeting. On the 17 February the Commission for
Racial Equality referred the case to the Standards Board for England which
adjudicates on alleged breaches of the local government code of conduct. It has
the power to suspend the mayor for a year or ban him from public life for five
years if he is found guilty of misconduct. The vote of censure and referral to the
board, however, had little impact on Livingstone and on 22 February he told the
capital's Jewish community he did not mean to offend them. He went on,
however, to condemn the reporter, his newspaper and its sister paper, saying
that he would take no lessons on anti-Semitism from the *Daily Mail*.

The whole affair had ended up in offending the Jewish section of the London
and elsewhere as well as many other groups and people who were normally
sympathetic to Livingstone. To some who had never wanted him back inside the
Labour party it was used as evidence to justify their views. At the same time it
provided an indication of the powerlessness the GLA has over the scrutiny of
the mayor's actions, an issue that GLA members had been raising almost since
its inception. What the affair also proved was that whatever the GLA and mayor

did on the policy or executive front it was the personality politics of Mr Livingstone himself that would always be the big story as far as the media was concerned.

Conclusion

Devolution in England has been dominated by two larger-than-life figures from the Labour party, both of whom seldom agree on much else but both of whom are committed to devolution for England. These two figures are the deputy prime minister, John Prescott, who had championed regional elected assemblies for England unsuccessfully and Ken Livingstone who had done likewise for London but successfully. Others have delved into the constitutional arena concerning devolved government in England but only as bit players compared with these two centre-stage politicians. Prescott was unable to get regional elected chambers off the ground, whilst Livingstone moulded the GLA around his own personal agenda. The GLA was often placed in a position of helplessness in seeking to keep Livingstone in check and therefore personality politics seemed on a number of occasions to dominate mayoral policy in London rather than any formal specific policy creation mechanism. Nevertheless, Livingstone's brand of politics brought notable successes, including the pioneering of the congestion charges and bringing the 2012 Olympics to London. These were successful projects, which were not only envied by towns and cities across Britain but in cities and capitals across the world. Yet there is no longer a clamour from English cities or regions for their own elected assemblies. The referendum defeat in the North-east has left regional devolution policy in a period of confusion with nobody being certain where it will go. It is certain to be more administrative than political in nature. English devolution therefore now looks to be the least certain devolutionary development to predict across the rest of the decade. The Labour government is in the processing of reviewing the scope and powers of the London assembly and at the same time it has to decide what will become of the regional chambers and RDAs.

Notes

1   *Hansard*, Vol. 939, Cols. 122–3, 14 November 1977 (quoted in Pilkington, 1997, p. 275).
2   In the Midlothian campaign of 1879 Gladstone declared: 'If we can make arrangements under which Ireland, Scotland, Wales, *portions of England*, can deal with questions of local and special interest to themselves more efficiently than parliament now can, that, I say, will be the attainment of a great national good' (quoted in Bogdanor, 2001).
3   The supplementary voting system is a variation of the alternative vote, developed for the Labour party in 1990 by the Plant Committee for possible future use if the

electoral system for Westminster were to be reformed. An absolute majority voting system rather than proportional, voters list the candidates in order of preference and, after the first ballot, if there is no outright winner, all but the top two candidates are eliminated and the second preference of these eliminated candidates redistributed until a winner is found.

4 Interestingly enough, the same division of union votes into those that balloted their membership first and those that did not was also true of the election of Alun Michael as Labour leader in Wales.

10

Conclusion:
how far have we come
and where do we go from here?

Much of the academic work undertaken on devolution has either been of an historical nature, recording the major events of devolution, of a political science nature, seeking to examine devolution from a series of theories or models, or a combination of both. This book is overwhelmingly one which examines devolution from an historical evolutionary viewpoint. Therefore if you examine the history of devolution it is quite apparent from the previous chapters in this book that, as former Welsh secretary Ron Davies stated, 'devolution is a process and not an event' (cited in Hazell, 2000, p. 276). For Scotland, Ireland and Wales devolutionary pressures have been building over the last three centuries. Over this time there have been many peaks and troughs on the devolutionary road but it is quite apparent that we are currently in a period of level progression.

For a development that had been so long in the preparation, devolution for Scotland and Wales when it happened came remarkably quickly. The whole process of referendums, consultative documents, legislation and elections leading to the official opening of the Scottish parliament and Welsh assembly was completed in little more than two years from the date of Labour's election victory. In Northern Ireland the process was a little more protracted, but then there were special reasons for that.

The first chapter set out the various notions around sovereignty and the concept of the nation state that help to define devolution in a British context. It also noted some of the other western nations' governmental systems on a union and federal level. In this respect devolutionary systems were normally the rule rather than the exception and Britain was not unique in developing its own system of politically devolved government. What did take place, however, was that the types of devolution that occurred in Britain meant that it became an asymmetrical nation in respect of the devolution of powers from Westminster to the Celtic nations. It has not become the federal system of nation states such as Germany or the USA. There are no unified principals and practice of territorial management. For each British nation this has meant a struggle to adapt to the settlement they had gained or, in the case of England, failed to desire. In each nation there were various challenges against the settlement. This challenge was most acute in Northern Ireland where some unionists rejected the settlement in its entirety and in Wales where most AMs pushed to remodel their assembly more on a parliamentary body, rather than corporate, with all that this involved.

Devolutionary models

In 2005, drawing upon the work of around twenty of the most prominent academics on devolution since the mid-1970s, Jennifer Todd highlighted three models of territorial politics from which we can rationalise devolutionary change.

The first concerned the concept of 'state realism'. Here the state has had adapted its state power and state sovereignty to take account of changing political realities. This new form of devolution is therefore simply 'the older dual polity whereby the centre allowed a certain practical autonomy on local issues to its peripheries, while retaining control over high politics'. There has been no radical change to the flexible 'British constitution'; it has only been bent partially to encompass the new devolutionary changes. The main problem with this notion of devolution is that the divide between the centre and the periphery is not clear and therefore the older 'mainframe' of the unitary state may be under intolerable strain and crack.

The second model considers devolution to be driven by 'European regionalism'. This indicates that nations within the UK move from state-centred to 'European determined linkage politics'. This means that, within a European context, nations such as Scotland, Wales and Northern Ireland need the UK parliament less and less as they can interact directly with the European Union without needing to go through Westminster. In turn the EU and European Commission require regions or nations in order to determine their policy output such as European regional development funding or support for cultural and linguistic policies. To participate in these programmes member states therefore have to be neatly packaged into differing regions. In the case of the UK, part of this packaging involves the identification of the constituent nations.

The final model sees devolution as a 'renewal of imperial legacies'. Here the Westminster government, just as it did with its colonies in the last century, transfers more and more interest and powers to the devolved nations. In time it will divest control of these and allow them to become independent within their own right. Those advocating this model point to Northern Ireland as an example of this. Here the Westminster government would be 'glad to rid of its responsibilities' for this troubled province. The main drawback to this theory is that all mainstream British political parties constantly advocate their commitment to maintaining the union.

Which model most closely fits devolution in Britain?

In the conclusion to the first chapter of this book it was stated that 'when devolution arrived on the policy agenda it was not viewed as yet another political process but instead a major and fundamental shift in the political structure of the British state and the engine by which the uncodified constitution and system of government evolved to match that of the other large European nations'. The reality of academic studies, however, has discovered that like the rest of the British system of government devolution has been a less radical step than most imagined. The ties to the centre are still very strong. In January 2005, after examining the process of devolution in Britain for the previous decade, the Economic and Social Research Council's Research (ESRC) Programme on Devolution and Constitutional Change was able to conclude six key points:

1　Relations between central and devolved government reveal minimal change from pre-devolution arrangement for dealing with Scottish, Welsh and Northern Irish matters, relying on bilateral and informal links largely amongst officials and not ministers.
2　There are few meetings between UK and devolved administrators, and special arrangements in some policy fields like agriculture and EU matters.
3　The Treasury retains considerable powers over devolved finance, though lacks levers like public service agreements, which it can use on Whitehall departments.
4　The apparatus for dealing with devolution at the centre is small and has a limited brief, and Whitehall departments have done little to differentiate between their England-only, England-and-Wales, and UK functions.
5　Neither Westminster nor Whitehall has sought to adapt the legislative process to create different categories of legislation according to which territories and functions it affects.
6　The pattern of minimal change has made major constitutional change a straightforward administrative and legal process, but one vulnerable to disputes created by future changes of government.

The ESRC's view therefore was that devolution in Britain had occurred along Todd's 'state realism' model. Devolution had resulted in modest and incremental change with minimal adaptation to cope with the demands devolution had created. Westminster had still maintained a legislative role in the devolved institution. This is true even in Scotland, where the Sewel motion enables Westminster to legislate for devolved matters with the Scottish parliament's consent. At the same time the home civil service remains loyal to no single devolved body but instead to the central government. The chain of responsibility for the civil service still lies within Whitehall through the cabinet secretary to the UK prime minister, as minister for the civil service. Neither has devolution seen the head-on clashes that were expected between the devolved institutions and government in Whitehall.

Initially it was hard for New Labour with its centralising tendencies to accept fully devolution to regions meaning a weakening of central control. Many saw the devolution legacy as having been that of the late Labour leader John Smith rather than Tony Blair. Sceptics believed that it would therefore not come around or that only a half-hearted effort would be made concerning its implementation. There were also attempts to select the leaders of the devolved institutions in both London and Cardiff, both of which resulted in eventual failure for Number 10.

After devolution settled down and didn't deliver the political meltdown of the United Kingdom that some political doom-mongers had predicated. 10 Downing Street concentrated on Westminster and international politics. Only in Northern Ireland, with its elusive movement towards a final peace settlement, was there continual interest. For Scotland and Wales there was only really concern from its MPs at election times. These devolved elections also caused distress in 10 Downing Street if Labour did badly. The clearest manifestation was perhaps in the Welsh assembly election of 1999 where Tony Blair reputedly attacked the 'f**king Welsh' for not electing a Labour majority (BBC News, 29 September 2005). In Westminster elections there was also interest if devolved government's policies were seen to adversely affect Westminster results. The problems with the NHS in Wales, the scrapping of some quangos such as the Welsh Development Agency and the rebanding of houses in Wales for council tax in 2005 were both negative issues that worried both Labour MPs in Wales and Westminster when the 2005 general election came around.

Another side-effect of devolution was the strengthening of cultural identity in Scotland, Wales and London for the inhabitants of each devolved area. Cultural identity had already been key to successfully establishing devolution (Gardiner, 2004) and where this identity wasn't apparent, such as in the North-east of England, the devolution failed to take root. At the same time, however, the political parties in Scotland and Wales which normally were seen as the manifestation of nationalism's political culturalism (the SNP and Plaid Cymru) suffered political setbacks. Far from opening the flood gates of nationalism and the subsequent break-up of the United Kingdom as had been predicated by devolution opponents, nationalism appeared in the mid-2000s to be going into something of an electoral decline as people voted instead for the pro-union parties. In a way nationalism had become diluted from the sole preserve of the nationalist parties to become part of the core of the divided national British political parties with their own national brands – Wales Labour, Scottish Conservatives or London Liberal Democrats being just three of many examples of the 'brand' change political parties undertook to make themselves appear more local.

Future policy direction

In the 2005 general election the British parties' election manifestos only briefly mentioned the devolved bodies (Constitution Unit, 2005a). Labour failed to mention Scotland but indicated it would give the Welsh assembly 'enhanced legislative powers' and 'reform' its structure and electoral systems. Labour also supported getting the Northern Ireland assembly back on track, something that enjoyed the support of the Conservatives and Liberal Democrats, as well. The Liberal Democrats also have wanted to have primary legislative powers for the Welsh assembly, elections there by STV and at the same time stronger powers for the Northern Ireland assembly and the chance to extend the role of the Scottish parliament.

The Conservatives remained the devolution 'sceptics' and put forward for a referendum with various options on whether the Welsh assembly should be abolished, stay the same or have enhanced powers. This then set the Welsh Conservative leader Nick Bourne, who was pro-increased powers to the Welsh assembly, against the shadow Welsh secretary Bill Wiggins who wanted the assembly scrapped. At the same time as squabbling about the Welsh assembly the Conservatives were more united in abolishing the English regional chambers and giving their powers to local government, in effect reversing their own previous governmental policy of taking power away from local government. The Liberal Democrats too would have given some of the power of regional councils to local government but kept them in a streamlined single agencies headed by executives comprising of elected councillors rather than government appointees. Labour itself was continuing to plan to put further responsibility for planning, housing and transport to the regional chambers. Just as the powers of the Welsh assembly had been reviewed, so Labour now planned to do the same for the GLA and the London mayor, which will no doubt highlight an over-reliance on personality politics concerning the holder of the mayor's post.

Both of the nationalist parties, the SNP and Plaid Cymru, continued with their aims of independence for each respective nation. To this end they would enhance their country's parliaments to enable them to take full control of the new nation states. At the same time, in common with the Liberal Democrats, both parties would have reduced the voting age to sixteen. Devolution therefore was still a political issue if no longer one in which the British parties devoted much time to. In this respect it seemed to have become part of the accepted framework of British politics. It hadn't led to the break-up of the United Kingdom as had widely been predicted, and with the exception of some Conservatives' views on the Welsh assembly and regional chambers there was no longer a political desire to return to the unitary system of government which revolved around Westminster. To this extent political devolution in Britain today is here to stay.

Appendix 1

Results of the referendum of 11 September 1997 in Scotland

In Scotland the SNP abandoned its 'nothing less than full independence' stance and supported devolution. Labour, the Lib Dems and the SNP worked well together for a 'yes-yes' vote, leaving the Tories, with no Scottish MPs, as the only supporters of a weak 'just say no' campaign. Only Tam Dalyell, poser of the West Lothian question, opposed devolution from the Labour side. In the event, over 60 per cent voted in the referendum and, although 10 per cent less voted 'yes' for taxation powers, only two areas – Orkney and Dumfries and Galloway – voted 'no'. Over 70 per cent of the total vote said yes to the parliament.

Results for Scotland by local government area

The first of the two figures given is a 'yes' vote for a devolved parliament, the second is a 'yes' vote for tax-varying powers. Votes are expressed as percentages.

Aberdeen	71.77	60.34
Aberdeenshire	63.88	52.27
Angus	64.66	53.43
Argyll and Bute	67.30	56.99
Clackmannanshire	79.97	68.66
Dumfries and Galloway	60.72	48.80
Dundee	76.00	65.50
East Ayrshire	81.13	70.48
East Dunbartonshire	69.77	30.23
East Lothian	74.19	62.68
East Renfrewshire	61.65	51.56
Edinburgh	71.93	61.96
Falkirk	79.95	69.19
Fife	76.08	64.68
Glasgow	83.59	62.05
Highland	72.58	62.05
Inverclyde	77.98	67.19

Midlothian	79.88	67.72
Moray	67.18	52.70
North Ayrshire	76.31	65.68
North Lanarkshire	82.55	72.17
Orkney	57.29	47.42
Perthshire and Kinross	61.74	51.30
Renfrewshire	79.06	63.59
Scottish Borders	62.79	50.73
Shetland	62.38	51.61
South Ayrshire	66.86	56.23
South Lanarkshire	77.81	67.61
Stirling	68.47	58.88
West Dunbartonshire	84.89	74.74
Western Isles	79.40	68.43
West Lothian	79.57	67.27

Appendix 2

Formula for working out the winners of regional seats in the additional member system (AMS)

Under AMS the electors vote for constituency representatives on a simple majority first-past-the-post system. They then elect the additional members through voting for parties, so as to make party representation as near proportional as possible. The additional members are elected from party lists according to a simple formula known as the d'Hondt method:

> The number of votes cast for each party list divided by the number of constituency members already elected plus 1.

In the Scotland bill there is a section in which this formula is explained by using as an example the actual votes cast for the four main Scottish parties in the 1997 election for the Euro-constituency of North-east Scotland, which was due to be represented in the Scottish parliament by nine constituency MSPs and seven additional members.

In the constituency vote

Labour won 113,021 votes and elected 5 MSPs.
The SNP won 95,493 votes and elected 2 MSPs.
The Liberal Democrats won 69,164 votes and elected 2 MSPs.
The Conservatives won 82,079 votes and elected 0 MSPs.

In the first division

- Labour's 113,021 is divided by 5 + 1   =18,837
- The SNP's 95,493 is divided by 2 + 1   =31,831
- The Lib Dems' 69,164 is divided by 2 + 1   =23,054
- The Conservatives' 82,079 is divided by 0 + 1 =82,079

Of these the Conservatives have the largest share and they receive the first added member.

In the second division

The Conservative's votes are now divided by $1 + 1$, giving a share of $41,039$.
This is still larger than the SNP and the Conservatives get a second additional member.

In the third division

The Conservative's votes are now divided by $2 + 1$, giving a share of $27,359$.
This is less than the SNP share so the SNP received the third additional member.

In the fourth division

The SNP's vote are now divided by $3 + 1$, giving a share of $23,873$.
This is once again below the Conservatives and it is they who get the fourth added member.

In the fifth division

The Conservative's vote are now divided by $3 + 1$, giving a share of $20,519$.
The largest vote is now the SNP and they get the fifth additional member.

In the sixth division

The SNP's votes are now divided by $4 + 1$, giving a share of 19.098
The Liberal Democrats now have the largest share and get the sixth additional member.

In the seventh and final division

Once again the Conservative share is largest and they take the last additional place.

Overall the distribution of seats is

	Constituency	Regional list
Labour	5	0
SNP	2	2
Liberal Democrat	2	1
Conservative	0	4

Appendix 3

Principles adopted by the National Assembly for Wales in government bills affecting the assembly (The Rawling Principles)

1 The assembly should acquire any and all new powers in a bill where these relate to its existing responsibilities.
2 Bills should only give a UK minister powers which cover Wales if it is intended that the policy concerned is to be conducted on a single England and Wales / GB / UK basis.
3 Bills should not confer functions specifically on the secretary of state for Wales. Where functions need to be exercised separately in Wales, they should be conferred on the assembly.
4 A bill should not reduce the assembly's functions by giving concurrent functions to a UK minister, imposing a requirement on the assembly to act jointly or with UK government/parliamentary consent, or dealing with matters which were previously the subject of assembly subordinate legislation.
5 Where a bill gives the assembly new functions, this should be in broad enough terms to allow it to develop its own policies flexibly. This may mean, where appropriate, giving the assembly 'enabling' subordinate legislative powers, different from those given to a minister for exercise in England, and/or which proceed by reference to the subject matter of the bill.
6 It should be permissible for a bill to give the assembly so-called 'Henry VIII' powers (i.e. powers to amend primary legislation by subordinate legislation, or apply it differently) for defined purposes, the test being whether the particular powers are justified for the purpose of the effective implementation of the relevant policy. Where such powers are to be vested in a UK minister for exercise in England, they should be vested in the assembly for exercise in Wales.
7 Assembly to have power to bring into force (or 'commence') all bills or parts of bills which relate to its responsibilities. Where the minister is to have commencement powers in respect of England the assembly should have the same powers in respect of Wales.

Appendix 4

Results of the referendum of 18 September 1997 in Wales

Without either legislative or tax-varying powers, the Welsh assembly could be seen as no more than an expensive talking shop. Many Labour party members, including half a dozen MPs, were strongly opposed and campaigned for a 'no' vote. After the vote, with a low turnout of only 50 per cent, the country divided in half, east and west. The largely English-speaking areas – along the Welsh Marches in the north-east near Liverpool, in Pembrokeshire and around Cardiff – voted 'no'. The largely Welsh-speaking Plaid Cymru heartland of the west, and the loyal Labour South Wales Valleys, voted 'yes'. The 'no' camp led throughout, until the very last declaration when a massive 'yes' vote in Carmarthen gave a majority of just 0.6 per cent to the pro-devolution campaign.

Turnout	0.12 per cent
'Yes'	559,419 (50.3 per cent)
'No'	552,698 (49.7 per cent)
Majority for 'yes'	6,721 (0.6 per cent)

Only a little over 25 per cent of the Welsh electorate voted in favour of devolution.

Yes		No	
Ynys Môn	1.80	Torfaen	0.32
Swansea	3.92	Wrexham	9.44
Bridgend	8.78	Cardiff	11.26
Caerphilly	9.40	Pembrokeshire	14.42
Blaenau Gwent	12.18	Powys	14.68
Merthyr Tydfil	16.42	Conwy	18.16
Rhondda Cynon Taff	16.94	Denbighshire	18.96
Ceredigion	18.40	Flintshire	23.60
Gwynedd	28.17	Newport	25.14
Carmarthenshire	31.08	Vale of Glamorgan	28.92
Neath Port Talbot	33.10	Monmouthshire	35.80

Note: The figures given are the percentage leads over the opposing view.

Appendix 5

The electoral regions and districts of Wales

Wales is divided into five electoral regions based on European parliamentary constituencies. Each region is then divided into a variable number of Westminster parliamentary constituencies. In elections to the Welsh assembly, each Westminster constituency elects one assembly member by first-past-the-post, while each European constituency elects four top-up members from a regional list. The proportion of assembly seats allocated to each region is intended to reflect the proportion of the Welsh electorate living in that region.

European constituency	Proportion of Welsh electorate	Number of seats
North Wales	21.6%	13 (21.7%)
Mid and West Wales	18.2%	12 (20%)
South Wales West	17.9%	11 (18.3%)
South Wales Central	21.6%	12 (20%)
South Wales East	20.6%	12 (20%)

Source: Figures taken from the *Government of Wales Act 1998* (Welsh Assembly, www.wales.gov.uk).

Note: Each region is divided as follows: North Wales (Ynys Môn, Caernarfon, Conwy, Clwyd West, Vale of Clwyd, Clwyd South, Delyn, Alyn and Deeside, Wrexham); Mid and West Wales (Meirionnydd Nant Conwy, Ceredigion, Preseli Pembrokeshire, Carmarthen West and South Pembrokeshire, Carmarthen East and Dinefwr, Llanelli, Montgomeryshire, Brecon and Radnorshire); South Wales West (Gower, Swansea East, Swansea West, Neath, Aberavon, Bridgend, Ogmore); South Wales Central (Vale of Glamorgan, Pontypridd, Rhondda, Cynon Valley, Cardiff North, Cardiff West, Cardiff Central, Cardiff South and Penarth); South Wales East (Newport East, Newport West, Monmouth, Torfaen, Islwyn, Caerphilly, Blaenau Gwent, Merthyr Tydfil and Rhymney).

Appendix 6

The single transferable vote (STV) electoral system

A system of voting developed by the British Electoral Reform Society as long ago as 1910 and proposed to the 1917 Speaker's Conference on Electoral Reform, STV was the electoral system used for the four university seats which existed between 1918 and 1949 as well as being adopted for the proposed Irish parliament of 1920. Its use in Northern Ireland elections was abandoned for local government in 1922 and for elections to Stormont in 1929, in order to safeguard the Protestant ascendancy. The system was recommended for devolved assemblies by the Kilbrandon Commission but was discounted in 1997 in favour of the additional member system for the Scottish Parliament and Welsh assembly. After 1922, STV had continued to be used in succession by the Irish Free State, Eire and the Republic of Ireland for all elections. After 1972, it was re-adopted for all non-Westminster elections in Northern Ireland in order to preserve proportional representation for the sectarian communities.

At the heart of STV is a multi-member constituency, electing up to six members to the parliament or elected body. For example, in elections to the Northern Ireland assembly voting takes place in the eighteen Westminster constituencies, each of which elects six members. Electors are faced with a long list of names since each party may nominate as many candidates as there are vacancies to be filled. The voter then places candidates in order of preference by writing 1, 2, 3 and so on alongside their names.

In counting the votes, the aim is to reach a quota calculated by *dividing the total number of votes cast by one more than the number of seats available, plus one*. For example, if 40,000 votes were cast in a constituency where three seats were available, the quota would be 40,000 divided by 3 + 1 plus one: i. e. 10,001. Any candidate reaching the quota with first preference votes is elected but very few are elected on the first count: in the June 1998 elections only one-fifth of assembly seats were decided by first-preference votes. There is a complex procedure for achieving the full number of members, involving the redistribution of first-preference votes surplus to the quota, as well as redistributing second-preference votes from those eliminated candidates who received the fewest first-preference votes, so as to eliminate wasted votes both in the sense of candidates who got more votes than were needed as well as candidates who got too few votes to count. This process of redistributing votes goes on until the necessary number of constituency members is elected.

Bibliography

Books and articles

Adonis, Andrew, *Parliament Today*, Manchester University Press, Manchester, 1993.

Alder, John, *Constitutional and Administrative Law* (2nd edn), Macmillan, Basingstoke, 1994.

Andrews, Leighton, *Wales Says Yes: the Inside Story of the Yes for Wales Referendum Campaign*, Seren, Bridgend, 1999.

Aughey, Arthur, *Missing England: Identifying the Eighty-Five Per Cent*, School Of Economics and Politics, University of Ulster at Jordanstown, PSA Leeds Conference, 2005.

Aughey, Arthur and Duncan Morrow (eds), *Northern Ireland Politics*, Longman, Harlow, 1996.

Awbery, A.W., *Pembrokeshire Welsh: a Phonological Study*, Gomer, Llandysul, 1986.

Bennett, Michael, John Fairley, and Mark McAteer, *Devolution in Scotland: the Impact on Local Government*, Joseph Rowntree Foundation, York, 2002.

Bogdanor, Vernon, *Devolution in the United Kingdom*, Opus, Oxford, 1999.

Bogdanor, Vernon, 'England may get its turn', *Guardian*, 23 April 2001.

Boyce, George, D. and Alan O'Day (eds), *The Making of Modern Irish History*, London, Routledge, 1996.

Brack, Duncan and Robert Ingham (eds), *Dictionary of Liberal Quotations*, Politicos, London, 1999.

Bradbury, Jonathan, 'English Regional Government', *Politics Review*, April 1996.

Bradbury, Jonathan, 'Yr Ie Bychan – the Little Yes', *Politics Review*, April 1998.

Bradbury, Jonathan and James Mitchell, 'Devolution: Between Governance and Territorial Politics', *Parliamentary Affairs*, Vol. 58, No. 2, 2005.

Bradbury, Jonathan and Meg Russell, *Learning to Live with Pluralism? Constituency and Regional Members and Local Representation in Scotland and Wales*, ESRC Research Programme Briefing No. 28, March 2005.

British-Irish Council Reports 1999–2003, British-Irish Council, London and Dublin, 2003.

Bristow, Gillian, 'Finance', in John Osmond and J. Barry Jones (eds), *Birth of Welsh Democracy: the First Term of the National Assembly for Wales*, Institute of Welsh Affairs, Cardiff, 2003.

Bristow, Gillian, 'Power of the purse', in John Osmond (ed.), *Welsh Politics Comes of Age: Responses to the Richard Commission*, Institute of Welsh Affairs, Cardiff, 2005.

Brogan, Hugh, *Longman History of the United States*, Longman Group, Harlow, 1985.

Broughton, David and Alan Storer, 'The Welsh assembly election of 2003: the triumph of "welfarism"', *Representation*, Vol. 40, No. 4, 2004.

Brown, Alice, 'Taking their place in the new house: women and the Scottish parliament', *Scottish Affairs*, No. 28, Summer, 1999.

Brown, Alice, David McCrone and Lindsay Paterson, *Politics and Society in Scotland*, Macmillan, London, 1996.

Budge, Ian, Ivor Crewe, David McKay and Ken Newton, *The New British Politics*, Addison Wesley Longman, Harlow, 1998.

Butler, David and Gareth Butler, *Twentieth Century British Political Facts 1900–2000*, Macmillan, London, 2000.

Cannon, Jon (ed.), *The Oxford Companion to British History*, Oxford University Press, Oxford, 1997.

Clark, David, 'A people's convention for London', *Guardian*, 14 August 2001.

Clark, Alistair, 'Between Iraq and a hard place? The Scottish local government elections of May 2003', *Representation*, Vol. 41, No. 1, 2004.

Clinton, Bill, *My Life*, Hutchins, London, 2004.

Coakley, John and Brigid Laffan, 'Institutions and modes of territorial management', in John Coakely, Brigid Laffan and Jennifer Todd (eds), *Renovation or Revolution? New Territorial Politics in Ireland and the United Kingdom*, University College Dublin Press, Dublin, 2005.

Cochrane, Feargal, *Union Politics and the Politics of Unionism since the Anglo-Irish Agreement*, Cork University Press, Cork, 2001.

Cole, John, *As it Seemed to Me*, Weidenfeld & Nicolson, London, 1995.

Cole, Michael, 'The changing governance of London', *Talking Politics*, Summer, 2000.

Constitution Unit, *Nations and Regions: the Dynamics of Devolution Monitoring programme: Second Draft, Quarterly Report*, University College London, London, 2000.

Constitution Unit, *Monitor Supplement: the General Election and the Constitution*, University College London, London, 2005a.

Constitution Unit, 'Monitor: Welsh devolution the next steps', *Constitution Unit Bulletin*, Issue 31, September, 2005b.

Cook, Chris and John Ramsden (eds), *By-elections in British Politics*, UCL Press, London, 1997.

Cooper, Marc-Philippe, 'Understanding subsidiarity as a political issue in the European Community', *Talking Politics*, Spring, 1995.

Coxall, Bill and Lynton Robins, *Contemporary British Politics* (2nd edn), Macmillan, Basingstoke, 1995.

Cunningham, Michael, 'British government policy in Northern Ireland 1969–89, its nature and execution', *Politics Review*, September, 1992.

Cunningham, Michael, *British Government Policy in Northern Ireland*, Manchester University Press, Manchester, 2001.

Curtice, John, *Public Opinion, Nations and Regions: the Dynamics of Devolution*, Quarterly Monitoring Report, Scotland, June, The Constitution Unit, University College London, London, 2003.

Curtice, John and Stephen Herbert, *STV In Local Government Elections: Modelling the 2003 Result*, SPICe briefing, 3 June 05/31, Scottish Parliament, 2005.

Curtis, Edmund, *A History of Ireland from Earliest Times to 1922*, Routledge, London 1936.

Dale, Ian, *Conservative Party: General Election Manifestos, 1900–1997*, Routledge, London, 2000a.

Dale, Ian, *Liberal Party: General Election Manifestos, 1900–1997*, Routledge, London, 2000b.

Davies, John, *A History of Wales*, Penguin, Harmondsworth, 1994.

Davies, D. Hywel, *The Welsh Nationalist Party, 1925–1945: a Call To Nation Hood*, University of Wales Press, Cardiff, 1983.

Davies, Norman, *The Isles, a History*, Macmillan, London, 1999.

De Paor, Liam, *Milestones in Irish History*, Mercier Press, Cork and Dublin, 1986.

Deacon, Russell, 'How the additional member system was buried and then resurrected in Wales', *Journal of Representative Democracy*, Autumn/Winter, Vol. 34, Nos 3 and 4, 1997.

Deacon, Russell, '"Early Days": the first year of the National Assembly for Wales (1999–2000)', *Talking Politics*, April, 2001.

Deacon, Russell, *The Governance of Wales: the Welsh Office and the Policy Process 1964–99*, Welsh Academic Press, Cardiff, 2002.

Deacon, Russell and Steve Belzak, 'Duw a Gadno Dywysog Cymru' – Brenhinfraint Cymru: a oes arnom angen, Tywysog Cymru o hyd? Caerdydd, Y Ganolfan Er Diwygio, 2000.

Deacon, Russell, Dylan Griffiths and Peter Lynch, *Devolved Great Britain: the New Governance of England, Scotland and Wales*, Sheffield Hallam University Press, Sheffield, 2000.

Denver, David, Charles Pattie, Hugh Botchel and James Mitchell, 'The devolution referendums in Scotland', *Journal of Representative Democracy*, Winter, Vol. 35, No. 4, 1998.

Electoral Commission, *Assembly Elections 2003: the Official Report on the Northern Ireland Assembly Elections 26 November 2003*, Belfast, April 2004.

Electoral Commission, *The National Assembly for Wales Elections 2003: the Official Report and Results*, Cardiff, November 2003.

Ellis, Berresford P., *Wales a Nation Again! The Nationalist Struggle for Freedom*, The Garden City Press, Cardiff, 1968.

ESRC, *Devolution and Constitutional Change, Delivering Public Policy after Devolution: Diverging from Westminster*, ESRC, Swindon, 2003a.

ESRC, *Devolution and Constitutional Change, Public Attitudes, Devolution and National Identity*, ESRC, Edinburgh University, Edinburgh, 2003b.

ESRC, *Research Programme on Devolution and Constitutional Change, Central Government's Responses to Devolution*, Briefing No. 15, ESRC, Swindon, January 2005.

Evans, Mark, 'Devolution to Scotland and Wales: is power devolved power retained?', in Steve Lancaster (ed.), *Developments in Politics Vol. 10*, Causewa, Ormskirk, 1999.

Falconer, Peter and Alistair Jones, 'Electing a Scottish parliament', *Talking Politics*, Winter, 1999.

Falkus, Malcolm and John Gillingham (eds), *Historical Atlas of Britain*, Grisewood & Dempsey, London, 1981.

Ferguson, Neil, *Empire: How Britain Made the Modern World*, Penguin, London, 2004.

Finlay, Richard, *Independent and Free – Scottish Politics and the Origins of the Scottish National Party 1918–1945*, John Donald, Edinburgh, 1994.

Finlay, Richard, 'The Labour party in Scotland 1888–1945', in G. Hassan (ed.), *The Scottish Labour Party: History, Institutions and Ideas*, Edinburgh University Press, Edinburgh, 2004.

Foulkes, David, Barry Jones and R. A. Wilford, *The Welsh Veto*, The University of Wales Press, Cardiff, 1983.

Fraser, D., 'New labour, new parliament', in G. Hassan (ed.), *The Scottish Labour Party: History, Institutions and Ideas*, Edinburgh University Press, Edinburgh, 2004.

Fraser, Lord, *The Holyrood Inquiry: a Report by The Rt Hon Lord Fraser of Carmyllie QC*, Scottish Parliamentary Corporate Body, Edinburgh, 2004.

Freedland, Jonathan, 'Livingstone's London', *Guardian*, 4 May 2001.

Gardiner, Michael, *The Cultural Roots of Devolution*, Edinburgh University Press, Edinburgh, 2004.

Gaffney, Angela, *Aftermath: Remembering the Great War in Wales*, University of Wales Press, Cardiff, 1998.

Graham Jones, J., 'The Parliament For Wales Campaign 1950–1956', *The Welsh History Review*, Board of Celtic Studies, Vol. 16, No. 2, 1992.

Graham Jones, J., 'The Peacemonger: David Davies', *Journal of Liberal Democrat History*, Issue 29, Winter 2000–01, 2001.

Griffin, Brian, 'A force divided – policing Ireland 1900–60', *History Today*, October 1999.

Griffiths, Dylan, 'The Welsh assembly', *Talking Politics*, Winter, 2000.

Griffiths, Jim, *Pages from Memory*, London, Dent, 1968.

Grigg, John, *Lloyd George: the Young Lloyd George*, Penguin, Harmondsworth, 1997.

Harvie, Christopher, *Scotland and Nationalism: Scottish Society and Politics 1707–1994* (2nd edn), Routledge, London, 1994.

Harvie, Christopher, 'The economic and social context of Scottish Labour', in G. Hassan (ed.), *The Scottish Labour Party: History, Institutions and Ideas*, Edinburgh University Press, Edinburgh, 2004.

Harvie, Christopher and Peter Jones, The Road To Home Rule: Images of Scotland's Cause, Polygon, Edinbugh, 2000.

Hassan, Gerry (ed.), *A Guide to the Scottish Parliament: the Shape of Things to Come*, Centre for Scottish Public Policy, The Stationery Office, Edinburgh, 1999.

Hassan, Gerry (ed.), *The Scottish Labour Party: History, Institutions and Ideas*, Edinburgh University Press, Edinburgh, 2004.

Hassan, Gerry and Peter Lynch, *The Almanac of Scottish Politics*, Politicos, London, 2001.

Hazell, Robert, 'Constitutional futures', *Talking Politics*, Spring, 1999.

Hazell, Robert (ed.), *The State and the Nations: the First Year of Devolution in the United Kingdom*, Imprint Academic, London, 2000.

Hazell, Robert, 'A purely English parliament?', *Guardian*, 3 January 2001.

Hazell, Robert (ed.), 'Introduction: the dynamism of devolution in its third year', in his *The State of the Nations 2003: the Third Year of Devolution in the United Kingdom*, Imprint Academic, London, 2003.

Hearn, Jonathan, *Claiming Scotland: National Identity and Liberal Culture*, Polygon, Edinburgh, 2000.

Henderson, Ailsa, *Regional Political Cultures in the UK*, Wilfrid Laurier University, PSA Leeds Conference, 2005.

Henderson, Ailsa and Amanda Sloat, 'New politics in Scotland? A profile of MSPs', *Talking Politics*, Summer, 1999.

Henderson, Ailsa and Amanda Sloat, 'New politics in Scotland? Evidence from Holyrood', *Talking Politics*, Winter, 2000.

Hennessey, Thomas, *Northern Ireland, Ending the Troubles?*, Palgrave, New York, 2001.

Heppell, Timothy and Rowan McCreanor, 'English regional governance: the next stage of constitutional change', *Talking Politics*, Vol. 15, No. 3, April, 2003.

Herbert, Stephen, Ross Burnside and Simon Wakefield, *UK Election 2005: in Scotland*, SPICe Briefing 10 May 05/28, Scottish Parliament, 2005.

Hetherington, Peter, 'Prescott gets half a cake', *Guardian*, 20 November 1998.

Hetherington, Peter, 'The benefits of regionalism', *Guardian*, 31 January 2001.

Hetherington, Peter, 'Scots and Welsh face subsidy axe', *Guardian*, 24 April 2001.

Hetherington, Peter and Emma Pinkney, *Nations and Regions: the Dynamics of Devolution*, Quarterly Monitoring Report, November, The Constitution Unit, University College London, London, 2004.

Heywood, Andrew, *Politics*, Macmillan, Basingstoke, 1997.

Hopkins, Stephen, 'The Good Friday Agreement in Northern Ireland', *Politics Review*, February, 1999.

House of Commons, *The English Regions and Referendums on Elected Regional Assemblies*, Standing Committee on Regional Affairs, London, 11 December 2003.

Hutchinson, I. G. C, *Scottish Politics in the Twentieth Century*, Palgrave, London, 2001.

Hunt, Steven, 'Peace in our times? Prospects and dilemmas after the Northern Ireland Assembly election results', *Talking Politics*, Winter, 1999.

Irwin, Colin, *Peace Building and Public Policy in Northern Ireland*, Centre for the Study of Ethnic Conflict at Queen's University Belfast and Joseph Rowntree Charitable Trust, Belfast, 2003.

Jackson, Alvin, 'The Irish Act of Union', *History Today*, January, 2001.

Jeffrey, Charlie, 'Judgements on devolution? The 2003 elections in Scotland, Wales and Northern Ireland', *Representation*, Vol. 40, No. 4, 2004.

Jones, Bill (ed.), *Political Issues in Britain Today* (3rd edn), Manchester University Press, Manchester, 1989.

Jones, Bill and Dennis Kavanagh, *British Politics Today* (2nd edn), Manchester University Press, Manchester, 1994.

Judge, D., *The Parliamentary State*, Sage, London, 1993.

Judges, David, *Political Institutions in the United Kingdom*, Oxford University Press, Oxford, 2005.

Keating, Michael, *The Government of Scotland: Public Policy Making after Devolution*, Edinburgh University Press, Edinburgh, 2004.

Keegan, Victor and Martin Kettle (eds), *The New Europe*, Fourth Estate, London, 1993.

Kellas, James G., *The Scottish Political System* (4th edn), Cambridge University Press, Cambridge, 2004.

Kennedy, Liam and David S. Johnson, 'The Union of Ireland and Britain, 1801–1921', in George D. Boyce and Alan O'Day (eds), *The Making of Modern Irish History*, London, Routledge, 1996.

Kingdom, John, *Government and Politics in Britain*, Polity Press, Cambridge, 1991.

Lee, Joseph, 'The Land War', in Liam De Paor, *Milestones in Irish History*, The Mercier Press, Cork and Dublin, 1986.

Labour Wales, *Shaping the Vision*, Labour Wales, Cardiff, 1995.

Lang, Mark S. and Alan Storer, 'The subject committee', in John Osmond and J. Barry

Jones (eds), *Birth of Welsh Democracy: the First Term of the National Assembly for Wales*, Institute of Welsh Affairs, Cardiff, 2003.

Laffin, Martin, 'The engine room: the civil service and the national assembly', in J. Barry Jones and John Osmond (eds), *Building a Civic Culture: Institutional Change, Policy Development and Political Dynamics in the National Assembly for Wales*, Institute of Welsh Affairs, Cardiff, 2002.

Laffin, Martin, Gerald Taylor and Alys Thomas, *A New Partnership? The National Assembly for Wales and Local Government*, Joseph Rowntree Foundation, York, 2002 .

London Assembly, *Report of Transport Policy and Spatial Development Policy Committee – Congestion Charging Scrutiny*, GLA, London, 2000.

London Assembly, *Alternatives to Congestion Charging*, proceedings of a seminar held by the Transport Policy Committee, 31 January, GLA, London, 2002.

London Assembly, *Congestion Charging: a First Review*, GLA, London, 2004.

Lynch, Peter, 'Labour, devolution and the West Lothian question', *Talking Politics*, Autumn, 1996.

Lynch, Peter, 'Devolution and a new British political system', *Talking Politics*, Winter, 1997/98.

Lynch, Peter, 'The road to a Scottish parliament', *Politics Review*, April, 1998.

Lynch, Peter, 'Petitioning the Scottish parliament: an experiment in citizen participation', *Talking Politics*, April, 2001a.

Lynch, Peter, *Scottish Government and Politics: an Introduction*, Edinburgh University Press, Edinburgh, 2001b.

Lynch, Peter, *SNP: the History of the Scottish Nationalist Party*, Welsh Academic Press, Cardiff, 2002.

Lynch, Peter, 'Toward an England of the regions? Devolution and the future government of England', *Talking Politics*, Vol. 16, No. 3, April, 2004.

Lynch, Peter and Steven Birrell, 'Grievances galore', *Guardian*, , p. 13, 7 May 2001.

MacClean, John, *The Vanguard*, December 1920, republished by the Revolutionary Communist Group, Glasgow, 1998.

Mackie, J. D., *A History of Scotland*, Penguin, Harmondsworth, 1964.

Madgwick, P. J., Non Griffiths and Valerie Walker, *The Politics of Rural Wales: a Case Study on Cardiganshire*, Hutchinson, London, 1973.

Major, John, *John Major: the Autobiography*, Harper Collins, London, 1999.

Mattingley, H. (trans.), *Tacitus on Britain and Germany*, Penguin, Harmondsworth, 1948.

Masterman, Neville, *The Forerunner: the Dilemmas of Tom Ellis 1859–1899*, Merlin Press, Monmouth, 1972.

Mawson, John and Spencer, Ken, *Whitehall and the Reorganisation of Regional Offices in England*, ESRC Whitehall Programme, London, 1997.

McAllister, Laura, *Plaid Cymru: the Emergence of a Political Party*, Seren, Bridgend, 2001.

McAllister, Laura, 'The Richard Commission – Wales's alternative constitutional cconvention?', *Contemporary Wales*, Vol. 17, pp. 140–61, 2004.

McAllister, Laura, 'The value of independent commissions: an insider's perspective on the Richard Commission', *Parliamentary Affairs: a Journal of Comparative Politics*, Vol. 58, No. 1, pp. 38–52, 2005.

McCormick, Donald, *The Mask of Merlin: a Critical Study of David Lloyd George*, Macdonald, London, 1963.

McLean, Iain, *The English Regions after Regionalism*, Nuffield College, Oxford, PSA Leeds Conference, 2005.

McLaughlin, Greg, 'The media', in *Nations and Regions: the Dynamics of Devolution,* Quarterly Monitoring Report, Northern Ireland, August, The Constitution Unit, University College London, London, 2003.

McVicar, Murray and Simon Wakefield, *Guide to the Scottish Budget – Subject Profile,* 22 April 03/24, Scottish Parliament, Edinburgh, 2003.

Mitchell, James, 'Reviving the union state?', *Politics Review,* February, 1996.

Mitchell, James, *Devolution in the United Kingdom – Revision Notes,* Politics Association Resource Centre, Manchester, 1999.

Mitchell, James, 'Politics in Scotland', in Patrick Dunleavy, Andrew Gamble and Gillian Peele (eds), *Developments in British Politics,* Palgrave, London, 2004.

Mitchell, James, 'Scotland: expectations, policy types and devolution', in Alan Trench (ed.), *Has Devolution Made a Difference? The State of the Nations 2004,* The Constitution Unit, University College London, Imprint Academic, London, 2004.

Mitchell, James and Jonathan Bradbury, 'Political recruitment and the 2003 Scottish and Welsh elections: candidate selection, positive discrimination and party adaptations', *Representation,* Vol. 40, No. 4, 2004.

Mitchison, Rosalind, *A History of Scotland* (3rd edn), London, Routledge, 2002.

Moran, Mike, 'Reshaping the British state', *Talking Politics,* Spring, 1995.

Morgan, Kenneth. O., 'Gladstone and Wales', *Welsh History Review,* Vol. 1, No. 1, 1960.

Morgan, Kenneth. O,. *Lloyd George, Family Letters 1885–1936,* Oxford University Press, Oxford, 1973.

Morgan, Kenneth. O., *Wales in British Politics 1868–1922,* University of Wales Press, Cardiff, 1980.

Morgan, Kenneth O., 'Divided we stand', *History Today,* May, 1999.

Morgan, Kevin and Steve Upton, 'Culling the Quangos', in John Osmond (ed.), *Welsh Politics Come of Age,* Institute of Welsh Affairs, Cardiff, 2005.

Mulholland, Marc, *Northern Ireland: a Very Short Introduction,* Oxford University Press, Oxford, 2003.

Nairn, Tom, *After Britain: New Labour and the Return of Scotland,* Granta, London, 2000.

National Assembly for Wales, *Assembly Review of Procedure, Final Report,* February, Cardiff, 2002.

Navarro, Marie and David Lambert, *The Nature and Scope of the Legislative Powers of the National Assembly for Wales,* ESRC Devolution and Constitutional Change Programme, Briefing No. 13, January, ESRC, Swindon, 2005.

Neunreither, K., 'Subsidiarity as a guiding principle for European Community activities', *Government and Opposition,* Vol. 28, No. 2, Spring, 1993.

Nelmes, Graham, V., 'Stuart Rendel and Welsh Liberal Political Organisation in the Late Nineteenth Century', *Welsh History Journal,* Vol. 9, No. 4, December, 1979.

Norton, Philip (ed.), *The Consequences of Devolution,* Hansard Society, London, 1998.

Nowlan, Kevin. B, 'Catholic emancipation', in Liam De Paor, *Milestones in Irish History,* The Mercier Press, Cork and Dublin, 1986.

Office of the Deputy Prime Minister, *Your Region, Your Choice,* ODPM, London, 2002.

Office of the Deputy Prime Minister, *Your Say,* ODPM, London, 2003.

Office of the Deputy Prime Minister, *Housing, Planning, Local Government and the Regions Committee. Government Response to the Committee's First Report of Session 2004–05, on the Draft Regional Assemblies Bill,* 1st Special Report of Session 2004–05, House of Commons, The Stationery Office, London, 2005.

Osmond, John, *Welsh Europeans,* Seren, Bridgend, 1995.

Osmond, John, 'The civil service', in John Osmond and J. Barry Jones (eds), *Birth of Welsh Democracy: the First Term of the National Assembly for Wales*, Institute of Welsh Affairs, Cardiff, 2003.

Osmond, John, 'Wales towards 2007', in Alan Trench (ed.), *The Dynamics of Devolution: the State of the Nations 2005*, The Constitution Unit, University College London, Imprint Academic, London, 2005a.

Osmond, John, *Nations and Regions: the Dynamics of Devolution*, Quarterly Monitoring Report, Wales, Institute of Welsh Affairs, Cardiff, 2005b.

Osmond, John, 'Virtual Parliament', *Agenda*, Institute of Welsh Affairs, Cardiff, 2005c.

Orwell, George, *Animal Farm*, Secker and Warburg, London, 1945.

Oxford English Dictionary, Oxford University Press, Oxford, 1992.

Patterson, Henry, 'Northern Ireland 1921–68' in Arthur Aughey and Duncan Morrow (eds), *Northern Ireland Politics*, Longman, Harlow, 1996.

Pearce, Graham and Sarah Ayres, *Decentralisation in the English Regions Assessing the Implications for Rural and Transport Policy*, Briefing No. 16, ESRC, Swindon, 2005.

Pilkington, Colin, *Representative Democracy in Britain Today*, Manchester University Press, Manchester, 1997.

Pilkington, Colin, *The Politics Today Companion to the British Constitution*, Manchester University Press, Manchester, 1999a.

Pilkington, Colin, *The Civil Service in Britain Today*, Manchester University Press, Manchester, 1999b.

Pilkington, Colin, *Britain in the European Union Today* (2nd edn), Manchester University Press, Manchester, 2001.

Pimlott, Ben and N. Rao, *Governing London*, Oxford University Press, Oxford, 2002.

Prebble, John, *The Lion in the North*, Secker & Warburg, London, 1971.

Privy Council, The Inner House of the Court of Session, Judgment of the Lords of the Judicial Committee of the Privy Council, delivered 15 October, Privy Council, London, 2001.

Preston, Peter, 'The break-up of Britain', *Guardian*, 23 April 2001.

Rallings, Colin and Michael Thrasher, *Why the North East Said 'No': the 2004 Referendum on an Elected Regional Assembly*, LGC Elections Centre, University of Plymouth, PSA Leeds Conference, 2005.

Representation, Arthur MacDougall Trust, Vol. 40, No. 3, 2004.

Richard Commission, *Report of the Commission on the Powers and Electoral Arrangements of the National Assembly for Wales*, National Assembly for Wales, Cardiff, 2004.

Robertson, David, *The Penguin Dictionary of Politics*, Penguin, Harmondsworth, 1986.

Robins, Lynton and Bill Jones (eds), *Debates in British Politics Today*, Manchester University Press, Manchester, 2000.

Rose, Peter, *How the Troubles Came to Northern Ireland*, Palgrave, London, 2001.

Rowlands, Ted, 'Whitehall's last stand: the establishment of the Welsh Office, 1964', *Contemporary Wales*, Vol. 16, 2004.

Russell, Meg and Robert Hazell, 'Devolution and Westminster', in Robert Hazell (ed.), *The State and the Nations: the First Year of Devolution in the United Kingdom*, Imprint Academic, London, 2000.

Sandford, Mark, 'The governance of London', in Alan Trench (ed.), *Has Devolution Made a difference? The State of the Nations 2004*, Imprint Academic, London, 2005.

Sandford, Mark and Peter Hetherington, 'The regions at the crossroads: the future of sub-national government in England', in Alan Trench (ed.), *Has Devolution Made a Difference? The State of the Nations 2004*, Imprint Academic, London, 2005.

Sandford, Mark and Lucinda Maer, *Scrutiny Under Devolution: Committees in the Scottish Parliament, Northern Ireland and the National Assembly for Wales*, Imprint Academic, London, 2003.

Schama, Simon, *A History of Britain: the British Wars 1603–1776*, BBC, London, 2001.

Scottish Office, *The Scotland Bill*, Scottish Office, Edinburgh, 1998.

Schlesinger, Philip, David Miller and William Dinan, *Open Scotland? Journalists, Spin Doctors and Lobbyists*, Edinburgh University Press, Edinburgh, 2001.

Scott, David, 'Barnett – a fair share of the cake', *Public Eye*, Issue 39, February, 2002.

Scottish Executive, *Making it Work Together: a Programme for Government*, Scottish Office, Edinburgh, 1999.

Scottish Office, *Scotland's Parliament*, Cm 3658, Scottish Office, Edinburgh, 1997.

Scottish Parliament, Finance Committee, 5th Report, Session 2, Stage 1 of the 2005-06 Budget Process, Volume 1 – Report, 2004.

Scottish TV, *Annual Report 2004*, Edinburgh, 2005.

Seldon, Anthony, 'Northern Ireland', in Bill Jones (ed.), *Politics UK* (2nd edn), Harvester Wheatsheaf, Hemel Hempstead, 1994.

Sell, Geoffrey, 'Scottish nationalism in the 1990s', *Talking Politics*, Spring, 1998.

Shephard, Mark and Paul Cairney, 'The impact of the Scottish parliament in amending executive legislation', *Political Studies*, Vol. 53, 2005.

Shortridge, Sir Jon, *ASPB Reform: Circular Letter to Chief Executive Officers*, Assembly Sponsored Public Bodies, 2 August, Cardiff, 2004.

Standards in Public Life, *The Funding of Political Parties in the United Kingdom, Vol., 1*, Report Cm 4057-1, TSO, 1998.

Steinberg, S. H. and I. H. Evans, *Steinberg's Dictionary of British History* (2nd edn), Edward Arnold, London, 1970.

Stenton, Frank, *Anglo-Saxon England* (2nd edn), Clarendon Press, Oxford, 1947.

Stoker, Gerry, Brian Hogwood and Udo Bullman, 'Do we need regional government?' *Talking Politics*, Spring, 1996.

Tanner, Duncan, Chris Williams and Deian Hopkins, *The Labour Party in Wales 1900 – 2000*, University of Wales Press, Cardiff, 2000.

Taylor, A. J. P., *The Struggle for Mastery in Europe 1848–1918*, Oxford University Press, Oxford, 1954.

Taylor, Brian, *The Road To The Scottish Parliament*, Edinburgh University Press, Edinburgh, 2002.

Taylor, Bridget and Katarina Thomson, *Scotland and Wales: Nations Again?*, University of Wales Press, Cardiff, 1999.

TEU, *Treaty on European Union*, Office for Official Publications of the European Communities, Luxembourg, 1992.

Tindale, Stephen, *The State and the Nations: the Politics of Devolution*, IPPR, London, 1996.

Thatcher, Margaret, *The Downing Street Years*, HarperCollins, London, 1993.

Thatcher, Margaret, *The Path To Power*, HarperCollins, London, 1995.

Thomas, Alys 'Liberal Democrats', in John Osmond and J. Barry Jones (eds) *Birth Of Welsh Democracy: the First Term of the National Assembly for Wales*, Institute of Welsh Affairs, Cardiff, 2003.

Todd, Jennifer, 'A new territorial politics in the British Isles?', in John Coakely, Brigid Laffan and Jennifer Todd (eds), *Renovation Or Revolution? New Territorial Politics in Ireland and the United Kingdom*, University College Dublin Press, Dublin, 2005.

Tomaney, John, 'The regional governance of England', in Robert Hazell (ed.) *The State and the Nations: the First Year of Devolution in the United Kingdom*, Imprint Academic, London, 2000.

Tomaney, John, Peter Hetherington, and Emma Pinkney, *Nations and Regions: the Dynamics of Devolution*, Quarterly Monitoring Report, The English Regions, The Constitution Unit, University College London, London, 2005.

Trench, Alan, *Better Governance for Wales: an Analysis of the White Paper on Devolution for Wales*, The Devolution Policy Papers No. 13, ESRC Devolution Programme, London, 2005.

Tonge, Jonathan, 'Politics in Northern Ireland', in Patrick Dunleavy, Andrew Gamble, and Gillian Peele (eds) *Developments in British Politics*, Palgrave, London, 2004.

Tonge, Jonathan, *The New Northern Irish Politics?*, Palgrave MacMillan, London, 2005.

Treasury, H. M., *Funding the Scottish Parliament, National Assembly for Wales and Northern Ireland Assembly: a Statement of Funding Policy*, HM Treasury, London 2004.

Wales Office, *Concordat between the Cabinet of the National Assembly for Wales and the Wales Office*, Office of the Secretary of State for Wales, London, 2001.

Wales Office, *Better Governance for Wales*, Wales Office, Cardiff, 2005.

Walsh, Richard B. 'The death of the Irish language' in Liam De Paor, *Milestones in Irish History*, The Mercier Press, Cork and Dublin, 1986.

Watkins, Philippa and Alys Thomas, *Welsh Assembly Government Bids for Primary Legislation*, National Assembly for Wales, Members Research Service, Cardiff, 2005.

Welsh Assembly Government, *Putting Wales First: a Partnership for the People of Wales*, Welsh Assembly Government, Cardiff, 2000.

Welsh Opposition Press Release, Issued on behalf of the leaders of the Plaid Cymru – the party of Wales, Welsh Conservative and Welsh Liberal Democrat groups in the National Assembly, 'Opposition Parties Hail Top-Up Fees Agreement', Tuesday 21 June, 2005.

White, Michael, 'How the mayor has performed ...', *Guardian*, 4 May 2001.

Wilford, Rick and Robin Wilson, 'A bare knuckle ride: Northern Ireland', in Robert Hazell (ed.) *The State and the Nations: the First Year of Devolution in the United Kingdom*, Imprint Academic, London, 2000.

Wilford, Rick and Robin Wilson, *Nations and Regions: the Dynamics of Devolution*, Quarterly Monitoring Report, Northern Ireland, August, The Constitution Unit, University College London, London, 2003.

Willetts, David and Richard Forsdyke, *After the Landslide: Learning the Lessons of 1906 and 1945*, Centre for Policy Studies, London, 1999.

Wilson, Robin, 'Political context', in *Nations and Regions: the Dynamics of Devolution*, Quarterly Monitoring Report, Northern Ireland, August, The Constitution Unit, University College London, London, 2001.

Wilson, Robin, 'Assembly', in *Nations and Regions: the Dynamics of Devolution*, Quarterly Monitoring Report, Northern Ireland, August, The Constitution Unit, University College London, London, 2003.

Wyn Jones, Richard and Roger Scully, 'A "settling will"? Public attitudes to devolution in Wales', in Colin Rallings, Roger Scully, Jonathan Tonge and Paul Webb (eds), *British Elections and Parties Review, Vol. 13*, Taylor and Francis, London, 2003.

Wyn Jones, Richard and Roger Scully, 'Minor tremor but several casusalties: the 2003 Welsh election', in Roger Scully, Justin Fisher, Paul Webb and David Broughton (eds), *British Elections and Parties Review, Vol.14*, Taylor and Francis, London, 2004.

Wober, J. M., *Watching Parliament on TV – Views from Scotland, England, Wales and Northern Ireland*, Hansard Scottish Parliament Programme, Edinburgh, 2000.

Wright, Alex, 'Scotland/UK relations', in *Nations and Regions: the Dynamics of Devolution*, Quarterly Monitoring Report, Scotland, August, The Constitution Unit, University College London, London, 2003.

Young, Hugo, *One of Us*, Macmillan, London, 1989.

Internet websites

General

The Constitution Unit, University College of London, produces four reports each quarter on the progress and development of devolution in respectively Scotland, Wales, Northern Ireland and England. The reports are posted on the internet in May, August, November and February each year and can be read at www.ucl.ac.uk/constitution-unit. The reports are found on the 'Nations and Regions' pages, where information can be found on how to receive the relevant reports by e-mail.

The Economic and Social Research Council has since 2000 run a multi-million-pound-funded 'Devolution and Constitutional Change Programme' which covers all of the areas within this book. Their website containing more details is: www.devolution. ac.uk/.

The BBC also runs a regional news service which contains details of all major political events concerning devolution. Their web link is: http://news.bbc.co.uk/1/hi/uk/default.stm.

British government

Office of the Deputy Prime Minister (responsible for English devolution): www.odpm.gov.uk/

Greater London Authority and London Mayor: www.london.gov.uk/

Scotland

Scottish Executive: www.scotland.gov.uk
Scotland Office: www.scotlandoffice.gov.uk/
Scottish Conservative and Unionist party: www.scottishtories.org.uk/
Scottish Green party: www.scottishgreens.org.uk/
Scottish Labour party: www.scottishlabour.org.uk/
Scottish Liberal Democrats: www.scotlibdems.org.uk/
Scottish National party: www.snp.org.uk/
Scottish Parliament: www.scottish.parliament.uk
Scottish Socialist party: www.scottishsocialistparty.org/

Wales

Institute of Welsh Politics: www.aber.ac.uk/interpol/IWP/
Institute for Welsh Affairs (Welsh think tank): www.iwa.org.uk/
National Assembly for Wales : www.wales.gov.uk
Plaid Cymru (The Party of Wales): www.plaidcymru.org/
Wales Office: www.walesoffice.gov.uk
Wales Labour party: www.welshlabour.org.uk
Welsh Conservatives: www.conservatives.com
Welsh Liberal Democrats: www.welshlibdems.org.uk/home_e.asp

Northern Ireland

Alliance party of Northern Ireland: www.allianceparty.org/
Democratic Unionist party: www.dup.org.uk/
Northern Ireland Office: www.nio.gov.uk
Northern Ireland Assembly: www.niassembly.gov.uk/
Northern Ireland Executive: www.nics.gov.uk/
Sinn Fein: www.sinnfein.ie/
Social Democratic and Labour party: www.sdlp.ie/
Ulster Unionist party: www.uup.org/

Index